A SERVANT'S
JOURNEY

A SERVANT'S JOURNEY

The Life and Work of Thomas Kilgore

Thomas Kilgore Jr.
with
Jini Kilgore Ross

Judson Press ® Valley Forge

A Servant's Journey
© 1998 by Judson Press, Valley Forge, PA 19482-0851
All rights reserved.

ISBN 0-8170-1297-4

Printed in the U.S.A.

06   05   04   03   02   01   00   99   98
10   9   8   7   6   5   4   3   2   1

I dedicate this book to my grandchildren,
Robin Raschard, Niambi Robinson Cade,
and Okera Robinson,
and to my great-grandchildren,
Justen Charles Cade and Joshua Simeon Kilgore Cade

Where I had wronged or hurt, I asked for forgiveness;

where I had failed, I asked for understanding;

where I had helped or enabled, I sought no reward;

where I had inspired or uplifted, I said, Give God the praise;

and where I had advocated a quality of life that is more excellent,

I implored all to follow that trend.

—Thomas Kilgore Jr.
1913–1998

Contents

Part I
MEMOIRS

Part II
SERMONS, SPEECHES, AND WRITINGS

APPENDIXES

Acknowledgments

The writing of this book has taken place over several years and with the assistance of the following persons: my wife, Jeannetta, to whom I am indebted for her interest, comments, and additions and for her patience over the years of my ministry, as I have given so much time away from her; my daughter the Reverend Jini Kilgore Ross, who is a journalist by trade and who has been extremely helpful in the writing of the book; my daughter Lynn Kilgore Hendy, for her concern and eagerness for the book's publication; and Mrs. Shirley Bell, to whom I extend much thanks and appreciation, not only for her efforts in typing the initial manuscript from my barely legible penmanship and making helpful suggestions for the book's content, but for her excellent service as my administrative assistant for more than thirty-one years. Her well-kept files of the work of my ministries through the years made possible the easy retrieval of information for this book. I am also grateful to my friends Dr. Hugh Gloster and Dr. J. Alfred Smith Sr. for their kind expressions in the Forewords.

•

After my father's death, several persons set aside their responsibilities and commitments to contribute to the timely production of this book. They are Lynn Kilgore Hendy, my sister, who retyped for computer format the sermons, speeches, and writings and helped select photographs; my son Okera Robinson and family friends Carolyn Neal, Rev. Gwenn Pierre, and Deborah Simpson, who helped in various capacities with the supplementary material and appendixes; and my husband, Earl Ross, who graciously took over some of my regular duties and didn't complain when others were left undone so I could complete work on this book. The assistance of these family members and friends is greatly appreciated.

JKR

Forewords

...a long and distinguished career...

When the history of the second half of this century is written, Dr. Thomas Kilgore Jr. will have an important place in religion, community development, civil rights, and higher education. During a long and distinguished career he became minister of several well-known churches and president of two national Baptist conventions and carried his message not only to Los Angeles and California but also to the United States and the world. His memoirs are important, therefore, because they give a first-hand account of his life and work.

I first met Tom during his undergraduate years at Morehouse, and we were good friends from that time. Even as a college student, Tom was a serious, scholarly young man who was determined to prepare himself for a life of service to humanity. I think I can correctly say that he tried to be a good Christian even during his undergraduate years. I remember seeing him frequently in the company of Dr. Charles D. Hubert, dean of the Morehouse School of Religion; and I believe he lived in Dr. Hubert's home during part of his college years. I know that he did not spend most of his time visiting the campus of Spelman College and rapping with the Morehouse brothers at the corner of Chestnut and Fair.

After completing our studies in Atlanta, Tom and I followed different careers in different places. He prepared himself for a career in the ministry at Howard University and Union Theological Seminary, and I prepared myself for a career in education at New York University.

During the early years of our careers Tom and I occasionally met each other, especially at Morehouse; but we began a close friendship and colleagueship when I returned to Morehouse as president in 1967 and found him on the Board of Trustees. This friendship and colleagueship became even closer when Tom was elected chairman of the board.

Tom and I came through some difficult times together at Morehouse. When I assumed the presidency in 1967, the college had limited cash reserves and the Atlanta University Center had been hit hard by student unrest, which culminated with demands to change the name of the Atlanta University Center to the University of New Africa and to oust white students, teachers, and trustees. Despite this difficult start, we managed to sextuple the endowment to more than $27 million, to raise funds for the construction of thirteen new buildings, to triple the enrollment and faculty salaries, to strengthen the academic program and administrative operations, to build the business enrollment to more than 900 majors, to start the Dual-Degree Program in Engineering with Georgia Tech and — most of all — to found and nurture the Morehouse School of Medicine until it first awarded the M.D. degree. In the 1970s, we also bought most of the land in the blocks in which the chapel and the stadium now stand, as well as several parcels across Fair Street, and also successfully conducted the college's first capital campaign, which had a goal of $20 million, including a drive for $1 million in Atlanta.

As I review the past, I can see Tom in five ways.

First of all, he was a Christian. He was outstanding as an individual who worshiped his God and loved his fellow man. In this life I have never known a better Christian than Tom Kilgore.

Second, he was a gentleman, a member of a rare and vanishing breed. A gentleman is born and not made. You can make a president or a king, but you cannot make a gentleman. Tom Kilgore had the class, the culture, the refinement, the dignity, and the integrity of a true gentleman.

Third, he was a good friend. In the course of working together, Tom and I developed a very brotherly relationship. He was my best counselor, not only in college business, but in personal affairs, as well. We shared joys and sorrows. Realizing what a good friend I had in Tom, I "grappled [him] to my heart with hoops of steel."

Fourth, Tom was an ideal husband and father. Over the years I frequently saw him in these two roles, and I must say that he was hard to surpass in these two capacities. He was a loving and devoted husband, and his love and devotion were returned by his wife, Jeannetta. He was also a loving and devoted father who did everything in his power to rear his daughters, Lynn and Jini, properly and to show his affection for them, and they replied by becoming fine young ladies in whom he was well pleased. And now I want to make my only negative comment about Tom. With Jeannetta in charge at home all of the time, he was not as dominating as head of the family as he was as chairman of the board.

Fifth and finally, Tom was a great Morehouse man — maybe the greatest if measured in terms of what he gave to the college. He gave his life, his love, and his loyalty. Moreover, although he was not a wealthy man, he gave generously of his money, probably to the degree that his wife criticized him severely. But, most of all, he contributed his leadership, which carried Morehouse through many trials and tribulations. He did, indeed, pledge his life to "dear old Morehouse," gave himself in loyalty, and was steadfast, honest, and true to Morehouse and her ideals in all things that he did.

This then was Tom Kilgore: a loyal Christian, a fine gentleman, a good friend, an ideal husband and father, a model Morehouse man. He enriched the experience of thousands of people, and all of our lives are better because he passed this way. This was Tom Kilgore. When will there be another?

HUGH M. GLOSTER

President Emeritus of Morehouse College

...a multiplicity of gifts...

Dr. Thomas Kilgore Jr. was a peerless person because of his excellence in so many areas of service. The average person is fortunate in accomplishing high achievement in one discipline, but Dr. Kilgore was given a multiplicity of gifts by God Almighty. Taking courage, commitment, and compassion to be companions with his boundless energy and incomparable optimism, Dr. Kilgore prayerfully disciplined his gifts to honor God and help humankind.

This pioneer blazed many new trails of progress. Generations unborn will reap rich benefits from his legacy. The many-talented Thomas Kilgore Jr. has an incredible record as administrator,

builder, civil rights leader, denominational leader, economic developer, family man, pastor, preacher, prophet, professor, and
pensman. From his pen we read the highest thoughts of American
clergy. Younger scholars seeking a mastery of American religious
history will be studying the life and thought of Thomas Kilgore Jr.

In his book *After Virtue*, Alasdair MacIntyre presents a philosophical discussion of the managerial and therapeutic corruption of
our culture. He writes about the need for our institutions to have
a moral consciousness. Practice must be guided by virtue. The high
point of the life and work of Dr. Kilgore was his integrity. He placed
moral values far above the values of numerical growth and financial
gain. His private morality and his public morality harmonized. The
institutions that he built, managed, and guided could pass the test of
Amos's plumb line of institutional integrity.

I write as a disciple of Dr. Kilgore. He adopted me as a spiritual
son. He was the one who installed me as pastor of Allen Temple
Baptist Church during his tenure as the first African-American presi-
dent of the American Baptist Churches, U.S.A. (ABC/USA). I needed
Dr. Kilgore's wisdom to help me survive the transition from serving
as a field representative of the Ministers and Missionaries Benefit
Board of ABC/USA to becoming an inner-city American Baptist pas-
tor. When I felt like resigning from my position as pastor, it was
Dr. Kilgore who inspired me to persevere. As I matured as a pastor,
Dr. Kilgore opened new doors for me with the Progressive National
Baptist Convention (PNBC).

During his presidency of Progressive Baptists, I was given the
high honor of preaching at the Shrine Auditorium in Los Angeles
at the annual meeting of the convention. Famous preachers like the
late Dr. Howard Thurman and Dr. Lloyd Ogilvie were among the
preachers. As a visionary, Dr. Kilgore always matched the younger
clergy with the senior clergy so that experience could enrich youth.
He taught me to support women in ministry and to train, encour-
age, and promote lay persons for ministry. When I became president
of the PNBC, I had the challenging opportunity not to present my
own agenda but some of the many goals that were introduced to us
by Dr. Kilgore.

The African-American pulpit has produced many matchless orators. Younger pastors and seminarians aspiring to be pastors often
imitate these pulpit giants. The travesty of this practice is that it

divorces prophetic ministry from the pulpit so that electronic messages are used to promote religious entertainment that focuses on making worship a commodity to sell rather than an event to encounter the God who calls us to righteous living and to spiritual intimacy with the Living Christ. Dr. Kilgore continues to teach me and many others through his persuasive and powerful writings that God has called us to be prophetic preachers and not "user-friendly talk show hosts." Dr. Kilgore is numbered among *Ebony* magazine's list of top fifteen great preachers and has been a consultant for the magazine's annual selections, but he was not an entertainer. He was a responsible pulpiteer.

As you read Dr. Kilgore's book, you will begin to appreciate even more the goodness and the greatness of the transforming message of this man. I assure you that this book will empower you for reflective and responsible living in an age that worships technology and neglects the spiritual hunger of the human heart.

J. ALFRED SMITH SR.
Pastor, Allen Temple Baptist Church
Oakland, California
Professor of Preaching and Church Ministries
American Baptist Seminary of the West
Berkeley, California

Part I

Memoirs

Chapter 1

Early Years
1913–1931

In early 1901, Thomas Kilgore migrated from Greenville, South Carolina, to the small town of Woodruff, South Carolina, to work in a cotton oil mill. At age twenty, he had become proficient in two areas: he was a good painter and a good farmer. But Tom, as he was called, was a victim of wanderlust.

He became restless in his Lowendes Hill community on the outskirts of Greenville, so having heard of job openings in the new cotton oil mill in Woodruff, he walked the twenty-eight mile distance, applied for a job, and was hired.

Tom had been in Woodruff but a short time before he met a sixteen-year-old young lady by the name of Eugenia Langston. She was the oldest of three children of Ella Langston, who was the cook and housekeeper of Dr. Posey and his family. Ella Langston's three children were fathered by Vandy Lanford, a prosperous landowner. As Eugenia, Herbert, and Daisy grew up on the Lanford plantation, there were conflicts between them and the Lanford children born to Vandy Lanford's wife. Ella Langston, who was only three generations away from her African slave foreparents, sensed this tension and took a position as cook and housekeeper for the Posey family in Woodruff. She later married George Miles and gave birth to two more children, Joseph and Jessie Mae Miles.

Ella Langston-Miles was my maternal grandmother; her daughter Eugenia was my mother, and Thomas Kilgore was my father.

By the early part of 1902, a courtship had developed between Thomas and Eugenia. He was twenty-two, and she was seventeen. Eugenia had finished seventh grade in the segregated school for black children, and Dr. Posey and Grandmother Miles had made plans to enter her in the academy at Benedict College in Columbia, South

3

Carolina. But the courtship grew stronger, and by midsummer, Tom had convinced Eugenia that she should become his wife instead of entering the academy. In the early fall of 1902, they were married. After their marriage, Tom and Eugenia established residence in a small house on the Coleman farm, and thus began a farming career for the family that lasted the next twenty-two years.

From the fall of 1902 until the summer of 1909, Tom and Eugenia were tenant farmers on the Coleman plantation. As tenant farmers, they furnished labor. Seeds, supplies, farm implements, and stock were furnished by the Colemans. The tenants had the privilege of cultivating a garden, raising chickens and hogs, and producing their own peanuts and sweet potatoes. The basic crops were cotton, corn, cane for molasses, sweet potatoes, peanuts, wheat, and oats. After all crops were gathered in the late summer and fall, there was a settlement. The commonly accepted division at that time was fifty-fifty. The landowner received 50 percent of the sale of all money crops, and the tenant family received 50 percent plus housing.

During the seven years of farming on the Coleman plantation, there were born to Tom and Eugenia the following four sons: Waymon, September 1903; Lamar, April 16, 1905; Frank, November 1, 1906; and Rockerfeller, October 26, 1909.

Tom's desire was to have his own farm, a desire that was never realized. But a development did take place that turned out to be the next best thing to ownership. In the late fall of 1909, he was approached by Matthew Gist, a neighbor. Mr. Gist and his family lived in a four-room house on a 150-acre farm that also had a three-room tenant house. This farm was not owned by Mr. Gist. He leased it from a white Baptist preacher, Rev. Brown. He then had the privilege to sublease the tenant house to whomever he desired. The tenant house was leased to Tom and Eugenia and family, and they moved to the Brown farm a few days before Christmas, 1909. Within a year the Gist family decided to move from the farm into the town of Woodruff, where Mr. Gist began to do public work. This move meant that my family would now occupy the main farmhouse. This also meant that a new lease arrangement was executed between my family and Rev. Brown.

Because my parents' seven years on the Coleman farm had been productive for them and the farm owner, they had a good reputation for honesty and productivity in the community. Therefore, they were able to work out an unusually good lease agreement on the Brown farm. For five bales of cotton a year, the 150-acre farm was leased to them to be farmed and developed as if owned by them. Stock, two mules and a horse, wagon, buggy, farm implements, and many other necessities were bought on credit as my father and brothers began to farm in this new pattern. The tenant house on the farm was rented to a family that leased from my family.

By the time they were well settled as the leasees of the Brown farm, the family began to expand. On October 14, 1911, another son, Wells, was born, and on February 20, 1913, I, Thomas Jr., was born. Sixteen months later, July 31, 1914, the seventh son, Harold, was born.

When I speak of my birth, I must relate a trauma that took place that was told to me by Mama. When I was two months old, I was the victim of a terrible cold that turned to double pneumonia. Our family physician, Dr. McCord, who was Mama's cousin, visited and examined me and stated that I would not live through the night. Aunt Callie, whose family lived in the tenant house on the farm, suggested to Mama that she try an oral medical remedy to see if it would give me relief. She stated that one of the Colemans' mares had recently given birth to a pony, and that a mixture of mare milk and calomel, a white tasteless powder, would break the fever and improve my breathing. The Colemans gave the milk, and Aunt Callie gave the calomel. The dosage was prepared and given to me, and miraculously, by morning, the fever had abated, and I was on the way to recovery.

By 1914, Papa was well in command of the farm. His diversified crops of cotton, corn, wheat, oats, sweet potatoes, cane, peanuts, and assorted vegetables were tended by him and the older sons, Waymon, Lamar, and Frank. The farm was also well stocked with cattle and hogs.

As the farm developed, so did Papa's and Mama's interest in the community. In New Bethel Baptist Church they were deacon and deaconess; they were lodge members, and both were active on the informal school board for the African-American children.

In the Woodruff school system, a typical southern one, the white children were housed in a fine brick steam-heated building, and the black children were housed in a four-room frame building, heated by a round pot-bellied stove. I can never forget the many cold mornings that my brothers and I went to school and had to make the fire in the stove and warm ourselves before we began our classes.

Before I started to school at the age of five and a half, I had learned to read and write and do simple arithmetic. I also formed the habit of asking Mama questions. I wanted to know why black and white children went to different schools, and why black and white people went to different churches. I raised other questions, such as, "How does Santa Claus come down the chimney?" and "What is the difference between a bull and an ox?" Even though such questions were puzzling, Mama always had a satisfactory answer.

In spite of our Christian grounding, superstitions abounded in our community. One of these was centered around our oil-burning lamps. It was thought that if you inhaled in the process of blowing out a lamp and the blaze seemed to come toward your mouth, you would swallow the blaze. The customary remedy to put out the swallowed blaze was to drown it with wine.

One hot summer's night, Mama and Papa went to a lodge meeting and left Waymon in charge of his six younger brothers. Because of the heat, we slept on floor pallets instead of our regular beds. Just before he went to bed, Waymon proceeded to blow out the lamp and inhaled in the process. As the light went out, he exclaimed, "I swallowed the blaze!" whereupon he aroused all of us from our pallets, and in our night clothes, with Jack, our dog, we walked through the quarter of a mile wooded area between our house and Aunt Callie's. Upon reaching her house, Lamar knocked on the door, and Aunt Callie responded, "Who is it?" Lamar answered, "The Kilgore boys." She opened the door and said, "What do you boys want?" Lamar answered, "Waymon was blowing out the lamp and swallowed the blaze." Aunt Callie said to all of us, "Come in here." She then took Waymon into the kitchen, took a jug of wine from a shelf, and poured a large glassful, gave it to Waymon, and said, "Drink all of it, boy." This Waymon did. Then she told us to go on back home. Needless to say, fourteen-year-old Waymon was drunk by the time we got back home. But beyond a doubt, the blaze had been extinguished.

•

As our family grew, we learned many good lessons. For the first seven boys, the farm life presented an opportunity to share, to cooperate, and to resolve sibling conflicts without doing any irreparable bodily damage. But there was one occasion when permanent damage was almost inflicted. It was a balmy spring day, and a heavy shower of rain came, leaving a little stream on the outer edge of our front yard. I was playing in that stream, and my brother Rockerfeller was about ten yards away from me, shooting at birds with a slingshot. He turned to look at me, and said, "Do you believe I will shoot you?" I answered, "No." By the time the word was out of my mouth, he had released a stone from the slingshot that found its target on the tip of two of my front teeth, breaking off about a third of each tooth. When Mama finished with him, he found different targets thereafter for his sling-shooting.

Even though we did many devilish things as farm boys, such as riding the neighbors' bulls in a nearby pasture and shooting rocks with slingshots at gamblers on the banks of a creek on our farm, we also learned many valuable lessons in the art of cooperation. There was wood to be cut for heating and cooking purposes; water to be drawn; mules and horses to be fed, watered, and groomed; hogs and chickens to be fed; cows to be fed and milked; and many other odd jobs inside and outside the house. These chores were divided among us, giving each one of us specific tasks to perform. Our major job in the late spring, the summer, and early fall was to be efficient field hands. This meant that each of us had to learn how to plow, plant and cultivate crops and, in due time, to harvest them.

While we were still on the farm, and before Harold, the seventh boy was twenty-six months old, our first sister, Malissa, was born on August 31, 1916. She was named for Papa's Aunt Malissa, an aristocratic matron who specialized in buying fine clothes, expensive china, crystalware and silverware, and other fine household artifacts. Her husband, Uncle Columbus Woodruff, was a first-class chef in fine resort hotels in upstate New York in the summers and in hotels in Florida during the winters.

Sixteen months after Malissa was born, Ella Maye arrived on December 31, 1917, and was named for Grandmother Ella Miles. On May 16, 1920, Herman, the eighth son was born. He was followed by Thaddeus Daniel, on February 16, 1922, and the third daughter, the last of the twelve children, was born March 16, 1924. She was named Mamie Beatrice. Thaddeus and Mamie were named for Papa's sister Mamie and her husband, Thaddeus.

Papa was Aunt Malissa's favorite nephew, and she almost demanded that the first girl in the family be named Malissa. As Malissa and Ella Mae grew up, Aunt Malissa created a problem in our family by lavishly spending money on fine clothes for her namesake and paying little or no attention to Ella Mae. This forced Mama, with her meager financial resources, to try to dress Ella Mae comparably to Malissa.

At the end of World War I, after the armistice was signed, Papa continued to succeed on the farm. Cotton prices were good, and other cash crops added to the family income. By 1922, Waymon, who had never liked to farm and who became ill while picking cotton and peas or pulling fodder from corn stalks, was given permission to take a job in a nearby cotton mill. He worked a fifty-five-hour week and earned twenty cents an hour. This weekly cash income in the family helped greatly. It also helped to make payments on the new 1922 Model-T Ford touring car that Papa bought. Our family was the second black family in the community to own a car, and it not only provided quicker transportation for our family than our horse and buggy had, but was also used to transport our neighbors.

From the mid-teen years to 1922, the farm had been productive, and the income from farm products had made possible a comfortable standard of living for us. All of us who were school age had attended school and were regular in our attendance at Sunday school and worship services each first and third Sunday when the preacher came.

My own experiences in church and Sunday school were somewhat different from my brothers' and sisters'. From the time I was five or six, I was fascinated by the presence in our home of ministers, teachers, and other public figures who partook of the hospitality of our guest room. The demeanor and language of these public figures ignited something in my psyche that made me want to emulate them. When I was four years old, I asked my parents if I could line a hymn in the church worship service. They received permission from Pastor J. C. Goode, and on the next Lord's day worship, I stood on the pulpit rostrum and from memory lined the stanzas of the hymn, "I Heard the Voice of Jesus Say," as the congregation sang after I repeated each line.

New Bethel Baptist was a gothic-type frame building with stained-glass windows. It had no of extra rooms, with the exception of the study for the pastor and one other small utility room. This meant that all Sunday school classes were held in the sanctuary. As a boy in the primary class, I was taught from picture cards, but I had a problem in this class because across the room from our class was the adult Bible class taught by Brother Samuel DeShields, who had a heavy voice and was very plain and explicit in his teaching. My parents and I soon discovered that my attention was not on the card class, but rather in Brother DeShields's class, and before long I was "promoted" from the card class to the adult Bible class.

As a boy, I was so enamored with church life that I started a "play" church with my younger brothers and sisters. When our cotton house was empty, after cotton picking season, we used it to play church. We sang hymns, I preached, and from time to time we held funerals for dead chickens and birds. The official mourner at these funerals was my sister Malissa, who could cry almost at the drop of a hat.

During the years 1922–23, some changes took place in our family life. My brother Lamar, after having finished the ninth grade (which was the highest grade taught at Woodruff Rosenwald School for "colored children"), was accepted at South Carolina State College, where he studied for two years. My brother Waymon married Ada Foster, and after a year their daughter Magnolia was born. They moved to Brevard, North Carolina, where Grandmother Ella Miles and her family had relocated. My brother Frank was busy collecting eggs from the chickens' stray nests and selling them. He was also cutting wood from the back side of the farm and selling it. His two older brothers often wondered why he seemed always to have more money than they.

In their mid- and late teens, my four older brothers had made professions of faith and joined the church, and in August 1922 my brother Wells and I made our professions and were baptized into church membership.

All did not go well between the late teens and 1923. As the country settled down after World War I, prices of cotton and other farm commodities dropped. To add insult to injury, the 1922 cotton crop was practically devastated by the boll weevil. In 1923, cotton farmers like Papa had somewhat abated the damage done by boll weevils by applying a mixture of arsenic and molasses to the squares of the cotton stalk, but this relief was undermined by another drop in cotton prices. During the good days, cotton had sold for forty to forty-two cents a pound. In 1923, it dropped to the mid-thirties. Papa held back the sale of eighteen bales of cotton, hoping for the price to go up. After holding it for two months, he was forced to sell. He sold it for eighteen cents a pound. This sounded the death knell for our farm life, so in early 1924 we moved from the Brown farm to the town of Woodruff. Aunt Malissa and Uncle Columbus had passed, after willing their six-room house and four acres of land to Papa, in trust for my sister Malissa.

The adjustment from farm life to small-town living was made smoothly because some of my brothers and I were able to find after-school jobs. One brother became a delivery boy for John Floyd's grocery store. The Floyd family was our closest neighbor, and when she entertained, Mrs. Floyd regularly borrowed Mama's fine linen, silverware, china, and crystal glasses, which had been inherited from Aunt Malissa. It is interesting that the segregated mores of the South permitted a white family to use a black family's dining materials although it was unthinkable for the two families to eat together.

At age eleven, I was given permission by my parents to work in the afternoon and on Saturdays for a white friend of my mother, Mrs. Eliza Rogers, the wife of the owner of the only men's clothing store in Woodruff. She was a kind and graceful lady. She paid me ten cents an hour and gave me gifts of ties and other clothing from time to time, and I responded to her as if she were a second mother. Two of her greatest interests, beyond her family, were her church work and her beautiful flower garden. Both of these interests impressed me greatly, and she also added to my parents' teachings the importance of integrity, hard work, beauty, and friendliness.

•

Uncle Herbert Langston, Mama's brother, and his daughter, Daisy, moved to Brevard, North Carolina, after the death of his wife, Aunt Marie, and my brothers Lamar and Frank left to find jobs in Brevard at the end of 1925.

In the absence of the many chores that farm life demanded, Mama found time to take a job cooking the dinner meal for a nearby white family. During the same time, Papa was doing odd jobs, and the responsibility for cooking and housekeeping was left to Rockerfeller and me.

In early 1926, Papa, Rockerfeller, and I left for Brevard, and in July of '26, the rest of the family followed. Months later, the house in Woodruff was sold, and we purchased a house in Brevard.

There is an interesting sequel related to our moving from Woodruff. The packing and preparation for moving was done mainly by Mama and Wells, with the help of some neighbors. Two trips were made on successive days. The first day's load was primarily furniture. The second load was made up of some furniture and barrels packed with linens, bedding, dishes, crystal, and silverware. When the second load was delivered by the movers, the barrel was missing that contained the fine china and crystal that the Floyds had often borrowed. To this day it is not known what happened to that barrel.

As we settled in Brevard, Lamar was working as an orderly in the hospital, Frank and Rockerfeller were working in the leather tannery, and Papa was looking for land to farm. In the meantime, he plied his earlier trade as a painter.

Brevard was a new experience for our family. It was a town just a bit larger than Woodruff, but very different in many ways. Mountainous Brevard's cool summer climate was attractive to tourists from the warmer southern states. There were only a few farmers in Transylvania County, of which Brevard was the county seat. The town and county's economic strength was bolstered by a tannery, a small cotton thread mill, a lumber company, a small resort hotel, many resort boarding houses, summer camps, and countless bootleggers. It was always a source of fun for us children to gather in front of the courthouse on Main Street and watch the revenue officers pour down the drain gallons upon gallons of "white lightning" that had been confiscated from one of the many corn liquor stills scattered throughout the mountains.

Church life in Brevard was different from that in South Carolina. Worship services were held each Sunday instead of each first and third Sunday. There were four churches in the black community, the largest and oldest of which was Bethel Baptist Church, organized in 1865. Our family chose to worship and work in Bethel. We became accustomed to attendance in Sunday school, two worship services, and B.Y.T.U. (Baptist Youth Training Union) every Sunday.

Rev. A. H. Wilson was Bethel's pastor, and he was assisted by three young ministers: Rev. Smith, Rev. Bailey, and Rev. Lloyd. My observance of these three young ministers functioning in the worship services and carrying out other church duties deepened my interest in becoming a minister. I became very active in the church. By the time I was fourteen, I was president of the B.Y.T.U., teacher of a Sunday school class, and financial secretary for the church. I also attended conventions and association meetings with Pastor Wilson.

The Rosenwald School for black children in Brevard was inferior in building and supplies to the white elementary and high schools, but teachers like Mrs. J. H. Johnstone, who taught four generations of Brevard children, her daughter, Coragreen, who taught me in the ninth grade, and Professor J. L. Jones, who was the principal during my eighth and ninth grades, were teachers who had proper credentials and were charged with a deep desire to motivate us to learn, regardless of the handicaps of segregation.

At the beginning of the summer of 1927, I became involved in a small business venture with a friendly white businessman, Mr. Moore, who owned a shoeshine stand on Main Street. The operator of the stand left town, and I was asked to operate it. Mr. Moore furnished all supplies and licenses, and I operated the stand for a split of the income, forty-sixty in my favor. Though a shoeshine was ten cents, many customers gave a quarter, and I felt that I was in a profitable business when my income on one Saturday was $10.20. When the summer ended, I had saved enough money to buy school clothes and supplies for myself and some of my younger sisters and brothers.

During the school year 1927–28, I competed with schoolmates Homer Kemp, Kemp Smith, and Cyrus Mooney for grades. Homer Kemp and I came out with the highest grade point averages. During that same year I also learned to be a good croquet player and, under the tutelage of teacher Coragreen Johnstone, developed a keen interest in English literature and poetry.

When school closed at the end of May 1928, public education for me ended, as it did for all black children in Transylvania County when they reached the ninth grade. The white children had the advantage of a standard high school. Because of this segregated arrangement, black parents who wanted to further the education of their children faced the burden of placing them in public or private high schools outside of the county.

A traumatic incident in my life led to my having to leave the county and in turn to my gaining admission to Stephens Lee High

School in Asheville, North Carolina. One afternoon in mid-August I was walking home from my summer job at the Wallace boarding house to rest a while before my evening shift there as a waiter serving dinner. I was stopped by a schoolmate, Herschell Thomas, who was driving his uncle's car with his girlfriend in the front seat and her older sister in the back seat. Herschell's permission to take his girlfriend for a ride was given by her mother only if the older sister went along. He asked me to go along with them for the ride, and I consented.

After driving a few miles out of town, we stopped on the roadside, and he and his girlfriend walked several yards away, and her sister and I got out of the car and talked. Suddenly, two cars drove up, and out jumped the county sheriff and three deputies. The sheriff confronted me and said, "You're under arrest for lewd and insulting remarks that you made to that white lady about forty minutes ago." I replied that I didn't know what he was talking about. He and one of the deputies threw me in his car, and the other two deputies were instructed to see that my friend and the sisters followed their car to the county jail. On the way to the county jail, Sheriff Tom Woods stopped at a house on the roadside, and a woman came out to greet him. They stood and talked for about ten minutes, and he returned to the car and drove into town.

When we arrived at the jail, my friend and the two young ladies were released, and I was locked in a jail cell. In a few moments the sheriff and one of his deputies came into the cell, and for two hours tried to force me to admit that I made lewd and insulting remarks to the woman. My constant answer was, "You may beat me, or even kill me, but I know that I have not insulted anyone, and I will not lie."

For three days I remained in jail. The first night was horrible, but after that I was calm and unafraid.

The reputation of Sheriff Tom Woods in the black community was about as low as it could be, and the community was much disturbed by my arrest. Papa had to be restrained. It was generally believed that my arrest was due to the sheriff's reaction to some transaction between him and the sheriff.

I was indicted, and a trial date was set. Papa retained a lawyer from a nearby town. At the trial, the woman that I was supposed to have insulted did not show, but the magistrate accepted the word of the sheriff and sentenced me to six months on the chain gang; however, he was sternly reminded by the lawyer defending me that I was a juvenile and therefore could not be sentenced as an adult. The magistrate then sentenced me to get out of the county for a year. My lawyer did not object to this, and that closed the case. Within two weeks, my parents found a place for me to stay in Asheville, and I entered Stephens Lee High School, where I was enrolled in the tenth grade.

I will always be grateful to my landlady, Mrs. Washington, a widow, her sister, Mrs. Shepherd, and her daughter for accepting me as a member of the family during my two years of high school work. My parents paid them $5 a week for my room and board. Subsequently, five of my younger brothers and sisters attended Stephens Lee High School and stayed in the Washington home.

For the first time in my life, I was away from my parents and my brothers and sisters. Accustomed as I was to small-town and country living, the "bigness" of the city of Asheville somewhat overwhelmed me at first and created a feeling of loneliness, but within two weeks an incident happened that changed this forever. Late one afternoon, when I was standing on Mrs. Washington's front porch feeling lonesome, a handsome young man across the street came out of his front door and stopped for a moment, looked at me, and said, "Hey, come over here." I walked over and met Bill Downs. That meeting was the beginning of a friendship that lasted for forty-eight years, until his death. Bill was the only child of his foster parents, who had raised him from a tiny baby that they found on their front doorsteps in Greer, South Carolina.

As our friendship developed, I was impressed with his friendliness, his sense of humor, his sartorial splendor in dressing, his beautiful voice, and his love for the church. I soon became a watchcare member in Nazareth First Baptist Church, where he was a member and sang in the choir. In due time, he got me a part-time job making $5 a week in a jewelry store where he was working. Bill was five years older than I and had finished high school three years before we met.

The two years at Stephens Lee High School were good years for me. My teachers, Mrs. Walker, Mrs. Martin, Mr. Arnold, Mr. Mc-Corcle, and Mr. Long, impressed on me the value of hard study and preparation, as well as the necessity of good moral character. I made many friends among the students, some of whom are still my friends.

Two of them, Johnnie Mae Humbert and the late Mary Brewer, married two of my brothers, Wells and Rockerfeller, respectively.

My scholastic average in high school gave me membership in the Crown and Scepter Club. In manual training, I won first place by building a porch set composed of a swing, bench, and chair. I also received a gold coin award for winning first prize in a declamation contest, speaking on the subject "Achieving Life's Goals through Education." Graduation from high school on June 6, 1930, was a realization of a goal that I had looked forward to achieving.

Parallel to my interest in school was my interest in the church. I attended worship services regularly, sang in the youth choir, attended Sunday school and prayer meetings, and in my high school senior year, was elected president of the Young People's Progressive Club. Of the forty-five or fifty members in the club, I was the youngest. Two of our club members knew some young people who lived in "Black Bottom," an area of town that was looked upon as a cesspool of gamblers, drunkards, and prostitutes. In one of our meetings, we decided that as young Christians, we were responsible for witnessing to the young people and others in Black Bottom, so our two members who knew youth in the area arranged for us to have one of our monthly meetings in one of their homes. The meeting was held and was well attended, and we were able to persuade some of the youth in the area to start attending church services.

The next Sunday in church, rumors spread that the Young People's Progressive Club met in Black Bottom and were playing cards, drinking, and dancing. All of these acts were considered cardinal sins. As president of the club, I called a special meeting, and we selected a committee to find out who started the rumor. A few days later, Pastor Gordon called me and said he wanted to talk with me. As I entered his house, with fear and trembling, he said to me, "I hear that your club met in Black Bottom." Starting to speak, I said, "But..." He cut me off and asked me if we were dancing, playing cards, and drinking at the meeting. My answer was, "No, sir." He then asked me about the committee we appointed. I told him that we wanted to know who started the false rumor. After I finished, he said, "My boy, I want you to remember what I am going to say. If someone starts a rumor on you and it's a lie, if you try to run it down, it will run you to death, but if you let it alone and forget it, it will die." I have never forgotten this advice from a moral genius.

A few days before Christmas, 1929, Bill Downs and I were walking home from a friend's house where we had participated in a lively card game of whist. I said to Bill, "I don't think that I should be wasting my time playing cards because I believe I have been called to preach." Bill answered, "Boy! Why did you say that? I have been thinking the same thing." On the second Sunday in January 1930, Bill preached his first sermon at Nazareth First Baptist Church. I followed by preaching my first sermon at Bethel Baptist Church in Brevard on the fifth Sunday in January 1930. My text was Matthew 21:22: "And all things whatsoever you shall ask in prayer, believing, you shall receive."

•

I had eagerly looked forward to entering Shaw University in the fall of 1930. I had been active in the Blue Ridge Educational Convention, of which my pastor, Rev. Wilson, was the president. The convention had accumulated $12,500 to be spent for scholarship assistance for young people going to college, and I was voted a scholarship to enter Shaw in the fall.

My family helped me to make preparations to leave for college, and a few days before the time of departure, Pastor Wilson and I went to the convention treasurer's home to get the money for my scholarship. I remained in the car filled with great expectations of what college would be like.

In about forty minutes, Pastor Wilson came out the door, and as he looked directly toward me, I perceived that all was not well. His usual open and friendly countenance was replaced with a look of utter frustration and disappointment. He got in the car and said, "Son, I hate to tell you this, but you cannot go to Shaw this fall because there is no money in the treasury." We then drove silently back to Brevard.

Later I learned the details of the empty treasury. The convention's treasurer had operated a coal yard for several years and was considered a prosperous black businessman. In an attempt to expand his business, he had used the convention's money but was planning to replace it; however, two mild winters had seriously reduced his income, and he was unable to do so. Now the treasurer was hoping that the coming winter would be much colder so he could replace the convention money. Alas, my request for funds came too early for his plan. Within a year, he had died. When his estate was settled, the convention received its portion: $218. Three years later the Blue Ridge Educational Convention went out of existence.

College education for me in the fall of 1930 was now out of the question. What next? I was determined to go to college, and I was just as determined to find a full-time job to earn some money to enroll in college the next school year. I went to Mr. Dickerson, the business manager of the jewelry store where I had worked part-time, and asked for a full-time job, but he said there was no opening; however, I knew that he was sympathetic to my desire to go to college. He then said, "My wife has an opening in our boarding house; go and talk with her about a full-time job." I went and talked with Mrs. Dickerson and was hired as a butler, waiter, and chauffeur for $8 a week and tips, plus a room on the premises.

As I reflect on the year and three months that I worked for the Dickersons, there are a few incidents worth mentioning. One day as I was serving tea in the parlor, I overheard a conversation between Mrs. Dickerson and a guest. The guest said, "This young butler of yours seems to be very competent and well mannered." Mrs. Dickerson answered, "Yes, and he is so different from the former butler, who often tried to engage guests in conversation, as if he was somebody." I was shocked by the comment and wondered whether she thought that I was "somebody."

A few weeks later, I emphatically demonstrated that I was somebody. One of my duties was to answer the telephone and the doorbell during meal hours. As I was serving lunch, the doorbell rang. I answered and was returning to take the tray of food to the dining room, but before I reached the pantry, the telephone rang. I answered, and by the time I did that and returned to the pantry, I heard Mrs. Dickerson's footsteps coming from the dining room. She opened the door of the pantry and in a harsh tone of voice said, "Tom, what is wrong? The guests have been waiting too long for their next course. Get it out there as fast as you can." When she entered the pantry, I had already picked up the tray, but after her command, I put the tray down and said, "The doorbell rang, and I answered it, and before I could return to serving, the telephone rang. There's the tray of food. If I am not serving it fast enough, you should get someone else." She turned and reentered the dining room, and I resumed serving the guests. As I carried out my duties in the dining room, I kept thinking about what she had said about Edward, the former butler, and how my response to her harsh command was to let her know that I was somebody. Evidently she understood, for after the lunch hour she came to the pantry and apologized for speaking so harshly to me.

Another unforgettable incident that took place at the boarding house involved Robert, the son of "Cookie," the eighty-six-year-old Mrs. Margaret Alexander, who for more than fifty years was the housekeeper and cook for the Dickersons. Robert was the handyman and was rumored to be Mr. Dickerson's son. He and his now retired mother lived on the premises as I did. Robert had a habit of celebrating his half day off on Thursdays by going off and getting drunk, then returning to the house in a highly inebriated state. On one Thursday, Robert came to work drunk as usual and encountered Miss Morning, the housekeeper for the boarding house, who was white, and who had a habit of her own that was resented by all of the black workers. When she passed one of us in a hallway, she would exhibit her bigoted authority by saying, "Step aside." Well, one of Robert's jobs was to see that the hallways were kept clean, so on this particular Thursday while Robert was doing his duty, Miss Morning came down the hall, met Robert, and said, "Step aside." Robert looked straight at her and said, "Step aside yourself," and added some expletives that are unprintable. Miss Morning had to take two days off to regain her composure, and afterward there was no more "Step aside." Though Robert continued to drink, Miss Morning's habit was forever broken.

The fifteen months at the boarding house seemed to pass quickly. I spent a few days with my family in Brevard, and on September 1, 1931, I boarded a bus with a friend and classmate, Corrette Woodward, bound for Atlanta, Georgia, and Morehouse College. I had saved enough money for one semester's tuition ($40), two months' room, board, and laundry ($22), and the student activity fee ($12).

Chapter 2

Morehouse College
1931–1935

The orientation ceremonies at Morehouse were inspiring and challenging. The faculty and staff were gracious and encouraging. But the sophomores were not so congenial. When Woodward and I arrived on the campus with our trunks, we were met by several sophomores whose trunks were also in the hallway of Graves Hall. Their greeting was, "Welcome 'dogs'; you are here in time to take our trunks upstairs." Of course we cooperated. Among those sophomores were two persons whom I thought I would hate forever. After all, for almost two years I had been a licensed preacher, but was now treated with the indignity of being called a dog. The hazing by the sophomores soon ended, however, and Herman Fields and Ghost Curry turned out to be two good friends.

Because it was necessary for me to work in order to stay in school, I took a job as the teachers' waiter. This made it possible for me to have the same bill of fare as the teachers and staff. To say the least, there was a real difference between theirs and that of the students, whose menu on Wednesday evenings was peanut butter, syrup, and bread.

Early in the second semester of my freshman year, an unforgettable dining room incident took place. I was standing behind the teachers' table, which was partially hidden by steps coming from the floor above into the dining room. Suddenly, there emerged from the kitchen a student with a fully loaded .32-caliber handgun. The day before, Dube, a Nigerian student, who worked in the kitchen, had been "roughed up" by the food service manager, Mr. Robinson, and was now in the process of settling the score. As he slowly walked toward the teachers' table, his roommate attempted to stop him, but Dube pointed the gun at him, and he quickly retreated. Fear and pandemonium permeated the dining room. Students rushed the main exit. In the meantime, Dube was moving slowly toward the teachers' table. I was standing close to a window. I raised it, knocked the screen out, and jumped out. Simultaneously, Mr. Robinson shielded himself with Dr. L. O. Lewis, and jumped out the window that I had raised. The students who had not been able to get out of the dining room said that Dube shook his head in disgust and disappointment when his intended victim escaped. Campus rumor had it that Mr. Robinson did not stop running until he reached his home in East Point, several miles from the campus. Dube quietly went to the president's home following the episode, told him what happened, and gave him the gun. The president dismissed Robinson and permitted Dube to continue his studies at Morehouse.

Early in my freshman year, I was invited by two seniors, Milton Curry and Ernest Jordan, to attend Sunday worship with them at Ebenezer Baptist Church. Rev. Martin Luther King Sr. had recently become pastor of the church following the death of his father-in-law, Rev. A. D. Williams. I was completely captivated by the friendliness and kindness shown to me by the King family. After I had attended worship services at Ebenezer for only a few Sundays, Dr. King gave me opportunities to teach Sunday school class and, because I was a licensed preacher, occasionally to deliver a sermon . Mrs. Williams and Mrs. King invited me to their home for Sunday dinner from time to time. Compared to Morehouse dinners, dinner at the Kings' house was a rare treat.

The visits in the Williams-King home afforded me the opportunity to interact with the children, Christine, Martin Jr., and A. D. At two years and nine months of age, Martin Jr. was the most outgoing and talkative of the three. At this early age, he showed evidence of an inquisitive mind.

My first year at Morehouse was a busy one. I was elected president of my class, was active in the campus YMCA, played forward on the freshman basketball team, and made the honor roll. George Smith and I were the only two freshmen admitted to the newly organized University Players. Both of us played in that year's production of Shakespeare's *Macbeth*.

•

As I entered my sophomore year at Morehouse, I had become deeply impressed with the "Morehouse mystique." This indefinable description for the demeanor of Morehouse students created in new students a desire to excel academically, to interact socially in a positive way, and to demonstrate genuine moral and spiritual values in everyday living. It didn't matter whether you were in Professor Dansby's math class, Professor Lewis's speech class, Professor Whitney's psychology class, or Professor Hubert's religion and philosophy class; you were challenged to excel.

During my years at Morehouse, practically all of the students had been negatively affected by racial segregation, but in spite of this damnable social scourge, the administration, faculty, and staff spared no pains in emphasizing to students that the quality of life was not determined by the color of one's skin. This position prompted Professor L. O. Lewis in a chapel service to correct Kendall Weisiger, the white chairman of the Morehouse Trustee Board, who on two occasions during his chapel remarks used the term "Negra." When he finished, Professor Lewis rose and commended him for his remarks. He then corrected him by saying, "Mr. Weisiger, the word "N-e-g-r-o" is pronounced "knee-grow" and not "Neg-ra."

My sophomore and junior years were years of hard study, many campus activities, and a new position that made it possible for me to remain at Morehouse. Because I did not have funds for tuition and room and board on the campus, Dr. and Mrs. Hubert permitted me to live in their home. In return, I helped with the house cleaning and cooking and drove their son, Jerome, to and from school.

•

For the first few months of my sophomore year, I experienced a feeling of real frustration. I had made the dean's list my freshman year and was hopeful that I would maintain a high scholastic average. Yet I needed to find a balance between the necessary hours for study, my responsibilities in the Hubert home, and time for campus activities, which included being president of my class, being active in the University Players, and being chairman of the campus YMCA. By the end of the first semester, I solved the problem by dropping some of my extracurricular activities and spending less time socializing. Near the end of the second semester, I pledged to become a member of the Omega Psi Phi Fraternity.

My junior year at Morehouse was a tough but fulfilling one. I was elected secretary of the Student Government Association (SGA), performed in two presentations of the University Players, and was elected president of the Atlanta Intercollegiate Association, an inter-racial group of students from Atlanta colleges. I also participated in a city-wide oratorical contest sponsored by the American Bible Society. The requirement for entering was to write an essay of fifteen hundred to two thousand words on the subject "The Bible as Liter-ature." I won first place. The new Morehouse president, Dr. S. H. Archer, attended the event and asked me later to present the paper in chapel.

In the spring of my junior year, I was elected president of the Stu-dent Government Association and basileus of my fraternity, and I moved back on campus. Mary McLeod Bethune had convinced Pres-ident Roosevelt to create the National Youth Administration, from which Morehouse received a grant and was appointed to develop a project that would involve twenty students in some kind of "upward bound" activities. Contact was made with twenty churches, each of which received a student who had to initiate programs for young people in the areas of drama, music, and athletics. Each student was paid $15 a month, and I was paid $20 a month as director of this program.

My senior year was not a great year for me academically, but it was productive in other ways. My highest grades were in two classes at Atlanta University, under the tutelage of Dr. W. E. B. Du Bois. The class in the spring semester, "The Reconstruction Period," was given just after Dr. Du Bois finished writing his book *Black Reconstruc-tion*. I was privileged to be one of four students in this spring class who were assigned to read the proofs. To have been exposed to the teaching of one of the world's greatest scholars was an opportunity I will ever cherish.

My studies and activities on the campus did not demand all of my time. Like most Morehouse men, I was attracted by the young ladies on our sister campus, Spelman. During my junior year, I developed a positive social relationship with a senior at Spelman, Eleanor Frazier, the daughter of a professional educator in Baton Rouge, Louisiana. However, after her graduation, she began teaching, our relationship waned, and she married Rev. H. Beecher Hicks Sr. (Many years later, after I married and my wife and I had two daughters, we had oc-casion to visit the Hicks family. Our younger daughter, who was about six years old, knowing nothing of my college courtship with the former Eleanor Frazier, wrote in the Hicks's guest book, "I love you." This brought much laughter from the Hickses and Kilgores. To add to the irony, our elder daughter, as a young woman living for a time in Washington, D.C., became a member of Metropolitan Baptist Church, pastored by Rev. H. Beecher Hicks Jr.)

Our Inter-collegiate Council held bimonthly public forums at a Methodist church in downtown Atlanta in which we presented outstanding public speakers. In the spring of 1935, Mrs. Eleanor Roosevelt accepted our invitation to address our council. As we gathered at the church for the meeting, we were confronted by city police and the American Legion. We were told that we could not follow our usual practice of nonsegregated seating. They were explicit and stated that blacks and whites could sit on the same floor, but in separate aisles, or either group could sit downstairs while the other group sat upstairs. We decided not to contest their ruling and quietly left the church and held our meeting on the Spelman campus. At previous meetings, our seating arrangement had always been nonsegregated. But at previous meetings, Eleanor Roosevelt had not been our speaker. Although Mrs. Roosevelt was not popular in the South, because she was the first lady of our country, our otherwise unnoticed meetings would have attracted the public's attention and possibly have made an issue of the students' integrated seating.

•

As the day of graduation drew near, I found myself moving in too many directions. First, there was the Spelman dance, the first one ever held on that campus. As president of the Morehouse SGA, I was asked to lead the dance with the president of the Spelman student body. Since I could not dance, I asked Miss Mildred Burch, the president's secretary, to give me a few lessons, which she graciously did.

The evening arrived for Spelman's inaugural dance. The hall was packed with Morehouse and Spelman students, and the Spelman student president and I moved to the center of the floor. I was greatly relieved when she led the dance, and I managed to follow properly. I was much more relieved when all of the other students came on the dance floor and joined us. After that dance, I took the position of President Archer, who often said in chapel that students spend too much time dancing and partying. He would conclude by saying, "I have two objections to dancing," looking sharply down at his feet. That is exactly how I felt about my first and last dance.

In addition to the Spelman dance, campus elections for the next school year were also taking place as final exams and graduation day were fast approaching. Student politics captivated my interest with the Alphas and Sigmas pitted against the Kappas and Omegas. John Long, a junior and an Alpha, was the most capable person for editor of the campus paper. Though I was an Omega, I believed that the welfare of the school should supersede student politics, so I supported John. The Omegas called a meeting and threatened to impeach me, but I convinced them that I was right. And John won.

Then there was the class play, with which I was also involved. Ann Cook and S. M. Ross, professors of drama at Spelman and Morehouse, wrote our class play and asked me to take the lead role. The play was a critique of the quality of fraternity politics at Morehouse. In the flux of activities, including final exams, I found it hard to concentrate on the play. Even though my ability to memorize was good, at this time it was overworked. On the day of the Class Day exercise, the play started off well, but as it moved along, I began forgetting and ad libbing. We finally made it to the end, and Professor Ross came to me and said, "Thank you, Tom." I said, "Thanks for what?" He answered, "For writing a new play."

The day of graduation came, and on that day I experienced a disappointment that seemed catastrophic to me. The highest honor that a graduating senior at Morehouse can receive is the Best Man of Affairs Award. It was generally conceded by my classmates and many of the faculty and staff that I would be the recipient. I had been superactive, a good representative for the school, and had kept a good grade point average — until the last semester of my senior year. On graduation day when all the other awards had been announced, President Archer made the appropriate remarks and then said, "The Best Man of Affairs Award for the Class of 1935 goes to Malachi Charles Darkins." My heart skipped a beat, my countenance fell, and I wanted to disappear. But Darkins was my best friend, and at the end of the exercises I congratulated him heartily.

I had prayed for this award, I had dreamed about it, and I wanted it more than anything else in the world, but I had failed to meet all the requirements for it. I had prayed hard, but my academic priorities were not in order. I had learned a lesson, and it taught me a new dimension in prayer. I walked around that graduation day, and many days afterward, praying a new prayer that I still pray at times even now. It is simply this: "Lord, help me never to seek honor, and help me to do my best at all times. Help me to put first things first and to choose priorities according to Your will." I have had many disappointments since the one at my graduation, but they have never hurt the way that one did.

Even though I experienced great disappointment on the day of my graduation, it was a day of great joy because Mama came to witness the first of her children graduating from college. I said to her that day that I was so glad that Papa came to Woodruff when he did, and that he persuaded her to marry him instead of going to Benedict College. If she had gone to college, it is unlikely that she would have given birth to twelve children, and maybe not even six, and where would I be now? She answered by saying, "All things work for good for those who love the Lord."

Chapter 3

North Carolina
1935–1947

The summer of 1935 was a busy one for me. Rev. Wilson, the pastor of our home church, asked me to serve as his assistant, with the responsibility of working with the young people of the church.

As we planned programs and events, I reflected on the humiliation of my arrest and trial in 1928. I asked the pastor for permission to invite the Morehouse Quartet that had performed for President Roosevelt along with violinist Drew Days, a senior at Morehouse, to present a concert in the auditorium at the county courthouse. Pastor Wilson gave permission, and the young people of the church and I sold tickets and saturated the county with handbills. On the evening of the concert, the auditorium was packed with a predominantly white audience.

During the intermission, I stood in the same spot that I had stood in seven years prior when I was sentenced to leave the county because I was falsely convicted for insulting a white woman. I surveyed the massive audience and said, "I stand in this spot, where I was falsely condemned, to say that I have forgiven everyone who took part in the kangaroo court action that was designed to destroy me, and I have invited my friends to give this concert tonight as a gift of beauty and inspiration for an act of ignominy and shame." For a moment there was complete silence and then a burst of applause.

Along with my work in the church, I was constantly looking for employment. Full-time employment was a great necessity for me. Even though the Depression had waned somewhat, jobs were still hard to find. I had earlier sent an application to the county superintendent of schools for a position of principal or teacher. There was a vacancy, but when I was interviewed, the superintendent said that I was too young for the job.

That summer there were six brothers and sisters younger than I, and two of them were ready and eager to enter college. To compound the financial problems, Papa, whose health had declined, was too ill to plant and cultivate his fifteen acres of corn, so with the help of Herman and Thaddeus, who were fifteen and thirteen years old, I volunteered to do the farming. We prepared the ground, planted the corn, and cultivated it, producing over six thousand bushels, the sales from which greatly aided the family.

Even though I was born on a farm and worked in the fields as a boy, this experience taught me some new lessons. In early July, when the corn was about three or four feet tall, a terrible storm swept across the mountains and valleys. The feeling I had when I went to the field and saw literally every stalk of corn prostrate on the ground was indescribable. My first thought was that all of the seeds and all of our labors had been wasted. I went home and told my family what happened. Papa, an experienced farmer, laughed and said, "Wait until the sun comes out and shines on the corn." I went to bed that night praying for the sun to shine all day long the next day. Sure enough it did, and when I went to the field in the middle of the afternoon, the corn was standing erect and tall, its very leaves seeming to be expressing thanks to the sun. I stood there and looked upon those shiny green leaves and thanked God. I have never forgotten this experience because it impressed upon me firmly that we must never despair when we are down, and we must never think that the storms in life have the ultimate say. More often, they are the prelude to a happier and more responsive life.

The summer's corn was harvested in September, and Papa died on October 26. I still did not have a job, but I had not lost hope. After the Thanksgiving holiday, I borrowed a car to take my sister-in-law back to Forest City, North Carolina, where she was teaching. On the way, she expressed a desire to stop in Rutherford to speak with the county school superintendent.

While I was sitting in the superintendent's outer office, the door opened, and out came a lady whose presence suggested dignity and culture. She spoke to me, and I arose and returned the greeting. She then asked me if I was a college graduate and if I was employed. I tried desperately to give an answer that would not give the impression that I was anxious. As calmly as I could, I answered that I was a recent graduate of Morehouse College, with a minor in education, and that I was looking for a job.

This lady, Mrs. Dennis, was the Jeans Supervisor (a special name given to supervisors for black students, named after someone in the area) for the black schools in Rutherford County, North Carolina. She informed me that there was a principal/teacher vacancy in a three-teacher rural school in the Doggetts Grove community and asked if I would like to apply for the position. I paused for a moment to subdue my anxiousness and then calmly stated that I would like to apply for the position.

This encounter with the supervisor took place on the Monday after Thanksgiving, and by the following Monday I was in place as the principal of Rutherford County's Doggetts Grove Elementary School.

The school was housed in a three-room frame building on an unpaved country road. Across the road and facing the school building was the house of Mr. and Mrs. Sam Goode. When the school was built, Mr. Goode bought an acre of land facing it and built a six-room house. His plan was to provide room and board for the Doggetts Grove schoolteachers, and it worked. One teacher lived in the community, and the other teacher and I boarded with the Goodes. My salary was $58 per month, and room and board was $15 per month.

The superintendent warned me that Doggetts Grove was a rough community and that I should refrain from having programs at the school at night. He informed me that during the previous principal's administration, hoodlums and disorderly men and boys had created disturbances at programs. I listened carefully to his advice, but at the same time, I was preparing my fifth and sixth grade pupils for a Christmas program, and the other two teachers were doing the same for their classes. The Christmas program was planned for a Thursday evening, the last day before the Christmas holiday break. Invitations had been sent to all of the families in the community, and by early Thursday evening the two classrooms that had been made into an auditorium by opening a folding wall were packed with parents and children.

Before the program began, I detected a fire burning at the edge of a wooded area about five hundred feet from the school. I left the building and went straight to the spot where a group of men had gathered and were gambling. I got their attention, told them that I was principal of the school, and invited them to come to the Christmas program.

In spite of the fact that two or three wanted to ignore the invitation and continue gambling, the majority accepted, and the whole group walked back with me, came in, and witnessed the program. I spent three years as principal of Doggetts Grove School, during which time we presented many programs without any problems.

The wide disparity between educational resources in Rutherford County's white schools and in its black schools was shameful and abominable. Our school had no library and scarcely any textbooks even though the state furnished textbooks for all schools. I requested textbooks for our school and was sent used and ragged books that had been discarded by the white schools. I sent them back to the superintendent's office and requested new books, which I received within a few days. We were not so lucky in acquiring library books.

In January 1936 I received a letter from Professor Darity, who preceded me as principal of Doggetts Grove School and was now principal of a two-teacher school in the village of Cliffside, about seven miles to the east. The letter was an invitation for me to deliver the dedication address for their new brick school building. I accepted the invitation and on the appointed date spoke to a large audience of parents and children.

As I spoke, I noticed two attractive ladies sitting near the rear of the audience. I had been particularly attracted by the hat of one of the ladies. At the close of the meeting, I was introduced and found that they were also county teachers. I did not see these ladies again until we met at a county-wide meeting of teachers. At this meeting, I spoke with the lady whose hat had attracted me at the school building dedication and indicated that I would like to call on her. Another month passed, and I saw her again at a teachers meeting. She rather cunningly said, "I haven't heard from you." That sparked the setting of a date on which I would call on her.

Miss Jeannetta Miriam Scott taught in a small school in the village of Henrietta, North Carolina, about five miles from Doggetts Grove School. I had no transportation, but the community had an informal taxi driver, Mr. Jim McIntyre, and on the set date, he delivered me at Miss Scott's boarding residence in Henrietta. To my dismay and utter disappointment, she had another gentleman friend visiting with her. We awkwardly participated in a three-way conversation until Mr. McIntyre returned at 10:00 p.m. to carry me back to Doggetts Grove.

Since there were no telephones for communication, my next encounter with Miss Scott was at another teachers meeting. Another date was set, and on the appointed day, Mr. McIntyre delivered me to Henrietta. On this date, there was no third person.

After a pleasant evening of conversation, the clock struck ten, and Mr. McIntyre had not arrived. I was now in the danger zone because the community mores looked with disfavor on any young lady who entertained a guest beyond 10:00 p.m., and this was especially true of public school teachers. Ten-thirty, eleven, and no Mr. McIntyre. At this point I rose to leave to walk the five miles back to Doggetts Grove. I bade Miss Scott good night and started on my trek home.

It was a balmy spring evening, with an almost full moon shining brightly. About a mile from my house, I came to a stream that was about six feet wide. The moon, reflecting in the middle of the stream, created the impression in the stream of a large stone. I decided to make a leap to the "stone" and then another leap to the other side of the stream. I made my leap, but instead of landing on a stone, I landed in a pool of water two feet deep. I made my way out of the stream and hastened my pace to reach home.

My landlord, Mr. Goode, never gave boarders a key to the house because he always wanted to know where we had been and what we had been doing. I knocked on the door. He opened it, looked at me and my dripping wet clothing, and in dismay exclaimed, "My Lord, 'Fesser,' what happened?" I was too wet and too chilled to tell him. The next morning, I explained the stream mishap.

By the time school was out in early June 1936, the relationship between Miss Scott and me grew to the point that we were talking seriously about our future lives together. In the midsummer of 1936, I visited her at home in Washington, D.C., and met her father, sister, and brothers. Her mother had died a few years earlier as a result of a tragic accident. During my visit, I asked her father for her hand in marriage. He consented when I assured him that we loved each other and that I was capable of taking care of his baby daughter.

As we returned to our schools in the fall, we began to make plans for our wedding. This blessed event finally took place on December 28, 1936, at our family home in Brevard, with my pastor, Rev. A. H. Wilson, performing the ceremony.

In August and October, prior to our wedding, two other important events in my life took place. On August 15, 1935, I was ordained into the Christian ministry by Bethel Baptist Church, but at Mt. Olive Baptist Church in Asheville, pastored by Rev. E. B. King. The ordination council was called by my pastor, Rev. A. H. Wilson of Bethel Baptist Church in Brevard. Dr. J. W. Hairston, pastor of Mt. Zion Baptist Church in Asheville, was the catechizer, and Rev. J. H. Smith, pastor of Liberty Baptist Church in Sylva, North Carolina, was the secretary. The other participating ministers were Rev. H. B. Ferguson, Rev. W. M. Hamilton, and Rev. Gudger.

In early October 1936 I was called to the pastorate of New Bethel Baptist Church in Asheville. New Bethel was considered a problem church. During the ten years before I was called, the church had been served by nine pastors. Most of the senior ministers advised me not to accept the call because I was only twenty-three years old and they felt that the church would "kill" me before I got started in the pastorate. But one minister, Rev. E. W. Dixon, pastor of Hill Street Baptist Church and moderator of the Mud Creek Baptist Association, said, "Son, take the church, and I'll stand by you, and you will make it."

After accepting the pastorate, I recalled vividly the advice given to me by an elderly shut-in lady. During a visit with her, she commended me for accepting the pastorate of the church. Then she frankly proposed this question, "Young man, is you married?" My answer was, "No." Then, speaking in a very high-pitched voice, she said, "Young man, if you are going to pastor that church" — her voice then dropped to a low bass pitch — "you better get you a wife." I assured her that I was engaged and would be married soon.

In many ways, 1937 was a year of new adjustments, including the transition from single to married life, accepting our living accommodations in the house of Rev. and Mrs. E. W. Dixon, getting acquainted with the officers and members of New Bethel Baptist Church, and commuting each weekend the sixty miles between Asheville and the Rutherford County schools where Jeannetta and I taught. At the beginning of 1937, my request to the county superintendent that my wife be transferred to Doggetts Grove school was granted.

Throughout 1937, the school work and church work blended well. The church accepted my recommendations for several organizational changes, and the membership grew steadily. These positive changes were made possible by the excellent cooperation of Deacons Wallace Kelly, Littlejohn, and Gilliard.

Deacon Kelly was a pullman porter who was converted and became a church member in his late forties. His conversion was a
dramatic experience, and he described it to me as follows: "I was
in a revival, and I found my Jesus. And when I found him, I left
the church and went from house to house to tell my neighbors that
I had found the Lord. I did this until almost daybreak, and then I
went home and went to bed, and I slept until noon. I should have
been at the train station at eight o'clock in the morning to take my
pullman car out to Cincinnati, but I overslept.

"When I went down for my next trip out, Mr. Parker, the pullman supervisor, called me into his office and said, 'Wallace, I am
certain that you know that you have lost your job because you permitted your car to go out two days ago without a porter.' I looked
Mr. Parker straight in the eyes and said to him, 'Sir, the night before
that car went out without a porter, I found my Jesus, and I spent
the night telling my friends and neighbors, and then went home and
went fast asleep. And I say unto you, Sir, if you can't understand
what this change means to me and you fire me the day you fire me,
is the day you die.'" Brother Kelly told me that after his statement
Mr. Parker stood before him trembling and said, "Wallace, your
Cincinnati car is waiting for you. Get on board."

One of the weaknesses that I discovered in my early pastorate
in New Bethel was in the area of music. This problem was solved
when Miss Gladyse Cowan, a public school teacher and musician,
accepted the position of director of music. Miss Cowan developed
a senior choir and a junior choir. My tenure at New Bethel lasted
two years, but as of this writing, Mrs. Cowan-Kennedy has directed
music in New Bethel for the past sixty years.

Our school work and church work prospered during 1937 and
through the school's closing in June 1938. In the summer of 1938,
I accepted the position of principal of the black public school in
Waynesville, North Carolina. This was a segregated three-teacher
school, with grades one through nine. As principal, I taught grades
seven through nine. At the beginning of this same school year,
my wife was transferred from the Doggetts Grove School to the
Grahamtown High School in Forest City, North Carolina.

In late September of 1938, I received a call to the pastorate of
Friendship Baptist Church in Winston-Salem, North Carolina. In

late November, I accepted the call and resigned from New Bethel and the Waynesville school.

I found no problem in resigning from public school work because I was ready to give full time to pastoring, but leaving New Bethel after two years was difficult. It was my first experience of the severing of relationship between pastor and people. When my resignation was read, there were tears and sobbing, and in the midst of the sorrow and disappointment, there was never a motion passed to accept it.

•

The acceptance of the call to the pastorate of Friendship Church in Winston-Salem was a major move for my wife and me. It meant adjustment to a larger church and a larger city, and it also meant the beginning of housekeeping. The transition went smoothly, and by the end of the Christmas season, we were in a comfortably furnished four-room parsonage.

Friendship Church and Winston-Salem offered new challenges for me. The church was larger, and under the leadership of my predecessor, Rev. Reid, who had died a few months prior to my calling, tremendous growth had taken place. The church with its many departments was well organized. This was especially true of the Sunday church school, which was properly graded and administered by officers and teachers who had been well trained.

After the Christmas holidays, my wife returned to her teaching position in Rutherford County, and I plunged into the duties of pastoring. I was utterly amazed at the quality of cooperation that was offered to a twenty-five-year-old pastor by deacons, trustees, and other church officers, most of whom were twice my age. This kind of cooperation opened the way for creative planning for ministry and service. In assessing our needs, the mutual understanding was that our greatest need was a new and adequate building. Our building facilities consisted of a wooden frame building, with a sanctuary and basement, and a small auxiliary house with five church school rooms. By the end of my first year as pastor, we had formed a building committee and retained an architect and builder, but before we began building, two other important developments took place.

Most of the persons in our congregation who were in the work force were domestic workers or employees of the R. J. Reynolds Tobacco Company. The tobacco company employees were paid from

$25 a week up to $45 for the skilled workers. Individual church contributions ranged from twenty-five cents to one dollar per Sunday, and my compensation as pastor was $20 a week, plus the parsonage. As we talked about building, a group began to raise money by selling chicken dinners and fish dinners and by conducting other fund raisers. I commended this in the beginning but soon came to realize that this was not the biblical way to finance the work of the church. Then an unusual thing happened: Rev. J. C. White, pastor of First Baptist Church in Winston-Salem, gave me a book, *Stewardship Revitalized* by Walt N. Johnson, which I read through fully two times. The reading of this book led to a revolutionary change in our method of financing the church.

In early 1940, I recommended an eight-week study course (one night weekly) on stewardship and financing the church. Deacons, trustees, church school and Baptist Training Union officers and teachers, and all leaders of church auxiliaries were requested to participate in the course. The response was tremendous, and for eight weeks about seventy-five persons attended the sessions regularly. By the end of the fourth week, over half of the group had increased their church offerings from the twenty-five cents to a dollar range, to a tithe of their earnings. By the end of the course, 60 percent of the working members were tithers. The Sunday church offerings had now quadrupled, and there were no more chicken dinners and fish fries. By the spring of 1942, we had torn down the old buildings and built a 450-seat sanctuary with appropriate offices and meeting rooms, facilities for a day care center, a stage and small auditorium for plays and programs, and twelve classrooms. This accomplishment was considered a miracle because of the scarcity of building materials occasioned by the Second World War.

The completion of the church building and the strengthening of programs of operation in the church put us in the position to view our responsibilities to the community and to our wider programs of missions and education.

•

The Second World War had its impact, both negative and positive. By the middle of 1942, more than a hundred members left Friendship Church to work in defense industries in Michigan, Illinois, New York, Connecticut, and the District of Columbia. This meant that almost one-fifth of the membership moved shortly after the completion of the new church building. The reduction in income from tithes and offerings was keenly felt, but for the next two years, through quarterly letters and the pastor's summer visits to members in the states mentioned above, the relocated members gave, and this helped considerably with mortgage payments and regular church expenses. In due time, the impact from the loss of members triggered by the war effort was softened by the addition of new members who soon raised the participation to its previous level.

After we built our new church facility, the first two new ministries were the establishment of an adult school and a child care center. We discovered that many adults could not read and write well enough to handle their business and personal affairs. There was also a great need for child care. With the assistance of the United Way, we opened the first publicly sponsored day care center for black children in Winston-Salem. This center served as a model for centers in six other churches.

The lack of black participation in political affairs and city government in 1942 was shameful. With a population of about sixty thousand, almost evenly divided between black and white, Winston-Salem had less than a hundred black voters. This was true notwithstanding the fact that the city was said to have the most harmonious race relations of any city in the state. In Friendship, we decided to do something about it.

We notified the community that we were opening voter registration school in the church. The law in North Carolina required that all voters had to be able to read, write, and interpret any part of the state and national constitution. We expanded our adult class to permit anyone old enough to vote to enroll for voter education. Class registration far exceeded estimates.

We set up model registration booths, with persons acting as tough "white" registrars who put the prospective voters through rigid examinations. A few weeks later, when the city's registration began, we decided to challenge the system.

On one Saturday, I carried five persons to register who had excelled in the tests. One by one, as they approached the registrar, each was denied. I asked them to leave, and I remained. I said to the registrar, "The persons that you denied were capable of registering, and I am going to stand here and observe every person who comes in to

register. If you register any white person who did not do as well as
my people, I'm going to have you arrested." The registrar looked at
me as if he thought I was crazy.

No other black persons came to register, but there was a line of
whites. The first couple he examined did well, and he registered
them. Another person did the same and was registered. The next
man and wife that sat to register were both practically illiterate.
They could barely read; their writing any portions of the constitution was completely out of the question. The registrar turned them
down, suffering a profane reaction from the man as he and his wife
left. I prepared to leave after he turned down two other persons,
saying to him, "I will be back next Saturday." The next Saturday we
were back with three carloads. Our people went in, got in line, and
each one was registered.

•

As Friendship's interest and concern for the community expanded,
the response from the community likewise grew. Even though our
church, compared to others in the city, was considered as small or
middle-sized, our ministries began to attract city-wide attention.

Our first vacation Bible school, with my wife, Jeannetta, as principal, drew over three hundred children from across the city. The
Sunday church school continued to expand, and we began to liberally support denominational associations and conventions. Our
liberal giving for missions and education caused us to be labeled the
"Mission Church."

Until the second year of my pastorate in Friendship, there had
never been a meeting of black and white clergy in the city. The first
meeting was arranged by some of the senior ministers of both races.
The theme for this interracial, ecumenical gathering was, "How can
the white pastors and churches be of assistance to the black churches
and pastors?" I was chosen to speak for the black pastors.

The meeting's planners had decided that the black preachers
would speak first. As I took my place at the podium, I properly addressed the group, then made the following statement. "I am going
to take the liberty to change the chosen subject for this gathering.
The subject for my comments will be, 'How can the black and white
pastors and churches be of assistance to each other in valid community ministry?'" There followed a "loud" silence for a few moments.

Then I proceeded with my speech. Among the many suggestions I offered were four that I will briefly mention.

First, I discussed the city's transportation system. The public was served by two bus companies: the Safe Bus Company, a black-owned business, and Duke Power Company. The Safe Bus Company principally served the black neighborhoods, and Duke Power buses served the larger city, which included some black communities. Safe Bus riders were integrated, but Duke Power riders were segregated, whites in front and blacks in back. In my remarks, I emphasized the folly, the inconsistency, and the racism that this mode of transportation reflected, and I challenged the white brothers to work with the black brothers to change this system. I was not disappointed when I got no "amens" from either side.

Second, I spoke of the unjust salary differences based upon race. In a conversation with me, a deacon in Friendship Church who was a cigarette manufacturing machine operator, a highly skilled job, related that he had trained his white machine partner, but the company paid his partner ninety cents more per hour than he received. I also reminded the group that I had been saddened by reading the obituaries of too many black women who had labored at tobacco work benches and died before they were fifty. By this time I perceived that I was losing some of my audience.

My third comment had to do with segregated news. The daily newspaper carried a column each day written by a black reporter entitled, "News of Colored People." This column was expanded to a whole page on Sunday. To the newspaper's credit, this column and page carried news of church services, funerals, school affairs, lodges, black businesses, etc. There were, however, some stories about black people that made the front page, but these stories were usually about murder or some other heinous crime. I challenged the gathered ministers to confront the publishers and demand that they provide fair and just coverage.

My fourth observation to an audience that by this time seemed to be totally turned off was that we should exchange services between black and white churches. This suggestion grew out of my conviction that the race gap of alienation could be more easily closed if Christians and religious persons of different races worshiped and prayed together; many racial tensions would vanish. I then stated that I was ready and willing to participate in exchange services with any white church that was ready to do the same. With this statement I brought my talk to a close.

I was a bit shocked by the aftermath. A few white brothers shook hands with me and spoke, but to my dismay, as the white ministers went their way, my black brothers huddled around me and scolded me for missing the mark of the meeting. I accepted the scolding and boldly said, "If the truth hurts, let it hurt."

Consolation came a few days after the meeting. I received a telephone call from one of the white ministers who pastored a church on the outskirts of Winston-Salem. He suggested an exchange of services, and within a month we had participated in a double exchange. However, a sequel to this exchange brought sadness to me and to this young Southern Baptist pastor whom I met in the post office about six weeks later. After we greeted each other, he told me that he was resigning from the church and taking a position as an army chaplain. He said that the congregation had turned against him after the exchange services and suggested that he resign. I expressed my sympathy and wished him well. As we departed, I said to myself, "He was free, but the congregation was still enslaved."

•

In the early fall of 1941, two new avenues for service were opened to me. I was called to the pastorate of the Rising Star Baptist Church in Walnut Cove, North Carolina, a village twenty miles northwest of Winston-Salem, and I accepted the position as chaplain of Winston-Salem Teachers College after the resignation of Rev. Kenneth H. Williams, a friend who was taking a position of chaplain in the U.S. Army.

The Rising Star Baptist Church was a unique small village church with an active adult membership of about thirty-two, plus ten or twelve children. The size of the church did not diminish her sense of pride. The members insisted that their pastor be trained and preferably be one who had pastored a medium or large church in Winston-Salem. By meeting these requirements and others, such as preaching ability and pastoral management, I was called, and I accepted the pastorate.

Worship services were held at 3:00 p.m. on the first and third Sundays of each month, with a communion service held on the evening of the third Sunday. For my initial worship service, I arrived at the church building at 2:45 p.m. To my dismay, no one was present, and the building was locked. Within five minutes, however, Deacon Scales, the church custodian, who lived within a stone's throw of the church, showed up, unlocked the church, and rang the bell. Within twenty minutes the whole congregation was assembled. For the next two worship services the same procedure was followed.

The week before my third worship service, I spent a day visiting all of the families in the church. During a conversation with Sister Sally Gray, the church clerk, I posed this question, "Why don't the members come to worship services on time, and why do they wait until the bell is rung to come?" "The answer is simple," she said. "The pastors that preceded you rarely came on time; therefore, the members decided that prior to each service the custodian would be on the lookout for the pastor's arrival and, upon his arrival, would ring the bell." At our next worship service, I announced that I would continue to be present for worship at or before the stated hour, and that there would be no further need to ring the bell to signal the arrival of the pastor. The suggestion was accepted, and the former practice ceased.

When I accepted Rising Star Church, I was informed that there was no money in the treasury, and there was an insurance premium due. My response to this was that we would hold some membership sessions on financial stewardship and develop a budget that would include operating expenses, mission and benevolent giving, convention and association expenses, and the pastor's salary. We would also establish a building fund. The last item to the budget was added because the church building was in woeful disrepair.

My pastorate in Rising Star Church covered a span of six years. During this period our membership grew from thirty-two to thirty-eight, but the overall growth of the church far outdistanced her growth in numbers. During these years we met all of our obligations, sent delegates to conferences and conventions, did community mission work, supported the unified budget of the General Baptist State Convention, supported Shaw University and the Lott Carey Foreign Mission Convention, and paid the pastor a salary of $50 a month. When I resigned from the pastorate in October 1947, a building fund of $6,000 had been accumulated.

The chaplain's position at Winston-Salem Teachers College afforded a new avenue of service for me. My basic responsibilities

consisted of preparing for and conducting a weekly Sunday afternoon vesper service, presiding at Wednesday chapel assemblies,
conducting a Sunday morning breakfast Bible class session, and
holding regular hours for student counseling. I was greatly encouraged and ably assisted in performing these duties by the director of
music, Professor James A. Dillard, and the president of the college,
Dr. Francis Atkins.

•

In the summer of 1942, Winston-Salem Teachers College received
a grant of $100,000 to fund the salary for a teacher to conduct
evening classes for local black ministers who had not finished high
school or college. The grant also provided for one religion course. As
chaplain, I was chosen to teach these classes. Two evenings a week I
taught a one-hour class in remedial English and a one-hour class in
New Testament principles.

The purpose for giving the grant, and particularly for instruct-
ing untrained black ministers, had a great deal to do with the
socioeconomic disparity in the wages paid white and black factory
workers. For this reason, I gladly accepted the position to teach the
classes because it would give me an opportunity to further explore
solutions to the problems I had addressed when the white and black
ministers met. Another reason that I welcomed the opportunity was
my personal knowledge of efforts in the community to unionize the
tobacco factory workers.

About a month after the classes started, something happened that
startled the city. A few moments after I had started to teach my New
Testament class, Attorney Jack Atkins, the college president's brother
and the executive secretary of the college, came into the class and
asked me to excuse myself for a few moments. In the hall he came
straight to the point, informing me that Factory No. 12 had gone on
strike. Then he added that he had received a call from Mr. Whitaker,
Reynolds Tobacco Company's personnel manager, who suggested to
him that because of my standing in the black community, it was possible that I was the only person in the city that could get the workers
to come back to work. (It is essential to know that practically all
of the two hundred persons who worked in No. 12 were black
women.) I listened to Mr. Atkins and said to him that I would have

to think and pray about the matter, and I would call him later in the evening. I went back and finished my class, and then hastened home.

My first act was to find a member of the church who worked in Factory No. 12. Annie Mae (whose last name now escapes me) lived a half block from our house. I hurried to her house and, finding her at home, told her that I had heard about the "walkout," and asked her to tell me in detail what she did on her job.

She said that the work at their work tables was not bad, but then she added that the worst part of her job, as well as that of the other women, was the rolling on dollies of two-hundred-pound hogsheads of tobacco from the landing platform to the work bench. As she finished her statement, I said, "Tell me no more."

I rushed back home to the telephone. My first calls were to four other ministers who along with me were considered "radicals." They were Rev. G. C. Crawford, Rev. A. H. McDaniels, Rev. Edward Gholson, and Rev. I. Logan Kearse. We all agreed that the time had come for greater justice and fair play for all of the tobacco factory workers. Subsequently, I called Attorney Jack Atkins and informed him that my colleagues and I had agreed that the time had come for significant changes and a restructuring of the work patterns and salaries for the tobacco factory workers, particularly the black workers. Therefore, I could not conform to Mr. Whitaker's suggestion. After this call, which was after midnight, I went to bed.

The next morning the first news that I heard on the radio was that all workers in Reynolds factories had gone on strike. My colleagues and I hurried to the factories and helped to organize the workers in orderly fashion. All around the factories leaders were chosen for bands of about fifty workers, and each band chose a song leader and a prayer leader. Each day for a six-week-long strike, the inner city around the factories was blessed with fervent prayers for justice and powerful renditions of Negro spirituals and gospel music. At the end of the six-week strike the company was ready to sit down around the bargaining table with labor leaders and factory workers. After many days of bargaining, the company and the union signed the first union contract with Reynolds Tobacco Company.

My colleagues and I did not escape the condemnation of some of the city's power structure, as well as that of a hastily formed company association that was created during the strikes.

The union operated for about a year. But McCarthyism was alive and well in 1942–43, and it was discovered that three of the union organizers had once been active in the Communist Party; therefore, the company was able to influence the National Labor Relations Board to abrogate the contract. There were some good results from the brief period of unionization, however. These included a restructuring of salary scales, the upgrading of black workers, and the promotion of some black workers to management positions.

As we turned our attention away from labor problems and job justice, the Friendship family along with other Baptist churches began to make preparation to entertain the forty-fourth annual session of the Lott Carey Baptist Foreign Mission Convention, which met in Winston-Salem in the late summer of 1942, with Friendship as host church. The Lott Carey Convention, begun in 1897, was named after former slave Lott Carey, who in 1821 became the first African-American missionary to West Africa.

The opening session was held in the sanctuary of Friendship, and Dr. E. C. Smith, pastor of Metropolitan Church in Washington, D.C., delivered the sermon. The host church's ability to entertain the convention messengers (delegates) was greatly enhanced by the very generous cooperation of Dr. Atkins, president of Winston-Salem Teachers College. After the opening session at Friendship, all other sessions and programs were held in the college chapel auditorium and various other meeting places on the campus. Since the city hotels denied accommodations to black people, we relied on the college dormitories for the housing of our delegates, and access to the college cafeteria and dining room made it possible to purchase meals at a reasonable cost and helped greatly in getting delegates to meetings on time.

The highlight of this session of the convention was the address delivered by Dr. Mordecai Johnson, president of Howard University. For one hour and forty-four minutes, he held the audience of some fifteen hundred listeners spellbound as he relentlessly challenged the audience to continue to do effective mission work in Africa and Haiti, but at the same time to rise up in rebellion against segregation and discrimination in America.

In 1943 we were in the middle of World War II. There was much fear for our sons and daughters who were in the armed services. This fear had a positive effect on many churches: worship attendance greatly improved, and churches received many new members.

Friendship was prospering as the congregation grew and as tithing and voter registration expanded.

By mid-1943, I began to take an inward look at myself. At the end of my college career I had turned down an offer made to me by Dr. John Hope, then president of Atlanta University. He had been informed that I was interested in Christian ministry and had offered to obtain a full scholarship for me at Crozer Theological Seminary, but after talking with my parents, who felt that I should get a job and help my younger brothers and sisters to go to college, I respectfully declined Dr. Hope's offer.

Eight years after my conversation with Dr. Hope, I was convinced that to reach my greatest potential I needed to enroll in a seminary and earn a divinity degree. With this in mind, I called a meeting of the officers of Friendship and asked them to recommend to the church that I be given a partial leave of absence to begin studies at Howard University School of Divinity, beginning in January 1944. The board acted, presenting the matter to the church, and the church approved it. The next approval came from Jeannetta, who was wholly in support of the idea.

After I was accepted by the Howard Divinity School, the arrangements with Friendship were as follows: Rev. Davis, my assistant pastor, was given additional pastoral duties and was to be assisted by an older minister, Rev. Jones. I would commute between Winston-Salem and Washington, D.C., every two weeks. With these arrangements, a new chapter opened in my life.

Even though it had been nine years since I had done any formal studying, I found little difficulty in keeping up with my classmates, most of whom were recent college graduates. I found the professors in the divinity school challenging and stimulating, and I ended my first quarter of study with a B-plus average. During my second quarter, I was chosen to represent my class on the seminary advisory committee.

On one of my semimonthly trips back to the church, I received a call from the chairman of the deacon board of New Bethel Baptist Church, one of Winston-Salem's largest churches. The pastor of the church, Rev. Gilmore, was ill, and a deacon asked me to invite one of my classmates to accompany me and preach for New Bethel on the weekends when I returned to Friendship.

My roommate at Howard was Jerry Drayton, a recent Morehouse

graduate. I conveyed the deacon's invitation to Jerry and asked him if he would like to join me on my next weekend trip. His answer was, "Yeah, man. When is the next trip?"

That trip opened up a whole new chapter in Jerry's life. After his first trip and sermon, he returned to New Bethel regularly. By the end of the spring quarter at Howard, Rev. Gilmore's physical condition had severely deteriorated, and in the early fall he died. Because Jerry's services at New Bethel had been so well accepted during the illness of Rev. Gilmore, Jerry was unanimously called as pastor at the beginning of his middler year in seminary. In 1994, Jerry Drayton celebrated his fiftieth year as pastor of New Bethel.

In late December of 1944, I finished my third quarter of studies at Howard. By this time, I had developed good friendships and relationships with many students, including Kelly Miller Smith, William "Rabbi" King, James Eaton, and two men whose first names now escape me, Quarterman and Wright. As a student who had about eight years of pastoral experience, I was called upon to counsel several of my fellow students. In addition, I related closely with administrators and faculty members. Among those whom I came to know more personally were Dean William Stuart Nelson, Dr. Farmer, Professor Keene, and Professor King.

•

My studies at Howard University were seriously interrupted after I registered for my middler year in January 1945. I received a call from a person representing a search committee for an executive secretary for the General Baptist State Convention of North Carolina. The call was a request for an interview. The Reverend C. E. Griffin, the incumbent secretary, had accepted a call to the pastorate of the First Calvary Baptist Church in Norfolk, Virginia. I consented to be interviewed by the search committee, and two days later we met in the conference room of the divinity school. After a two-hour meeting, I agreed to give an answer within ten days.

I had already delayed my theological training for nine years after finishing college, and I was literally hounded for my procrastination by Dr. Benjamin E. Mays whenever we met. My studies at Howard had gone so well that I did not want to disrupt them, but over against these factors, there was an inward gnawing about the North Carolina Baptists' offer that I could not overlook. I therefore decided to do three things. I would consult with my wife, I would spend some time in prayer, and I would confer with Dean Nelson and Dr. Farmer. I would also have to consult with Friendship Church and Winston-Salem Teachers College, where by the good graces of Dr. Atkins I still held my position as chaplain and rendered services on the weekends when I returned from school.

My first call was to discuss the matter with my wife, whose reaction was that the decision was basically mine and that she would adjust to whatever changes I chose to make.

My next move was to talk with Dean Nelson and Dr. Farmer. Dean Nelson strongly suggested that I continue my studies, but Dr. Farmer, a United Methodist and an ardent believer in denominational loyalty, felt that if my denomination needed me, I should take the position. I accepted his counsel, and on my next weekend trip to the church, I put the matter before the congregation and received their approval. Then I informed the search committee that I would accept the position.

Accepting the position as executive secretary of the state convention did not require my resigning from the pastorate of Friendship Church. Arrangements were made for the assistant pastor to become acting pastor while I served the state convention.

On February 1, 1945, I became the third full-time executive secretary of the General Baptist State Convention of North Carolina. The president was Dr. A. A. Bishop, pastor of five small-town and rural churches in eastern North Carolina. His residence was in Rich Square, North Carolina, where his father had been mayor of the town during the reconstruction period. Dr. Bishop was a versatile businessman, educator, and pastor. He was the principal of a rural school, a manufacturer of caskets, an undertaker, and the secretary of an eastern North Carolina burial society.

Dr. O. S. Bullock, pastor of First Baptist Church, Raleigh, North Carolina, was chairman of the convention Board of Directors. He and Dr. Bishop were characterized by Dr. Miles Mark Fisher, pastor of White Rock Baptist Church, Durham, North Carolina, as "the most 'selfish' unselfish leaders of any religious movement." By this Fisher meant that they gave their time, energy, and money to influence other pastors and churches to liberally support the mission work of the convention, but they expected nothing in return for their labor.

The headquarters of the convention was in the Leonard Building on Shaw University's campus in Raleigh. The staff consisted of Otis Hariston, editor of the *Baptist Informer,* Leon C. Riddick, director of Christian education, Drucilla Lee, secretary, Rev. Johnson, part-time field worker, and me.

The North Carolina General Baptist Convention was the mission, education, and social service instrument for the outreach ministries of 17,110 African-American Baptist churches in the state. These churches were pastored by 1,247 pastors, many of whom pastored two, three, and four churches; one pastored five churches. The convention was, and is, one of the few in the country that served, and serves, all of the black Baptist churches in the state. This unified position has been in place for almost a hundred years.

The primary goals of the convention were the financial support of Shaw University, the Lott Carey Baptist Foreign Mission Convention, a state mission program, and the Oxford Orphanage. A unified program for financial support was accepted by the fifty-five district associations and the member churches. Churches were given quotas according to size to underwrite the state budget and were asked to give monthly, quarterly, semiannual, or annual contributions. The funds were distributed as follows: one-fourth for Shaw University, one-fourth for state missions, one-fourth for the Lott Carey Convention, and one-fourth for office operations. Special offerings were also received for the Oxford Orphanage, Shaw University, the Lott Carey Convention, and other causes.

The strength and effectiveness of the convention was due largely to its active auxiliaries, the Women's Auxiliary, the Christian Education Congress, the Ushers Department, and the Laymen and the Youth Departments, which involved thousands of people of all ages in conferences, retreats, seminars, and training institutes throughout the state.

Within a year after my tenure as executive secretary began, our staff had grown to eleven. Rev. John White joined the staff as Baptist Training Union director, Louella Edwards filled the position as director of vacation Bible school, and Rev. O. L. Sherrill joined the staff as assistant to the executive secretary.

The two years and nine months of my tenure witnessed phenomenal growth in the convention. Support for convention causes was greatly increased, and land was purchased for the building of convention headquarters.

While I was serving the convention, my wife was given the position of director of the Child Care Laboratory School of Shaw University's Department of Teacher Training. Jeannetta and I had been married nine years and were childless. In fact, we had discussed adopting a child, but this step proved unnecessary because she became pregnant, and on July 11, 1946, our daughter Lynn Elda was born. Perhaps Jeannetta's daily dealing with the lab school children helped turn the tide.

Chapter 4

New York
1947–1963

In the summer of 1947, I received a call to the pastorate of Friendship Baptist Church in New York City, which I accepted because I had not planned to work for the convention more than three years. Jeannetta, Lynn Elda, and I moved back to Winston-Salem, I resigned from Friendship Church, and following the convention's annual session in October, we moved to New York.

The acceptance of the pastorate of Friendship Baptist Church afforded a new challenge for me. The crowded Harlem community was far different from the open spaces of Winston-Salem, but the adjustment to serving in the nation's largest city was made easier by the several vacation periods that my family had previously enjoyed in the city and in worship services at Friendship Baptist Church.

In 1926, Rev. John I. Mumford had resigned from the pastorate of Friendship Baptist Church in Winston-Salem and moved to New York City. He was called to Baptist Temple Church, which he pastored until 1936. He resigned from Baptist Temple and led in organizing Friendship Baptist Church in Harlem. The 103 charter members had grown to 850 when Rev. Mumford died in the late fall of 1946. The winsome personality of Pastor Mumford, his encouragement of people to serve, and his love and care for church members greatly enhanced the growth of the church.

Rev. Mumford possessed a kind of folk psychology that effectively facilitated the solution of problems. If a member became dissatisfied with the leader of a group, such as the deaconesses, ushers, or choir, and complained to the pastor, he had a simple solution: "Daughter, don't worry; start your own group." This method led to the church having seventy-six organizations by the time I arrived as pastor.

I witnessed another demonstration of Pastor Mumford's folk psychology in a Friendship worship service during one of my vacation trips to New York. On the Saturday before my Sunday visit, the Friendship Church annual boat ride up the Hudson River was held. About thirty minutes after the boat left the dock, it sprang a leak and had to return to the dock, so the ride was cancelled.

Since each person on the boat had paid $5, the boat company refunded the money to the church person in charge. On Sunday there was murmuring from the members, asking for the return of their $5, which was reported to Pastor Mumford. In his pastoral moment's presentation, he spoke of the aborted boat ride and said, "Yesterday many of you started up the Hudson River on our annual boat ride. The boat sprang a leak, and the ride had to be cancelled, and the money was refunded. When I heard about this my mind began to wonder. Imagine what would have happened if the boat had gotten in deep water and sunk before it could return to shore. This coming week would be a sad week. Hearses would be rolling from all sections of Harlem, and the whole city would be clouded with sadness. And now some of you are asking for a refund of $5. When you think of what could have happened, you ought to freely give that $5 to the church as a 'thank you' offering." At this moment a lady in the balcony rose and said, "Pastor, keep my $5, and add this $5 to it." This was followed by scores of others who said, "Keep mine, and add this gift to it." Needless to say, there was no further murmuring for a refund.

Two and a half months after our arrival in New York, there was a welcome change in our family. On January 18, 1948, our second child, Jini Medina, was born. The birth took place on a Sunday morning while I was in my study preparing for the worship service. The phone rang, and a hospital nurse said, "Your wife has just delivered a beautiful baby girl." For a moment I felt some disappointment because I had chosen the male name Brian for our second child. However, suddenly I offered a prayer of thanksgiving for the healthy birth of a new baby girl.

The beginning of my pastoral ministry in Harlem was very different from my pastorate in North Carolina. The great days of the Harlem Renaissance reached their climax in the 1930s, and by 1947 serious deterioration enveloped large segments of the Harlem community. But in spite of these negative changes, church life and

Harlem were alive and vibrant. This vibrancy challenged me to move forward with restructuring the organization of Friendship Church.

We began to make changes by inviting all members who desired to participate in the reorganization of the church to attend classes on the nature and mission of the church. The response was overwhelming. The emphasis of the classes was that the church is the Lord's church, the members are His witnesses, and our goals are to worship, fellowship, witness, evangelize, and develop as good stewards. The result of these classes was a radical reduction from seventy-six organizations in the church to the following: deacon board, deaconess board, trustee board, three choirs, two usher boards, Sunday school, B.T.U., and a few auxiliaries for special purposes. In due time these groups functioned well, and Friendship continued as a force for good in the Harlem community.

As the members adjusted to the reorganization of the church, Friendship grew in membership. By midspring of 1948, however, we realized that all of our problems had not been solved when the tithes and offerings gradually began to decline from Sunday to Sunday. One Sunday morning a member came to me and explained that she had put in her purse a five-dollar bill and a twenty-dollar bill. The twenty-dollar bill was to pay her weekly room rent, and the five-dollar bill was her gift for the church, but she had mistakenly put the twenty-dollar bill in the church offering envelope. When she made this known to the counting committee, no one had seen a twenty-dollar bill. This raised a red flag in my mind, especially since I had noticed a small decline in our weekly offerings over a ten-week period and had directed the secretary to run tapes on the offering envelopes. Each of the ten weeks, the tapes showed from $60 to $80 more than the offering amount reported by the counting committee. At the end of the ten weeks, I decided that we had to resolve this problem. One of the trustees and a local minister, members of the counting committee, routinely took the offering trays downstairs to the counting room just before the closing hymn and the benediction at each service, but this particular Sunday, when the appointed time came to pick up the trays, I calmly said to the trustee and the minister, "Please leave the trays there until after the benediction. I want to go down with them."

In the counting room, I stated that a problem existed. I explained that for ten weeks the secretary had run a tape on the offering

envelopes, and each week the tapes exceeded the gifts from the envelopes by $60 to $80. The shortage was always in multiples of five.
At this point one of the committee members who was also a trustee
said, "Pastor, we called you here to perform pastoral duties, such
as preaching, baptizing, giving communion, performing weddings,
conducting funerals, visiting the sick, etc., and it is our responsibility to handle the money and business of the church." I thanked
Brother Walden and looked him straight in the eye and said, "I have
been the pastor here for only seven months, and I may not be pastor
for another month, but as long as I am here, I am going to pastor every area of the church from your soul to the last penny given
the church." I followed this statement by informing the committee
that the secretary would work with the committee each week and
run a tape on the offering envelopes as they retrieved money from
them. The committee agreed, but this was not the end of the matter
for two of its members, the trustee and the minister who normally
carried the offering trays to the counting room.

Shortly after the encounter with the committee, my family and I
left for our summer vacation. When we returned, I received a call
from "Mama" Jackson, a member of the trustee board. She stated
that the devil had been busy while I was away. She informed me
that the trustee and the minister who usually took the offering from
the sanctuary to the counting room had canvassed the membership
with the message that the church secretary and I were stealing the
church money. She also told me that the trustee had developed a
new financial plan for the church, and that he would present it in
the upcoming church meeting. She followed this by saying, "I told
you when you came to the church to watch this man because I am
convinced that he has no religion."

After the conversation with Mama Jackson, I called Attorney
Joseph Dyer, the chairman of the trustee board, and asked if he
had called a meeting of the board and if he was familiar with a
new financial plan to be presented in the upcoming church meeting. Brother Dyer assured me that there had been no board meeting
and that he knew nothing of a new financial plan for the church.

The early fall church meeting was held, and in attendance were
about three hundred members, roughly a third more than in the
usual church meetings. As usual, I moderated the meeting, and when
I called for the report of the trustees, Chairman Dyer said, "We have

no report." At this point, the disgruntled trustee, along with the minister, rose and stated that the trustees would like to make a report about finances. I informed him that I had talked with the chairman of the board and was told that no meeting had been held, and he knew nothing of a new financial plan. For this reason, I stated, I cannot hear your report. He immediately appealed my decision. I accepted his appeal and put it before the church for a vote. He received seventy-seven votes, which was far short of the two-thirds of the house needed to sustain his appeal. He walked out of the meeting with his report and never came back to Friendship during the next fifteen years that I was pastor.

•

The early years of my ministry in Harlem were a unique period of change. The Harlem Renaissance of the '20s, '30s, and early '40s, had come to a climax. The emigration from the South of the late '30s to the mid-'40s had waned, and the exodus to the suburbs was increasing. Public housing projects were drawing hundreds of families from the almost century-old brownstones. But in spite of all of these changes, the Harlem community was still crowded and still offered a challenge to its churches to accelerate their ministries. In Friendship we took this challenge seriously.

Initially, we tried to address the needs of the youth in the community. Our first effort was the creation of a group of teenagers (twelve to seventeen years old) in the church who gave themselves the name the TK Teens. They became a regular organization in the church, focusing on music, dramatics, Bible study, and tutoring. Most of this group are now in their early sixties and occasionally still get together. Two young ladies from the group, Carolyn Bowman and Dorothy Robinson Tucker, have kept in constant touch with our family over the years.

In the early 1950s, Friendship created a weekday after-school program for community children (seven to sixteen), with part-time paid staff members. Forty to fifty children came each day after school, benefitting from a curriculum composed of tutoring, games, positive self-image training, and African-American history.

Because of limited space in our church building on 131st Street, we bought a four-story brownstone around the corner on 130th

Street, where we created the House of Friendship, which was in operation seven days a week. On Sunday, church school classes were held there. During the weekdays, there was gymnastics, a health clinic, an antidrug program, and other community programs. In 1963, we shared two floors of the House of Friendship with the March on Washington staff, and it was in this location that all of the planning for the historic march took place.

Friendship did not try to do community ministry alone. There was cooperation with other Harlem churches. Among these were Salem United Methodist, pastored by Rev. John Williams; Metropolitan Baptist Church, pastored by Rev. Stamps; Shiloh Baptist, pastored by Rev. Leslie Wainwright; and Williams Institutional C.M.E. Church, pastored by Rev. White. These churches with about a half dozen others, worked together in a community organization called the Heart of Harlem Neighborhood Church Association. This group sponsored concerts, presented Dr. Martin Luther King Jr. on two occasions, held joint Good Friday and Thanksgiving services annually, and conducted summer vacation Bible schools. One summer we registered 1,003 children.

In the mid-'50s, a group in Friendship Church created and legalized Friendship Enterprises. This legal entity operated two laundromats profitably until the city built public housing projects nearby and installed free laundromats.

I could not write about Friendship Church without mentioning the valuable aid I had from assistant ministers. Rev. Hunson Green, who as of this writing pastors Baptist Temple Church in New York City and is president of the New York City Baptist Ministers Conference, was my chief associate minister for all of my sixteen years at Friendship. His loyalty was without question. Rev. James Eaton, a fellow classmate at Howard Divinity School in 1944, was an effective director of our House of Friendship program. Rev. Earl Barnes, a talented musician and writer, was faithful and very helpful. In 1955, Rev. George Lawrence joined the ministerial staff as director of Christian education and associate minister. During my sixteen years at Friendship, the records of the activities of the church were well kept by secretaries Mary Greene, Drucilla Lee, Hattie DeBrix, and Serena Duncan. The music continued to be worshipful and inspiring under the direction of Dr. James Dillard, William Mercer, Aaron Clarke, Eugene Thamon, Reginald Parker, and organist Helen Deusberg.

Jeannetta was a fine helpmate at Friendship and, indeed, in all of my pastorates. She brought to our marriage an extensive background in church leadership and Christian education from her home church, Vermont Avenue Baptist, in Washington, D.C., pastored during her girlhood by Dr. C. T. Murray. She continued this training through courses at three conventions. Constant throughout the years have been her excellent memory, allowing her to call by name almost all of our hundreds of church members; her quiet leadership ability, keen insights, quick wit and humor, and genial nature; her God-given gift for knowing just how to help and support others; her enduring beauty and poise, impeccable habits, good taste, and style, which have served as a model for hundreds of young women; and her genuine concerned commitment for the mission of the church.

Jeannetta has also been a consummate hostess, and many persons have graced our dinner table and home. Some of them stayed for a while. We count as a daughter the late Cora Langston Hurley, who came to New York from North Carolina to obtain her college education, just shortly after Jeannetta and I moved there. She lived in our home during her college years and thereafter until she married and began her own family. At various times during our marriage, relatives and students have lived with us, so life in our home was quite lively with two young girls growing up and with their cousins, uncles, and grandmother, who came at intervals to live with us.

I enjoyed some special times with my wife and daughters. We challenged each other in parlor games, like "Monopoly" and "Dig," a word game; we looked at horror movies on television on Friday nights (without Jeannetta). We made preparations for Sunday on Saturday nights: the girls studied their Sunday school lessons, Jeannetta prepared Sunday's outfits and dinner, and I meditated on my sermon after I polished everyone's shoes. We went to Broadway plays; among them we saw the original Broadway cast in Lorraine Hansberry's *A Raisin in the Sun*. We had a number of pets, including a stately Dalmatian whom we named Kilgore's Duke of Morehouse, or Dukey, and a friendly terrier named Scott's Trixie of Miner, after my wife's teachers college alma mater in Washington, D.C. Because we lived in the bedroom community of East Elmhurst, in the borough of Queens, we were able to have a sizeable garden, and I taught the girls how to harvest fruits and vegetables. Each year, our peach tree yielded plentiful bushels of peaches, which we distributed among the Friendship members.

We hung a swing in the garage and built a see-saw, both of which attracted the neighborhood children, so our house became a gathering place, and the girls spent many carefree days with their friends playing hopscotch, dodge ball, and tag, climbing a low tree with large limbs in our backyard, and jumping double Dutch. In the summers, Jeannetta took them to the library to stock up on good reading, and she insisted that they read the Bible for a period of time each day. The summer fun culminated each year when our block was closed off for the annual block party, and all the neighbors enjoyed the festivities together.

The girls attended public and private schools in New York, beginning at a private school that was way ahead of its time in its approach to education, the Modern School. The headmistress was Mildred Johnson, daughter and niece of Hall Johnson and James Weldon Johnson, respectively.

•

Friendship was supportive of its pastor in his ministries beyond the local congregation. Some of these involvements included membership on the Board of Directors of the Harlem YMCA, vice president of the Harlem branch of the NAACP, and member of the Board of Directors of the American Baptist Home Mission Society. I served also as a member of the board of the Harlem Christian Educational Center, directed by Dr. Horatio Hill and assisted by Dr. Olivia Stokes.

The Empire State Baptist Convention, under the leadership of Dr. George Simms, pastor of Union Baptist Church, operated a small rest home for the aged in the upper Bronx. Dr. Simms discovered a thirty-room mansion on five acres of land in Tarrytown, New York, adjacent to the Rockefeller estate. The lady who owned it had heard that the convention was looking for larger quarters for its rest home, and she offered this property to the convention for $60,000. The convention closed the deal for its purchase, put down a small deposit, and was given time to raise and pay the remainder. I was chosen by the convention to conduct the fund drive to pay for the property. In order to stimulate giving, I arranged to have busloads of persons to visit and view the property on weekends. This was a mistake because the property was in an upper-middle-class white neighborhood, and the thought of blacks moving in for any reason was out of the question for them. When it was revealed to the community that the mansion would be used for a rest home for mostly black residents, the surrounding citizens influenced the zoning authorities of Tarrytown to deny our convention a zoning variance. Racism won another battle, and we sold the property to our insurance company.

In 1952, I felt that the pastorate of Friendship was well enough established that I could continue my seminary studies that had been interrupted in 1945, when I went to work for the North Carolina black Baptists. With the consent of the church, I registered at Union Theological Seminary for the fall semester, and after five years as a part-time student, I received my M.Div. degree in the spring of 1957.

•

In December 1955 Rosa Parks sparked a revolution by refusing to yield her bus seat to a white man. The first phase of this revolutionary movement was the Montgomery Bus Boycott, led by Martin Luther King Jr. Having known Dr. King since he was two years old, and having had him as a guest preacher for Youth Day in Friendship in 1953, I resolved to give some assistance to the movement. I called Dr. Sandy Ray, who was also a friend of the King family, and suggested that we raise some funds for the Montgomery movement and go see first hand this brave experiment for freedom. We succeeded in raising about $6,000, and the third week in January 1956 Dr. Ray and I were in Montgomery.

The fact that the bus boycott started in Montgomery was somewhat prophetic because that city was the capital of the confederacy. During our five-day stay in Montgomery, Rev. Ray and I observed the empty buses, the few black passengers who still rode them, but with their heads bowed, and the orderly demeanor of those who walked to their jobs or rode in the fleet of vans provided by the leaders of the movement. But the pinnacle of interest for us was demonstrated by the overflow crowds who attended the biweekly freedom rallies in local churches. Rev. Ray and I returned to New York with a determination to continue this movement for freedom, and I was so deeply impressed with what I saw happening in Montgomery that I decided to write my dissertation (a requirement for an M.Div. degree from Union) on the Montgomery protest movement.

•

By early 1957, the Montgomery protest movement had forced federal action to outlaw segregation in public transportation. This positive action created a climate for change in other sections of American life where segregation still existed. To take full advantage of this climate, a group of national black leaders decided to call the nation to accountability in the area of jobs and freedom. A. Philip Randolph, president of the Brotherhood of Sleeping Car Porters; Roy Wilkins, chief executive of the NAACP; Martin Luther King Jr., president of the SCLC; Whitney Young, president of the Urban League; and Dorothy Height, president of the National Council of Negro Women, all decided to sponsor a national March on Washington, May 17, 1957. The march was entitled "A Prayer Pilgrimage for Jobs and Freedom," and I was chosen to direct the march, with Bayard Rustin as my assistant. Friendship Church released me for six weeks to give full-time attention to the preparation for the march, which was attended by more than fifty thousand people from across the country. The major speeches, delivered by A. Philip Randolph and Martin Luther King Jr., challenged the federal government to accelerate efforts to eliminate segregation and to cooperate with states, businesses, and industries in reducing the jobless rate in the country. The black leadership group also met with President Eisenhower and urged him to give national leadership for the goals of the march.

•

In the spring of 1958 I was chosen by the board of the Harlem Baptist Educational Center to attend an international conference on Christian education hosted by Christian churches in Tokyo. In early July, I met in San Francisco with twenty-six other persons chosen from other sections of the country to attend the Tokyo gathering. After a day's briefing, we boarded a flight for Tokyo, with a brief stop in Honolulu.

The conference was in session for five days, and our delegation was a part of over six thousand persons from around the world in attendance. This experience in Tokyo was my first trip out of the country, except for brief visits to Mexico and Canada. With all due respect for changes that were taking place in our country, I felt a sense of freedom during the days in Japan that I had never felt in America.

As we attended the conference and spent twelve days touring the cities of Nara, Kyoto, Yokohama and areas on Japan's largest island, there were many exciting events. The first occurred during the conference meetings when I overslept one afternoon and missed joining the guide and groups as they left the hotel for the meeting assembly. When I woke up, I hurriedly left the hotel, made it through the crowded streets, and boarded a subway train to go to the meeting. I knew the direction to take, but I did not know the station nearest the meeting place. I was deeply concerned about the station where I should get off. Suddenly a young man in the seat next to me turned to me, his breath reeking with alcohol, and said, "Sorry, I drinking sake." Before I could answer him, I said to myself, "Young man, I don't care if you are dead drunk; you can speak English, and I am lost." Then I told him where I was going, and he stated that he knew the proper station. When we reached the stop, he asked if he could go with me. We sat together through a two-hour program featuring children. When we came out, he said, "Thanks for inviting me. This was the greatest experience I have ever had." He showed me the train to take back to the hotel, and we parted.

•

During 1958 and 1959, Martin Luther King Jr. was the guest of Friendship Baptist Church and other Harlem churches on several occasions. When he was stabbed by a demented woman while he was signing books in a department store on 125th Street, he had spoken the night before at Williams Institutional C.M.E. Church as a guest of the Heart of Harlem Neighborhood Council. When I met Coretta King at the airport after the stabbing, I found her to be obviously concerned about her husband, but just as obviously composed. Skilled surgeons at Harlem Hospital with the help of God saved his life. But outside the operating room until the wee hours of the morning New York Governor William Averell Harriman and I sat at a table praying for Martin. After several days in the hospital, Dr. King recuperated in Brooklyn, at the home of Dr. Sandy Ray.

•

In early 1961, Dr. King came to New York to set up an office of the SCLC. He met with A. Philip Randolph, Bayard Rustin, Jack Odell, and me. Later, Maya Angelou joined this group. The office, operating out of the headquarters of the Brotherhood of Sleeping Car Porters on 125th Street, was established principally to raise funds to support the overall programs of the SCLC. The funds were raised generally through letter solicitations and ads in the *New York Times*. At the height of the confrontation between the SCLC protesters and the Birmingham police, who turned fire hoses and dogs on the protestors, we carried a $6,500 full-page ad in the *New York Times,* with pictures of the police brutality. This ad generated gifts from across the nation that totaled some $362,000. Most of the money was used to post bonds for about three thousand young people who were arrested by the Birmingham police. The New York office continued to raise funds for the SCLC through the mid-1960s.

As the New York director of the SCLC, I worked closely with the movement. On one occasion when Dr. King came to New York, my wife hosted a lunch for him and a few others at our East Elmhurst home. At the lunch, Dr. King mentioned that our daughters had shown him the litter of puppies that Cuzzin, our mixed-breed dog, had given birth to. He said that he would like to have one of the puppies for his children. I promised that when they were weaned, I would send him one. When the time came, I shipped one of the puppies to him by air. A few months later I was in Atlanta and was invited to lunch at the King home. After lunch, I inquired about the puppy and said that I would like to see him. Martin's answer was, "Tom, why didn't you tell me that the puppy was not 'nonviolent'?" He said that the puppy had bitten a visitor, and for fear that the puppy might harm the children, he had gotten rid of the puppy.

His comment that the puppy was not "nonviolent" epitomized Dr. King's unusual sense of humor, which was further demonstrated on an occasion when he participated in a discussion with New York Governor Nelson Rockefeller and some clergymen. The meeting ran over two hours, it was 5:27 p.m., and Dr. King needed to catch a flight from Kennedy airport at 6:10 p.m. At that time of day it usually took forty-five to fifty minutes to go from 59th Street and

Central Park to Kennedy Airport. We made it in exactly thirty-eight minutes. As Dr. King dashed out of the car with Rev. George Lawrence carrying his luggage, he looked back at me and said, "Tom Kilgore, you are the greatest civil rights driver in the world." As they entered the terminal, the plane to Atlanta was backing out from the gate. Rev. Lawrence yelled, "Stop that Atlanta plane for Governor Rockefeller and Dr. Martin Luther King!" Even though Governor Rockefeller was back in his office, the plane taxied back, and Dr. King boarded.

•

By the early 1960s, Friendship's membership had grown beyond a thousand, and our church building and facilities were woefully inadequate. For the purpose of expansion we purchased seven brownstone houses on 130th Street that were back-to-back with the church building that faced 131st Street. Plans were drawn for building a four-story community house and educational building with the two top stories for much needed apartments for low- and middle-income families. These plans failed to materialize because in the late spring of 1963 I was called by the membership of Second Baptist Church in Los Angeles to accept the position of senior pastor of this historic African-American Baptist church, the oldest in southern California (see the Appendix, p. 219, for the history of Second Baptist Church). After much prayer and consultation with officers and members of Friendship and with my family, the decision was made to accept the call of Second Baptist Church.

The move from the East Coast to the West Coast that fall was made less difficult because both of our daughters were living in dormitories on their school's campuses. Lynn Elda had finished high school and was accepted as a freshman student at Antioch College in Yellow Springs, Ohio; and Jini was entering her senior year at her preparatory school, Palmer Memorial Institute, in Sedalia, North Carolina, where she and Lynn Elda both spent their last two years of high school.

•

Friendship was greatly disappointed with my decision to resign but at the same time was gracious and cooperative in the planning of a formal dinner and other appropriate ceremonies. On Thursday, October 7, 1963, my family and I were honored at a farewell dinner in the public dining room of Riverside Church. Over five hundred persons attended the dinner, and Deacon Vernon Dunlap, chairman of the board of deacons of Second Baptist Church, represented the church to which I had been called. On the Sunday following the dinner, I preached my farewell sermon at Friendship, and the following Tuesday my wife and I boarded a train at Grand Central Station for the three-day trip to Los Angeles. On Friday we arrived in Los Angeles and were met at the station by a delegation of Second Baptist Church members led by Deacon A. H. Spalding.

Chapter 5

California
1963–1985

My first sermon as pastor of Second Baptist Church was delivered at the 11:00 a.m. worship service, on Sunday, October 17. The title of my message was "We Have Come among You." The sanctuary and chapel were packed with more than a thousand persons. Among those who participated in the order of worship were Deacon Vernon Dunlap; Thelma Taylor, church secretary; Madame Mozelle Te Outley, church visitor; Anna G. Morrow, choir director; and Reverend Ulysses S. Donaldson.

The remaining months in 1963 were days and months of adjustment. These adjustments included a search for a parsonage or house and a series of installation services, which involved the following pastors and churches: Mt. Sinai Baptist Church, Rev. H. B. Charles, pastor; First A.M.E. Church, Rev. H. H. Brookins, pastor; Zion Hill Baptist Church, Rev. T. M. Chambers, pastor; and Holman United Methodist Church, Rev. L. L. White, pastor.

The first full year at Second Baptist was a productive one. As a new pastor, I found the work exciting, challenging, and at times difficult, but I also found responsiveness from officers and members of the church that was satisfying beyond my expectations.

Statistics often say in a few words what many paragraphs would be needed to tell. In my first full year, it was a pleasure for me to preach 79 sermons, visit 211 sick and shut-in members, hold 278 conferences with members and nonmembers, and attend 196 church organization meetings. I traveled more than 37,350 miles, mailed upward of 5,204 letters, met with 21 official boards, and held 10 staff meetings. And during this first year, we received 177 new members in Second Baptist and, by death, lost 26 members.

The ministry of Second Baptist Church went beyond the church borders as the pastor and designated members represented the church in the Los Angeles Baptist City Mission Society, the Southern California Baptist Convention, the American Baptist Convention, the Metropolitan Baptist Association, the Progressive Baptist State and National Convention, the National Council of Churches, the Los Angeles Church Federation, and many other religious and civic organizations. In addition, Second Baptist joined with six other community churches during the Lenten season in 1964 in establishing a community "Seven Last Words" worship service on Good Friday. This program has drawn large audiences each year since its beginning.

When I made the decision to accept the pastorate of Second Baptist Church, Dr. Martin Luther King Jr. asked me to open a Los Angeles SCLC office. In April of 1964, the office was opened at 2400 S. Western Avenue. Dr. King came and participated in the opening of the office, which was attended by a large number of SCLC supporters. As director of the office, I was assisted by Rev. Mansfield Collins, assistant director; Rose Carter, secretary, and Shirley Bell, assistant secretary. The major responsibilities of the office were to promote voter registration and raise funds to support national SCLC programs.

•

The year 1965 was an eventful one for the country, Los Angeles, and Second Baptist Church. In the church, we celebrated the eightieth anniversary, highlighted by a pageant that depicted the progress of the church under the leadership of its seven pastors. This event was climaxed by the last sermon preached by the venerable Rev. Jesse Jai McNeil, when on May 16, he preached on the topic "The New People of God."

That same year, 1965, brought the renovation of Griffith Hall, Second Baptist's fellowship hall, at the cost of $106,502, the operation of the largest Teen Post in the community, and the feting of nine hundred children in the community Christmas party.

In March, Selma, Alabama, had the attention of the nation, and I found myself there, working with Dr. King and the SCLC to help make preparations for the march from Selma to Montgomery to demonstrate for the right to vote. Before I arrived, a march had been attempted by about 250 persons, but they were brutally turned back by police wielding tear gas cannisters. While I was there, I joined about 1500 persons who attempted to march again, crossing the Edmund Pettus Bridge out of Selma, only to face a U-shaped contingent of armed police blocking the highway. The SCLC staff minister Hosea Williams said, "Let's march into them," but Dr. King said, "No, let us stop and have a prayer meeting." For one hour, we prayed on the highway and then went back to the church in Selma. At this point, Alabama's Governor George Wallace acquired a federal injunction barring the march, and Dr. King was severely criticized for retreating, especially by the young militants. After some reflection, he decided that the march must go on. Believing in safety in large numbers, Dr. King made a national appeal for clergypersons and others of good will to come in mass to Selma to attempt yet a third time the march to Montgomery. I returned to Los Angeles and worked with our SCLC office in organizing two planeloads of people who flew to Selma in response to King's appeal. Within a few days, President Johnson federalized the Alabama National Guard and committed four thousand army troops to Alabama to guard the marchers. On Sunday, March 21, two weeks after the second march attempt, Dr. King led the march from Selma to Montgomery. This episode resulted in the passing of the Voting Rights Act, securing for all citizens the right to vote without intimidation.

In August 1965, Dr. King called for a march around the county courthouse in Birmingham, which was considered by the SCLC to be the most segregated city in the country, to protest the unfair hiring practices that excluded African-Americans from clerical and other positions in the courthouse. The march was planned to take place during the meeting of the Board of Directors of the SCLC. Since I was in attendance at the board meeting, I participated in the march around the courthouse. As I marched with a young man who had tuned in his small radio, I heard something that attracted my attention, so I asked him to turn the volume up, and as he did I heard these words: "Los Angeles is experiencing a riot, and Watts is burning." I immediately left the picket line, checked out of the hotel, and caught a plane for Los Angeles.

High above Los Angeles, preparing for landing, I counted thirty-one buildings that were ablaze. I rushed home from the airport and immediately called H. H. Brookins and Jim Hargett. The three of us called together other ministers and community leaders and hurriedly developed a plan to go in pairs to talk with the young radicals to curb the violence and burning. We were able to get pledges of abatement. Our next step was to talk with public officials, including Governor Brown, the lieutenant governor, and others. While we were having these conversations, Dr. King called and stated that he was prepared to come to Los Angeles to help quiet the disturbance, but the governor and his advisors thought that King's presence would not help.

In the midst of these discussions with state and city officials, Rev. Billy Graham came to the city and flew over the riot areas in a helicopter. When Dr. King received the news of Billy Graham's helicopter visit, he called me and said, "Tom, if Billy Graham can come out there and fly over the city in a helicopter, surely I can come and sit down and talk to the young rioters." My answer was simple and to the point, "Come on, Martin."

The next day Martin and Bayard Rustin arrived, and we hastily set up a meeting with Mayor Sam Yorty and Police Chief William Parker. In the meeting, Brookins, Hargett, and I carefully outlined the plan we felt was already curbing the riot, and we suggested to the mayor and police chief that tensions would be lessened if the excessive number of police in the riot area would decrease. We also felt that Dr. King's presence would help greatly. After a lengthy conversation in which Dr. King and Bayard Rustin supported our suggestion, Chief Parker spoke. In a defiant and dictatorial manner he said, "I am the chief enforcement officer of this city, and I know what it takes to curb riots and lawlessness. I will not withdraw any officers, and if need be, I will send more police into the area." At this point, Bayard Rustin said to Dr. King, "Let's go to Watts and talk to the young people." Our conversation with the mayor and chief ended, and we waited until the next day. The chief's decision to send more police into Watts that Thursday evening increased the rioting, and the death toll rose.

On Friday we met at the Westminster Neighborhood Center, and Dr. King dialogued with about a hundred young African-American militants. He was well received by the group, and they listened with attention to his plea for nonviolence. But when he asked the group why they burned and destroyed property, one young fellow

answered, "They wouldn't listen any other way." Dr. King and Bayard Rustin left the next day, and we began the process of rebuilding
the city.

•

I was signally honored on October 10 to preach the 110th anniversary sermon of Bethel Baptist Church in Brevard, my home church
where I was licensed. I was grateful, too, for the opportunity to
be one of the American Baptist ministers who delivered twelve sermons on the Laymen's Hour radio program during 1965. I was
humbly honored when my messages were chosen with three other
persons who had spoken during the past three years as part of a
book entitled *Four Minute Talks for Laymen,* published by Judson
Press.

Although I was heavily involved in community activities locally
and nationally — in April I had been elected to the Board of Trustees
of Morehouse College — I was still able to perform important pastoral duties in Second Baptist Church. During 1965, 175 members
joined, increasing the membership to 2,035.

•

The beginning days of 1966 were busy ones for Second Baptist. We
held a Lenten series of services called "Voices of Living Faith" and
were challenged by powerful sermons from Rev. Ralph Abernathy,
Rev. James Hargett, Rev. J. H. Jackson, Dr. Carl Sagerhammer, and
Dr. H. H. Brookins.

On April 4, representatives from the U.S. Health, Education, and
Welfare Department, the State Department of Social Services, and
the Welfare Department of Los Angeles County Bureau of Public
Assistance, plus city and county officials and friends of the community and church members, gathered at Second Baptist to participate
in the opening and dedication of the Second Baptist Children's Center. With a grant of $97,200 under Title V of the Office of Economic
Opportunity (OEO), we opened the nation's pilot project for training at all levels for day care work. At the same time, we began
operating a child care center that accommodated ninety-two children daily from 6:30 a.m. to 6:00 p.m. The program also had

a jobs training component for the parents of the enrolled children. Jeannetta became the director of this nationally recognized center.

In addition to attending local, state, and national conferences and conventions and fulfilling preaching engagements around the country, I worked with Rev. E. V. Hill and others in organizing and developing an OIC Program (Leon Sullivan's Opportunities Industrialization Centers) for the recruitment and training of unemployed and underemployed persons. I was honored to participate in the President's White House Conference, "To Fulfill These Rights," during May and June. In general, 1966 was a year of much travel; I logged 262,269 miles.

•

The next year, 1967, Second Baptist and I were very busy. We continued to try to witness effectively in a very complex society, succeeding in some areas and failing in others. Our membership increased to 2,175. From contributions of $186,408, we gave $17,329 for local social service ministries and $29,329 for Christian missions, Christian education, and benevolences.

Second Baptist presented many outstanding preachers and speakers to the Los Angeles community. On January 30, Dr. Benjamin E. Mays was the guest speaker and guest of honor for a Morehouse Scholarship dinner. Later in the year, Rev. George Lawrence spoke for Men's Day, and Dr. Marion Wright Edelman was our guest speaker for Civil Rights Sunday on July 23.

My outside activities included the centennial sermon for the General Baptist State Convention of North Carolina, a lecture series at the California Baptist Seminary in Covina, and the conducting of a Social Action Evangelism Project with Lakeshore Avenue Baptist Church in Oakland. In the spring of the year, Jeannetta, Jini, and I motored across country to Yellow Springs, Ohio, to attend Lynn Elda's graduation from Antioch College. After her graduation, Lynn Elda returned to New York to head up a community program in Brooklyn for disadvantaged children, and except for brief periods of time during her adulthood in which she lived in Washington, D.C., and New Jersey, she has remained an ardently loyal New Yorker. She and her husband now own a brownstone home in Harlem and a getaway beach home on Long Island at Sag Harbor in the Hamptons. Their subdivision, named Azure Rest, celebrated its fiftieth anniversary as a community in 1997 and was lauded as the first beachfront resort community in the United States organized and owned by African-Americans.

•

In late 1966, I called the dean of the California Baptist Seminary and requested two students for internships at Second Baptist. He promised to call me back in a day or so. When he called back, he said that he was sorry that he could not help me because all his black students had been assigned to churches. I said that I did not ask for black students; I asked for students. He apologetically said, "I'll call you back," which he did, and the day after that two white students, Ellis Keck and Val Sauer, showed up at Second Baptist for interviews. Both were assigned duties as interns.

Keck and Sauer were well received by the congregation. Sauer remained with Second for a year, then transferred to another church. Keck remained through his graduation and then was given a full-time position as associate pastor, which he fulfilled for three years until he was called to the pastorate of First Baptist Church in Salt Lake City.

Two weeks before Thanksgiving, I received a call from a young man who was known in the community as "Brother Crook." He was affiliated with the militant, under-thirty young blacks of the middle and late 1960s. He said to me that the older black militants who had met in Jersey City in 1966 would not be meeting in 1967, but about nine hundred young black militants from nine central and western states wanted to meet in Los Angeles during Thanksgiving weekend. His problem was that he could find no place to meet. "What can you do, Reverend?" he asked. I told him that I would return his call.

I polled the fifteen members of the church trustee board and suggested that we permit this group to use our sanctuary and other facilities. I received fourteen positive answers and one negative one. I immediately called "Brother Crook" and told him that I had found a place to accommodate their group. When I told him that it was Second Baptist, he was momentarily breathless. The conditions for their using the church were as follows:

1. They would come in after our regular Thanksgiving service on Thanksgiving Day.

2. They would have access to the sanctuary, social hall, rest rooms, etc.

3. They would not smoke in the building.

4. My white associate pastor would be assigned as their contact person.

5. I would address and welcome the group.

6. There would be no profanity used in their deliberations.

7. They would have to finish before midnight Saturday.

The meetings were carried out smoothly. Rev. Keck reported to me that on only four occasions did the presiding persons have to speak to presenters about improper language. At 1:00 a.m. on Sunday, their conference ended.

This gesture on the part of Second Baptist of permitting the group to use its facilities free of charge made an impression on community militants that paid off in great dividends just a few months later following the assassination of Dr. Martin Luther King Jr.

The year ended with a children's Christmas party on December 21, held in the court of our community center and attended by 850 community children.

Sadness came to the Kilgore family in late December when the first of the twelve brothers and sisters in my family passed. Waymon Kilgore, the firstborn of the family, was funeralized on December 11.

There was triumph and tragedy in 1968, a never-to-be-forgotten year for our country and the world. On the credit side, we witnessed great and thrilling achievements. Nationally, we saw the Poor People's Campaign move our nation to do something about poverty, and we looked with awe as three astronauts orbited the moon. We observed some degree of saneness and progress in solving our problems in education, police protection, and job training. The community ministries of Second Baptist took a new giant step in the dedication of the Pueblo Christian Action Center, a youth development and training program in a densely populated low-income housing project.

The debit side of 1968 presented a sadder picture. The evilness of the crucifixion of Jesus was put into sharp focus by the assassination of Dr. Martin Luther King Jr. just a few days before Easter. The murky waters of hate that flow in our country at times came to the forefront in the assassination of Senator Robert Kennedy in a hotel in Los Angeles in June. The tragic deaths of these two great and good men left the whole world poorer, indeed. Added to these tragedies was the continuation of the no-win war in Vietnam that ultimately snuffed out the lives of fifty-four hundred Americans and countless hundreds of thousands of Vietnamese.

On March 12, Dr. King preached his last sermon in California from the pulpit of Second Baptist Church on the subject "Hope." When he was killed three weeks later in Memphis, where he was leading a protest against the city in behalf of underpaid garbage collection workers, violence broke out in almost a hundred cities and towns across the country, but not in Los Angeles. On the evening of his assassination on April 4, the religious and black militant leaders met and planned a mass meeting to be held at Second Baptist Church the following evening. The call for the meeting went out by word of mouth, radio, and television. The next night, more than eighteen hundred people packed the church. The featured speakers were Rev. James Hargett and Dr. Maulana Ron Karenga. Young men of the US organization served as ushers, and the Second Baptist choir sang. The message of the meeting was simple yet profound: Dr. King had given his life for a nonviolent society; therefore, let us honor him by keeping Los Angeles a nonviolent city.

The mass meeting on Friday night was followed by a hastily planned city-wide meeting in the Los Angeles Coliseum the following Sunday afternoon, which drew sixteen thousand persons, and Los Angeles moved through the weekend without any violence.

The meeting of the young black militants over the Thanksgiving weekend in 1967 had helped to create a bond between the churches and the militants in the community. In large part, this was why Los Angeles was saved from the riots and devastation that many U.S. cities suffered after Dr. King's assassination.

Two days after Dr. King's death, my mother, Eugenia Kilgore, died. Mama had been a widow since Papa's death in 1935. She had had some proposals to remarry, but she had avoided them all by saying, "I have nine husbands," referring to her nine sons. My family and I traveled to Atlanta to attend the funeral and memorial services for Dr. King. I offered the prayer at the service held on the campus of Morehouse College, which was attended by some seventy-five thousand persons, after helping to guide the mule cart that carried his body from Ebenezer Church, where the funeral was held, to the Morehouse campus for the mass service afterward. As we marched to Morehouse, the wheel on my side of the mule cart became loose, and I had to keep pushing it back on its axle to prevent it from falling off. Somehow this seemed a fitting metaphor for the instability that arose in our country following Dr. King's assassination.

From Atlanta we went to Brevard for Mama's funeral the next day.

•

In the passing days of 1968, I was guest preacher and counselor in late April for the "Design for Living" week at Maryland State College, Princess Anne, Maryland. In May, I delivered the commencement address and received an honorary degree from Morris College, in Atlanta, and Jeannetta, Lynn Elda, and I attended Jini's graduation from Occidental College, just outside of Los Angeles. In June I visited and worked for two days in Resurrection City in Washington, and in September I was elected to the Board of Directors of the Bank of Finance in Los Angeles. As 1968 came to a close, I was honored by Second Baptist for having served for five years as senior pastor.

The exciting '60s came to a close when the curtain went down at midnight, December 31, 1969. The decade began with hope in the election of President Kennedy and ended in a series of confrontations and polarizations centered around color and national priorities. In between were triumphs and tragedies, progress and problems, advancement and retrogression.

Some of the best minds, spirits, and lives were snuffed out in the '60s: John F. Kennedy, Robert F. Kennedy, Malcolm X, Martin Luther King Jr., Medgar Evers, Tom Mboya, and Viola Liuzzo, to mention a few. But over against these tragedies, there were significant triumphs. The legal back of segregation was broken, and the civil rights bills and other progressive bills at the national and state levels were passed. The March on Washington and the Poor People's

Campaign helped to clear our vision so we could see the plight of the poor in America. Either in folly or triumph, we spent multiplied millions of dollars to explore the moon and, tragically, billions of dollars fighting a sinful and senseless war in Vietnam.

During all of the successful movements and mistakes, the triumphs and tragedies of the 1960s, Second Baptist remained vibrant and kept developing as a true church. In March, under the leadership of Kathryn Anderson, we delivered seventeen hundred new and renewed memberships to the local branch of the NAACP. In that same month, we repeated our annual speakers series, "Voices of Living Faith," with presentations by Dr. Kelley Miller Smith, outstanding pastor, and Dr. Jitsuo Morikawa, educator.

During the week of May 14–18 the annual session of the American Baptist Convention was held in Cincinnati. Under the leadership of President "Cubby" Rutenber, the meeting as a whole followed the pattern of dynamic speakers, great music, and intense dialogue on religious and social issues. Two events added another dimension to the meeting that made it different from any previous ones.

The first of these events was the appearance of James Forman, former executive director of the Student Nonviolent Coordinating Committee (SNCC) and representative of a radical militant group, the National Black Economic Development Conference. The NBEDC had created the "Black Manifesto," a document demanding a half billion dollars from white American religious organizations for the development of neglected black communities in the country. The target projects of the manifesto were the strengthening of black colleges, the building of a network of radio and television stations, the opening of jobs at upper- and middle-management levels, and other changes for the advancement of black people.

When President Rutenber heard that Jim Forman was on the meeting ground, he sent for me and said, "Tom, Jim Forman is here and wants to address the convention, but the program is already set. What should we do?" I said to him calmly and positively, "We must unset the program and permit him to speak." My suggestion was accepted; Forman spoke for forty-five minutes, outlining the reparations program, and requested $60 million from the convention. His speech pointed out the great disparities between whites and blacks in America, in all fields of endeavor. He made sensible suggestions on how gaps could be closed and received a more than mild ovation at the close of his speech.

The American Baptist Convention did not comply with the Forman request, but his presentation ignited a movement. By the middle of the next year, the ABC and the Progressive National Baptist Convention formed a partnership and created a program called the Fund of Renewal with a goal of $12 million to support black and other minority colleges and Christian community centers operated by churches in various urban and rural areas. The goal was not reached, but during a period of two and a half years, more than $9 million was received for the Fund.

The next unusual happening at the Cincinnati meeting was my election to the presidency of the convention. For more than a dozen years prior to my election, I had been a faithful supporter of the convention. I had served as western vice president of the Home Mission Board and on various committees. I had some ambivalence about being called the first black president of the convention and would rather have been looked upon as a pastor and member in the convention whose support and talents had added to the strength of our mission.

As president from May 1969 to May 1970, I was away from Second Baptist roughly 60 percent of the time. The pastoral ministries were carefully and efficiently performed by Associate Pastor Ellis Keck and Assistant Pastors Ulysses S. Donaldson, Seth T. Toney, and Gerald Adams.

The novelty of being the first black president of a predominantly white religious group was evidenced in many ways. The person who planned my travel and engagements reported that I traveled more miles and preached to and addressed more audiences than any previous president. The facts are these: I traveled 179,249 miles, delivered 69 sermons and addresses in churches, state and regional meetings, and other gatherings, and spoke in 29 states and 43 cities.

•

I was considered by some of the more conservative persons in the convention to be a radical militant. Some of this grew out of my urgent appeal for the convention to hear James Forman. Some people had read a news release that went out when I was elected that said a black militant had been elected.

On October 19, 1969, I was guest preacher at First Baptist Church, Grants Pass, Oregon. Following the service, there was a dinner reception at which I was to speak. The address was followed by a question and answer period. The first question came from a man in the back of the dining room, and as I stood to receive his question, I noticed that he was holding two books. It turned out that one was a Bible, and the other was a dictionary. He began his question with this statement: "When you were elected, I read in the newspaper that you were a militant. Is that true?" He followed his question by reading from his dictionary the definition of a militant. My first answer to his question was a correction. I said, "If you read the news release correctly, it said, 'The new black president described himself as a militant with love.' " I followed this statement by asking him if he believed in the Baptist religious principle that after our conversion, we are in a church militant, and when we leave this earth we go to a church triumphant. He said he believed that principle. I followed by saying to him, and all present, that my militancy was "against sin of all forms, segregation, discrimination, and all actions that prohibited any person from exercising his or her given rights." The background to the brother's question was revealed to me by the pastor of the church, Rev. Brown, after the dinner reception. The questioner was a retired policeman from the Los Angeles police department. He was one of the many policemen who were deputized to quell the Watts Riot in the summer of 1965. His basic concept of a militant was one who starts riots.

•

In the summer of 1969 I was invited to address the American Baptist Laymen's annual meeting at the American Baptist Retreat Center in Green Lake, Wisconsin. About a thousand laymen were in attendance, and I was well received in spite of the fact that this segment of the convention was considered as its most conservative group. As the meeting began, there was some very spirited singing, and many brothers gave their testimonies of faith, but I was shocked when the brother who gave the prayer for the occasion prayed for me in this manner: "Lord, have mercy on our new president, give him a clear vision, and save him from his communist leanings." I responded to his prayer by including in my speech a strong appeal to that predominantly white laymen's group to use their influence as Christian men to help eradicate from America and the world all forms of segregation and discrimination and help build a society of peace and love for all people of all races, creeds, and colors.

In the fall of 1969, I addressed the American Baptist Conventions of Ohio, New Jersey, Colorado, Wisconsin, New York, Southern California, Oregon, Kansas, Northern California, and Massachusetts. I also spoke at the National Council of Churches meeting in Detroit. In between my participation in American Baptist meetings, I served as a consultant to the black ecumenical committee at Grotonwood, Massachusetts; attended the Morehouse trustee board meeting in New York; spoke at a citywide community Thanksgiving service in Nashville; and served as the general chairman of "A Salute to Mrs. Coretta Scott King" at the Coconut Grove in Los Angeles. This event generated some $56,000 that was divided equally between the Los Angeles SCLC office and the Atlanta Martin Luther King Jr. Center for Non-Violent Social Change.

As the curtain closed on 1969, I had finished six years as pastor of Second Baptist Church. In the performance of my priestly, prophetic, and pastoral ministries in 1969, I administered 13 communion services, conducted 13 funerals, performed 6 weddings, dedicated 12 babies, and attended 104 church group meetings, 17 staff meetings, and 6 board meetings. I also attended 79 civic and community meetings and 76 church-related meetings, counseled 175 persons, visited 92 sick persons, and presided over 3 church conferences.

•

During 1970, Second Baptist Church continued its involvement in various ministries. We tried to remain conscious of the changing times, and as we analyzed the black spirit movement, the war in Vietnam, and the polarization of races and groups, we tried hard to find what the gospel had to say to these conditions. In the early part of the year, most of my time was given to the work of the American Baptist Convention. I addressed city, state, and regional meetings in Chicago, Cincinnati, Kansas City, and New York City, as well as in Charlotte, North Carolina; Richmond, Virginia; Providence, Rhode Island; Burlington, Vermont; New London, Connecticut; Washington, D.C.; and Arizona.

In early April, I attended and presided at a meeting of American Baptist leaders in Charlotte, North Carolina. For years, some churches in the southern states had been affiliated with the convention. The Charlotte meeting, held at Myers Park Baptist Church, organized the southern churches into a new American Baptist region, which has grown from twenty-five churches to over two hundred.

I completed my tenure as president of the American Baptist Convention, as I presided over the annual meeting in Seattle, Washington, May 13–17, 1970. Our program theme was "God Speaks in Revolution, Reconciliation, and Renewal: Listen and Respond." Major program presentations were made by Carl F. H. Henry, Evans E. Crawford, Harvey E. Cox, and Coretta Scott King. Special music was rendered by the Alderson-Broadus choir, Second Baptist Church choir, and Rose Battle English. The four-day meeting was attended by more than three thousand messengers, including my wife and daughter Jini.

I will ever be grateful to Edwin H. Tuller, general secretary; Frank Johnstone, associate general secretary; Claude Black, program chairman; and William Elkins, chairman of the Resolution Committee, for their professional cooperation in making the annual session of the convention a memorable one.

Another experience worthy of note that took place in the summer of 1970 was the attendance of twenty-seven Second Baptist members, including my wife, and me at the 12th Congress of the World Baptist Alliance in Tokyo. But in June, just before we went on our trip, we stopped by my hometown, Brevard, where I officiated at the wedding of our daughter Jini, held at Bethel "A" Baptist Church. She married Dennis Robinson, a singer and bandleader with "The Tams," a popular rhythm and blues group that my brother, Rockerfeller, had managed for a number of years. During the fourteen years of their marriage, Jini and Dennis had two children, daughter Niambi Ayanna, born in 1973, and son Okera Damani, born in 1975.

In Tokyo, I was called upon to stand in for a panelist who didn't show for a panel on "Racism." In my remarks, I stated that in America some improvement had lessened racism, but our country was still a victim of racism in almost every segment of life. Needless to say, my frankness did not please the conservative U.S.A. Baptists.

We left Tokyo for Taiwan, Hong Kong, Thailand, India, Kenya, Ethiopia, Greece, Israel, Italy, France, and England. The forty-two-day trip through twelve countries and three continents was of great educational value. It was one in which new friendships were made, and in which some old ones were broken. When twenty-seven people travel and live close together in planes and hotels for forty-two days, they either bond more closely or lose what they thought was a good friendship. Both of these experiences took place on our tour. The following persons experienced the unforgettable three-continent tour: Roberta Austin, Grace Beasley, Guinevere Bland, Mable Brown, Ann Collins, Ola Mae Dailey, Edna Dilworth, Alma Dotson, Walter Dotson, Ruth Ficklin, E. W. Fisher, Vila Hancock, Jolaine Harkless, Zola Harkless, Annie Kilgore, Herman Kilgore, Jo-Helen Johnson, Zula Lee, Anna Mallory, Faye Mattox, Bernice McNair, Barbara Moore, Pearl Price, Kathryn Smith, Gussie Spiller, Jeannetta, and me.

As a result of contacts made in Ethiopia by our tour group, the next year six students were brought to Los Angeles to further their education. Members of the tour group invited them to stay in their homes until they could secure campus or other housing. The students were Fisseha Tsion Egziabher, Tseboat Mengesha, Ketsela Meshesha, Girma Berhone Selassie, Rahel Tamrat, and Senaite Trehai. After graduating from colleges, universities, and technical schools, the majority of these students became citizens and remained in the United States. Two of them, Fisseha and Girma, stayed with Jeannetta and me and became our unofficial sons. Both married and began their own families. Fisseha headed up international student housing at the University of Southern California for a number of years before moving to another state, and Girma and his wife developed a very successful business: a medical diagnostic laboratory.

After a very busy year's service as the president of the American Baptist Convention and the forty-two days of world travel, the activities in the fall of the year included attending and addressing the Nebraska Baptist Convention in Grand Island and the Indiana Baptist Convention in Fort Wayne. In early September I attended the Lott Carey Foreign Mission Convention in Fayetteville, North Carolina. On September 6, I was guest preacher in New York City's Riverside Church. I spoke from Genesis 42 and 43 and Acts 9 on the topic "Barriers, Brothers, and Bread."

The remainder of the year was spent in pastoral duties in the church and community. In sum 1970 was eventful, challenging, and frustrating, but, in the end, it was a rewarding year.

•

Life in Second Baptist Church in 1971 was highlighted by several novel events. At the beginning of the year a study commission was created for the purpose of executing a self-study of the church and its ministries. The goal of the commission was to recommend to the church a structure and thrust for a ministry that would involve each member in the highest level of spiritual worship, evangelism, social action, religious education, and local and global mission support. The commission was divided into eight subgroups: Audit, Budget and Finance, Christian Education, Communications, Community Relations, Service Organizations, Memorial and Historical, Scholarship and Awards, and Worship. Each of these study groups was mandated to do an in-depth study and report periodically to the commission. This procedure was in process for two years and nine months.

On the third Sunday in March, Dr. Benjamin E. Mays was the guest preacher at Second Baptist. His sermon topic was "The Least of These." Following the worship service, Dr. Mays was honored at a dinner and autographed 275 copies of his autobiography, *Born to Rebel.*

In the early summer, we learned that Rev. Ellis M. Keck, our associate pastor, had been called to the pastorate of First Baptist Church, Salt Lake City. This was sad news for the Second Baptist family. Rev. Keck was one of two young men — both of them white — who had served as ministerial interns, then as staff ministers in our church. In four years, the Keck family had warmed its way into the hearts of the Second Baptist family and the Los Angeles community. As the Kecks prepared to take leave for their new appointment, we honored them with a program and reception that lasted for four and a half hours and was attended by over seven hundred church members and friends.

Among the highlights of the program were expressions from the church youth group, several of whom gave complimentary remarks about the effectiveness of Rev. Keck's special work with them. But the most dramatic and unforgettable moment came from Larry Elkins. Larry was a young church member who was deeply involved in the Black Power movement and was very skeptical about my judgment in selecting white intern ministers at Second Baptist. When he arose to speak, he made a statement that reflected his complete acceptance of Rev. Keck as youth minister. He said, "I questioned Pastor Kilgore's judgment in bring white ministers into our church, but having worked with Rev. Keck for four years, I have only one statement to make, and it is, 'I found him to be a real dude.' "

Rev. Keck laughed about that comment and others similar to it. He remembered that once when he visited a member who had been sick and unable to attend church for a long time, the man, totally surprised to see a white man, said, "No, you can't be from Second Baptist Church."

There were three ministerial additions to the staff in 1971. Into the life of the church came David Morris as a ministerial intern, William Campbell, student minister, and Rev. Marvin Robinson, a pastoral consultant.

A pall of sadness encompassed the Kilgore family when Mamie Beatrice Harris, my baby sister, died at age forty-seven, a victim of cancer. She was funeralized at Bethel Baptist Church in Brevard on September 11.

Three extraordinary events took place near the end of 1971. On October 18, our first grandchild, Robin Jeannetta Raschard was born to our elder daughter, Lynn Elda. Robin brought a lot of joy to Jeannetta and me. She lived with her mother and father, James Raschard, first in New Jersey, then in New York. At the age of two, when she was sent to Los Angeles to spend a good portion of the summer with us, a lifelong loving relationship was formed. Every summer thereafter, into her teen years, Robin spent the summer with us and was joined by her cousins, Niambi and Okera, Jini's children, born in 1973 and 1975, who lived in northern California, about four hundred miles away. They began coming when Jeannetta determined that they were old enough (two years and one year, respectively), a little younger than what might have been my determination, but I soon found out that this was one area where I was not in charge. Jini's family also spent most Christmases with us, and Jeannetta and I spent several Thanksgivings with them. This, along with the Kilgore family reunion, held every other year, gave us opportunities to bond with our grandchildren. Among the grandchildren, Robin took a special liking to me, and I enjoyed seeing her whenever I happened to be in New York. Naturally, I was greatly pleased when she chose to attend Spelman College, Morehouse's sister school. My frequent trips to Morehouse made it possible for me to stay in touch with her during her college years. She graduated in 1993 and began medical studies at the New York Institute of Technology, College of Osteopathic Medicine, Long Island. Our granddaughter Niambi is married to Charles Cade Jr., and they have given us two great-grandsons, Justen Charles Cade and Joshua Simeon Kilgore Cade. In 1997, grandson Okera is a senior at Texas Southern University in Houston.

•

A second event occurred on December 21, 1971, when Second Baptist climaxed the year with an event called "70 Anniversary Bells at Christmas." Church members Brother Ben and Sister Minnie Underwood were honored as we celebrated with them their seventieth wedding anniversary. Sixty-three couples, most of whom had been married thirty-five-years or more, joined the procession and were a part of the vows repeating ceremony. Jeannetta and I were one of the sixty-three couples, and she chaired the event. The third event took place on December 26, when ground was broken for the construction of a thirty-nine unit housing project for senior citizens and small families. In less than twelve months the development was completed and named Griffith Gardens in memory of Dr. and Mrs. Thomas L. Griffith, the fifth pastor of the church and his wife.

•

In 1972 fifty-two new members were received at Second Baptist, and twenty members were claimed by death. Among that number was Dr. U. S. Donaldson, the associate pastor. Dr. Donaldson made a great contribution to the life and work of Second Baptist and is remembered for his diligence, scholarship, thoroughness in discharging his duties, and love for people.

After attending the midyear board meeting of the Progressive National Baptist Convention, my wife and I relaxed for an eight-day winter vacation in Nassau, Bahamas. When we returned from vacation, our attention and interest were focused on old and new ministries of the church. The eight subunits of the Study Commission were busy analyzing and critiquing every segment of church life. The Griffith Gardens board members were keeping watchful eyes on the completion of the housing project. The deacons were busy conducting a new registration of church members.

From mid-February to the early part of the summer, I was kept busy in fulfilling engagements and receiving unexpected honors. I gave a presentation in the C. D. Hubert Lecture Series at the Inter-denominational Theological Center in Atlanta and taught a class on "The Black Church," at the American Baptist Seminary in West Covina, California. On May 7, I was guest preacher at the Fifth Street Baptist Church, Richmond, Virginia, where Rev. Henry Gregory was the pastor. In the afternoon, Virginia Union Seminary conferred upon me the honorary LL.D. degree. From Richmond I flew to Denver for the annual meeting of the American Baptist Convention.

During the summer and fall months of 1972, our Second Baptist tour group traveled to Canada, New England, the southeastern states, and the Blue Ridge Mountains of western North Carolina. In mid-October, I completed nine years of service as senior pastor of Second Baptist Church. A complete new chapter opened in my life on June 7. Earlier in the spring, I had been visited in my home by the chaplain of the University of Southern California, Dr. Alvin Rudisill. He had come to extend an invitation to me on behalf of President John R. Hubbard to deliver the sermon for the annual baccalaureate service. I gave an oral consent, and within a few days a letter of invitation came from Dr. Hubbard. The letter stated that it was customary for baccalaureate speakers to receive an honorary degree at the commencement exercises. I began to prepare my sermon, "Toward a Soul-Full Community" (see below p. 156). On June 8, I marched in the commencement procession and, along with two other persons, received the honorary L.H.D. from the university.

A few days after the commencement, I received a call from Dr. Hubbard inviting me to have lunch with him. I consented and joined him on the appointed day in his private dining room. As we sat down at the table across from each other, he looked straight at me and said, "Your sermon at the baccalaureate service upset me." I looked straight at him, and said, "One of the purposes of a sermon is to upset persons." He then said, "You were on target, and you were right, and we must do something to change our image." He further stated he would like for me to take a position at the university, maybe a vice president for community affairs. I answered that my base of credibility in the community was in my pastorate of

Second Baptist Church, but I would consider giving some time as a consultant until he could find someone to take the position. At this point we agreed that I would consult the church and he would consult the university trustees. If there were mutual agreements, I would become a part-time member of his staff and would proceed to create an Office for Community Affairs.

•

Our country and the world experienced many changes in 1973. Some were good; others were bad. A satellite kept speeding toward Neptune; curtains were drawn on a phase of the Vietnam war; the floodgates of Watergate were opened wide; Tom Bradley, Maynard Jackson, and Coleman Young were elected as mayors of major cities; White House worship services ceased for a season; and the presidential tapes were lost or erased.

In Second Baptist Church, it was a year of some excellent endings and some fine new beginnings. Griffith Gardens was dedicated and formally opened during an impressive ceremony on Sunday, May 6. A large crowd of church members and civic and community persons joined in. The highlight of the occasion was the cutting of the ribbon by the children of Dr. and Mrs. Thomas L. Griffith, the pioneer former pastor and wife of Second Baptist (1921–40) who were memorialized in the naming of the housing complex. The ribbon was cut by Anna Griffith Morrow, Esther Griffith Merriweather, Thomas L. Griffith, and Lloyd Griffith. Councilman Gilbert Lindsay, Jeannetta, and I joined in the ribbon cutting.

On May 11, Pastor Emeritus J. Raymond Henderson and Mrs. Henderson were honored by members and friends of Second Baptist on the occasion of his seventy-fifth birthday.

My ministries outside of the church during the first six months of '73 were many and far apart. They began in January with preaching engagements at First John Baptist Church, Chicago, and as guest speaker for the Chicago Sunday Evening Club, on January 8. In mid- and late February I attended the Morehouse School of Religion board meeting and the executive committee meeting of the Fund of Renewal. In March, I was guest lecturer at California Baptist Seminary and participated in the OIC (Leon Sullivan's Opportunities Industrialization Centers) Pilgrimage in Washington, D.C. In April I attended the Morehouse College Trustee Board meeting, was guest preacher at Trinity Baptist Church in Aiea, Hawaii, spoke at the annual dinner of Salt Lake City's branch of the NAACP, and later in the month attended the annual meeting of the American Baptist Convention in Lincoln, Nebraska.

At the early summer business meeting of Second Baptist Church, the General Board recommended my taking a part-time position as director of community affairs at the University of Southern California. The recommendation precipitated much discussion. Many expressed misgivings about Second Baptist having a part-time pastor. A conclusion was reached when Trustee Ernest Shell stated that I already spent at least 30 percent of my time in community relations that my acceptance of the part-time position at the university would add a new dimension of community service to the ministry of Second Baptist. His statement ended the discussion, and a vote was taken of the 276 persons voting. Nine voted negatively.

On July 1, 1973, the Office of Special Community Affairs was opened and began operating out of the campus religious center. I served as director, and Aurora Banks was my assistant and secretary.

Prior to the creation of the Community Affairs office, the university had received a federal grant for two campus programs: the Black Students Service Center and El Centro Chicano, but the federal grant money was running out, and I was asked to find a new source of funding for the two student programs. Our office applied to the City of Los Angeles and Los Angeles County for block grant funds. For the next two years the programs were funded by these public funds.

By the late fall of 1973, the Office of Special Community Affairs was well known on the campus. As community affairs advisor to the president, I reported our programs in the president's senior staff meetings each month.

As the community became aware of the community affairs office at USC, the office was flooded with calls and requests for interviews. A case in point was a call from John Lamar Hill, the owner of Angelus Funeral Home and Radio Station KJLH. Radio station KIIS had registered a complaint with the Federal Communications Commission stating that KJLH's signal was interfering with theirs. KUSC, the university's station, had signed the complaint with KIIS. Mr. Hill asked me to set up a meeting with the manager of KUSC. This I did, and in the meeting Wallie Smith, KUSC manager, and his engineer met in a two-hour discussion with John Lamar Hill and his engineer and came to an agreement that KUSC would withdraw its complaint. This they did, and the Federal Communications Commission dropped the case against KJLH. Mr. Hill, a generous philanthropist, later included the university among his charities.

In the fall of 1973, USC chaplain Dr. Alvin Rudisill and I visited four college and university campuses to study their community relations programs: the University of Pennsylvania, Temple University, Bronx Community College, and Detroit's Wayne State University. The findings of this trip were greatly helpful in strengthening the work of the Office of Special Community Affairs.

As the curtain closed on 1973, I had finished my tenth year as pastor. We had received that year 61 new members, lost 38 by death, and ended the year with 1,605 active members, 197 delinquent members, and 60 shut-in members. Four families remembered the church with bequests and gifts. Brother and Sister Precious Lawton and Sister Annie McNeal left the church bequests of over $4,000. Brother Mack Covington gave the church land in San Bernardino, and Brother Walter Doston gave the church twenty-five shares of Sears Roebuck stock.

●

Historians have had great difficulty in trying to set 1974 in true focus. It was a year of a plethora of unusual happenings. The Irish Catholics and the Irish Protestants continued to kill each other. Starvation advanced at a rapid rate in Asia, Africa, and other parts of the world. The Middle East remained a powder keg. The oil-producing Arab nations flexed their muscles, raised their voices, and sent the white-dominated world into a financial spin. A president resigned in shame, and we got a new president without electing him. A satellite made its way to Venus, and 25 million Americans were still ill housed and living in poverty. One Watergate trial after another took place, and a deposed, sick president was pardoned.

In the flux of these changes and problems, Second Baptist Church stayed alive and made some progress. We spent the first six months of the year getting used to our new organizational structure and emphasizing our evangelistic responsibilities. This new structure, StEM (Stewardship, Evangelism, and Mission) was designed to involve all church members, including children, in geographical cell groups in which the church ministry of stewardship, evangelism, and mission would be carried out.

A new venture in the life of Second Baptist Church was inaugurated in the fall of 1974. We began, through the Second Baptist Men's Breakfast Club, the "Religion and Life Forum Series," which would take place annually. The theme of the first forum was "The Quality of Life — Toward a Survival of Excellence." The speakers for this inaugural forum were Dr. C. Eric Lincoln, then professor of the sociology of religion at Fisk University and a noted author, editor, lecturer, and authority in the area of race relations; Rev. Jesse Jackson, then president of Operation PUSH and a civil rights activist; Vernon Jordan, then national executive director of the Urban League; Los Angeles Mayor Tom Bradley; Dr. Robert McAfee Brown, then professor of religion at Stanford University; Dr. John Bennett, president emeritus and Reinhold Niebuhr Professor Emeritus of Social Ethics at Union Theological Seminary; and Dr. John R. Hubbard, president of the University of Southern California.

During 1974, I was elected in April as chairman of the Morehouse College Trustee Board, a position which I kept for the next seventeen years, and second vice president of the Progressive National Baptist Convention. At Second Baptist, I baptized 36 new members, blessed 13 babies, conducted 31 funerals, performed 9 weddings, and traveled 72,009 miles.

By 1974, the Office of Special Community Affairs at USC had expanded greatly. Gloria Cohen joined the staff as secretary, and Betty Carmichael became assistant director. One day Eugene Brooks, an assistant professor in the USC School of Architecture, and Levi Kingston came to the Community Affairs office to discuss parcel D-2 in the Hoover Redevelopment Project. D-2 was five and a half acres of land that the Community Redevelopment Agency had tentatively agreed to permit the Los Angeles school system to utilize for the construction of a school building for handicapped children. The development of the University Village shopping center, adjacent to USC, was completed, and our office of Community Affairs felt that the proper usage of the remaining acres in the Hoover Redevelopment Project would be for housing. I contacted the Community Redevelopment Agency and requested a hearing. The request was granted, and USC Vice President for Business Affairs Anthony Lazzaro, Vice President for Community Relations Leonard Wines, and

I made our plea before the agency, convincing them that the better use of the land was for housing. School Superintendent Johnston's reaction was that he was greatly disappointed that I, as a minister, would influence a vote against children. Within a year following the agency's action, construction was started for 150 units of housing. When it was finished, Century Gardens offered affordable housing for USC students and families of the community.

•

The year 1975 was marked by many religious conflicts and conferences. Protestants and Catholics continued to clash in Ireland. Civil war broke out in Angola, and Christian-Moslem conflicts in Beirut turned that paradise of the Middle East into a bloody heap. But while these destructive conflicts were taking place, world religious conferences were attended by thousands, for the paradox of the human species is that we are so fragile on the one hand and so able to abide change on the other. We, therefore, still carry on in spite of all that is happening to us, about us, in us, and around us. So, in this year of conflicts, the Baptist World Alliance met in Stockholm, Sweden, and I was privileged to deliver one of the major addresses; the World Council of Churches met in Nairobi, Kenya, and I was one of the five delegates from the American Baptist Convention.

As I look at 1975 chronologically, it was an uncommon year for me. For the month of January, I was visiting professor at Southern Baptist Seminary in Louisville, Kentucky. I taught a course entitled "The Social Mandate of the Gospel." At the first class session, two students dropped the course, stating that what I was teaching had nothing to do with the Christian religion. Thirty-two students remained in the class for the term, one of whom remained out of curiosity. My examination asked the students to evaluate positively or negatively the contents of the course. The curious young man took the opportunity to criticize everything that I had said and stated that he had wasted his time by remaining in the class. I agreed with him and gave him an "F."

Second Baptist celebrated its ninetieth anniversary from January through May. A hundred-person committee, chaired by Jeannetta, Charles R. Anderson, and Albert D. Matthews, devised a nine-component anniversary celebration. Three of the segments reflected the spirit in all of them. The first of these, held in the early part of the year, was an Emancipation Celebration, featuring Atlanta Mayor Maynard Jackson and baseball's superstar Henry (Hank) Aaron, who was in Los Angeles to serve as Grand Marshall of the Rose Bowl parade. The Emancipation Celebration culminated in a great revival service led by the Reverend Charles Butler of Detroit.

The second major event of our ninetieth anniversary celebration was our Ecumenical Convocation. This event was held in the morning on Founders Day, May 13. Fifteen denominations and four religions participated. Together in worship were Anglicans, Catholics, Jews, Muslims, and Protestants. A colorful robed procession of over 150 choir members, deacons, and clergy marched into the sanctuary where more than 600 worshipers were seated. The sermon for the occasion was given by the Reverend Sterling Carey, president of the National Council of Churches.

The deep spiritual solemnity of the Ecumenical Convocation was balanced by the third event, the vibrant and joyful Tribute Dinner held at the Hyatt Regency Hotel on the same day at 6:30 p.m. More than 875 members and friends witnessed a unique tribute paid to fifty individuals, businesses, institutions, and organizations that for over a period of ten years or more had made creative contributions toward the development of a better quality of life in Los Angeles. Mayor Tom Bradley and President John R. Hubbard of the University of Southern California responded for the recipients of the tribute.

In May, Jeannetta and I attended Jini's graduation ceremony at the Graduate School of Journalism, University of California, Berkeley, where she received her master's degree in journalism.

During the month of July, our tour group traveled to Europe. We toured and visited Norway, Denmark, Finland, Russia, the Netherlands, Sweden, Germany, Austria, and Switzerland. In Stalingrad (now St. Petersburg) we spent hours in the Heritage Art Museum. When we entered, we were told that the king and queen of Belgium were guests in the museum. As we were leaving, we saw the king and his attendants driving away. We surmised then that the queen and her attendants were still inside, and we waited at the gate. In a few moments, Queen Rabiola and her attendants came out of the gate near where we were standing. An attendant opened the door of her limousine. Before she entered, she looked in our direction. She then left her attendants, walked over to our group, and greeted me with a handshake. After a brief conversation, she returned to her limousine and drove off. My group teased me and wondered how I was able to attract the attention of the queen of Belgium.

From Russia we went to Stockholm, where we attended the meeting of the Baptist World Alliance. At this gathering of twelve thousand messengers from 124 countries, I delivered an address entitled "Fellowship beyond Frontiers" (see below p. 163).

From Stockholm we went to Amsterdam, and from Amsterdam we traveled by train to a small town in Germany on the Rhine River where we boarded a boat and sailed down the Rhine to Ausmanshasan. There we were to board a bus for Frankfurt. Lo and behold, no bus was there. In the midst of this quandary, I began to recall my limited German vocabulary that I had developed in a German class at Morehouse College forty-one years prior to this time. When an old man happened by, bowed and smiled, I said to him, "Haben Sie Kinder?" (Have you children?) He answered "Ya, ya!" (Yes, yes!), and demonstrated with his hands the heights of his grandchildren. He then helped us arrange transportation to Frankfurt.

Our European tour was completed after we spent two days in Austria and four days in Zurich and Geneva, Switzerland.

The second Fall Forum Series brought to the Second Baptist pulpit and the community four outstanding speakers: Dr. Walter E. Fauntroy, United States Congressman; Marcia Ann Gillespie, then editor in chief of *Essence* magazine; Dr. Mary Olivia Ross, president of the Women's Auxiliary of the National Baptist Convention, U.S.A., Inc.; and Dr. Hugh M. Gloster, president of Morehouse College. The theme for the series was "A Bicentennial Retrospective: The American Society and Century III."

From November 17 to 24, my daughter Lynn Elda and I were guests of Bishop H. Hartford Brookins in Lusaka, Zambia. Lynn Elda was employed by CBS Television, on her way to becoming a high-level television industry executive. We would primarily be visiting Nairobi, Kenya, site of the Fifth Assembly of the World Council of Churches, where she would be assisting some of her CBS colleagues in covering the event for two of the network's religious programs, "Look Up and Live" and "Lamp unto My Feet." Bishop Brookins was the presiding prelate of the Seventeenth Episcopal District of the A.M.E. Church. When I informed him that I would be a delegate from the American Baptist Convention to the

World Council of Churches meeting in Nairobi from late November to mid-December, he invited me to spend some days with him and address his annual conference, meeting in Lusaka. More than two thousand delegates from Zambia, Mali, and Rhodesia were in attendance at the conference. The business sessions and powerful and expressive worship services covered a period of four days. The singing was harmonious and robust; the shouting and dancing were accompanied by the artful use of many types of instruments. The preached message was interpreted in three different dialects. Having been a preacher for more than forty years, I thought I understood the "call and response" thoroughly, but I found new dimensions of it when I preached in Bishop Brookins's conference.

The delegates from Rhodesia were not given permission by their white government to attend the conference. Bishop Brookins's strong stand against white racism and domination in that central African country had made him persona non grata, so it was impossible for him to visit churches and for church members to leave the country to attend meetings called by him. However, eleven delegates secretly crossed the border and were active participants in the conference.

The ministry of Bishop Brookins in Africa was radically different from that of the average prelate. Along with his preaching, teaching, and spiritual nurturing of his constituents, he manifested a keen interest in their economic welfare. He made a deal with an English widow, who had recently lost her husband, to transfer her 150-acre farm to his conference for 50 million kwachas, about forty thousand American dollars. So impressed was she with what he desired to do for his congregants that she signed a contract for the purchase of the farm, only to find that the bishop did not have the 50 million kwachas or the down payment. The bishop was given ten days to raise the money; he succeeded, and the deal was closed.

Bishop Brookins, with the assistance of an American developer, built a large housing development for low- and moderate-income families. The farm and housing development and other innovative economic ventures deeply endeared him to his constituents. As he was nearing the end of his four-year term as bishop of the district, a group of his constituents begged me to influence him to remain another four years. I talked to the bishop about their desires, but he felt that four years in Africa was enough.

After a five-day visit with the bishop, Lynn Elda and I left for

Nairobi, Kenya, where we would spend twenty-one days at the Fifth Assembly of the World Council of Churches. More than twenty-five hundred messengers and delegates, representing Protestant and Orthodox Christians from more than a hundred countries, gathered in the spacious and well-appointed Nairobi conference center.

A major and essential part of the Assembly's life was worship. The work of the various Assembly committees was greatly enhanced by the sensitivity of what God was saying through powerful praise and thanksgiving. Then there was the "sound of silence," organized periods of silence to apprehend the presence of God. Assemblies are by nature wordy affairs at which, as in the bustling of our routine lives, silence has to be practiced and relearned in order that we may be able to listen and speak from greater depths. Even though the delegates and messengers spoke many and diverse languages and dialects, there was a depth of oneness in the worship services. The worship was further enhanced by the reproduction of paintings and sculptures of the one who frees us and unites us, Christ our Savior. The discussion groups and plenary sessions focused on the global problems of economic imbalance, racism, viable ecumenism, and world peace.

Two experiences enjoyed by most of us were an outdoor party given by President Jomo Kenyatta for the Assembly delegates and a reception at Nairobi City Hall hosted by the mayor, President Kenyatta's daughter. President Kenyatta personally greeted each delegate who attended the party, and at the reception that followed, the refreshments were delicious and plentiful. The drinks ran the gamut from mild orange juice to the strongest alcoholic beverages. I chose my drink from what I thought was orange juice, and imbibed it freely. Within a few moments my head began to swim and my feet staggered. I soon found a seat, and was told by a friend that what I thought was orange juice was, in fact, vodka.

On December 10, Lynn Elda and I boarded a plane for London and New York. On the eleventh, I was back at my desk at Second Baptist Church. As the curtain closed on 1975, we received fifty-five new members and gave $18,310 in our Christmas Eve offering to feed the hungry and $53,902 for missions and benevolences.

•

In the Apostle Paul's letter to the Philippian church, he disavowed any perfection, but he was determined to keep going. He said to his brothers and sisters of the church that even though he had not made it, he would forget his failures, leave them behind, and strain forward to those good things that lie ahead (paraphrase of Philippians 3:13–14).

The year 1976 was not one of great happenings in Second Baptist Church. We were aware that the nation was celebrating its bicentennial and were equally aware that our participating as a black church in the bicentennial celebrations had to be a correcting and history-adjusting task. Hopefully, as our nation entered the third century, it would be free of racism, poverty, and discrimination. In the fall of the year a new wave of hope came across the country when Georgia Governor Jimmy Carter was elected president.

Brother Claudious Bell was feted on January 18 by the church and community in recognition of his retirement from twenty years of faithful service as chief custodian and maintenance person at Second Baptist.

Between January 30 and May 23, I addressed the Long Beach Council of Churches; served on Mayor Bradley's Blue Ribbon Committee for the Central Business District development; installed Bobby Joe Saucer as dean of the Morehouse School of Religion; presided over the first distribution of American Baptist Churches FOR (Fund of Renewal) monies; and delivered the baccalaureate sermon and received an honorary degree (L.H.D.) from Redlands University in California. On Friday, September 10, I was elected president of the Progressive National Baptist Convention (see the Appendix, p. 223, for a history of the PNBC).

The Kilgore family held its biennial reunion in Los Angeles in the latter part of July. My remaining nine brothers and sisters — Lamar, Frank, Rockerfeller, Wells, Harold, Malissa, Ella Maye, Herman, Thaddeus — and I and our spouses, children, grandchildren, great-grandchildren, and friends invaded the city for seven days of exciting activities. These included exotic dinners, the Malissa Kilgore/Gerald Briley wedding, receptions by Mayor Bradley and USC President John R. Hubbard, a picnic in Compton, and a spirit-filled worship service held at Second Baptist Church, in which the Reverend Willie Moses Downs, my boyhood friend from Asheville, North Carolina, was the guest preacher.

The family reunion was climaxed by a benefit dinner at Town and Gown, an exclusive banquet hall on the USC campus. The dinner was cochaired by Mayor Tom Bradley, Attorney Thomas Griffith III, Mr. John Lamar Hill, Dr. Alvin Rudisill, and Mrs. Ruth Washington, publisher of the *Los Angeles Sentinel* newspaper. This excellent midsummer event and benefit netted over $6,000 for student financial aid and was coordinated by the Reverend Gerald Adams, Mrs. Shirley Bell, and Mrs. Betty Carmichael.

The organized Kilgore Family Reunion began in 1971, three years after my mother, Eugenia Kilgore, died. An informal reunion had begun in the 1950s, when the Kilgore children gathered annually at Mama's home on her birthday, July 28. Keeping this same date every two years, we decided to continue meeting in the even-numbered years to keep the family ties strong. At every reunion, we begin on Thursday evening with dinner in the host family's home. This is an informal gathering that has been enhanced over the years by the display of photo albums compiled by my sister Ella Maye for each of the family units. We have a formal banquet on Friday evening; a picnic and family business meeting on Saturday, at which officers are elected for the next two years and reunion coordinators and the city where the next reunion will be held are chosen; and a service of memory for the deceased members of the family during or before our worship service on Sunday. Because of the reunion, the family ties are strong even among the third and fourth generations of the descendants of Mama and Papa, and family members who live close to each other regularly see one another between reunions. Off and on through the years, Jeannetta and others have maintained a semi-annual family newsletter, which has also helped us keep abreast of each other's milestones and trifles.

The family reunion also reinforces family values and serves as a means of passing these values on to each succeeding generation. My brothers and sisters and I received from Mama and Papa some important life lessons: to attend to our business; to respect all people; to hate no one and to love all; and to work and to do our work well. We were rewarded when we did well, and we were punished when we did wrong. We were taken to church and Sunday school and were kept in public school. We were taught to be good neighbors and to share what we had with others, especially those who had less than we had. Most of all, Mama and Papa emphasized that we were all God's children.

•

In 1976, my ministry outside of Second Baptist Church continued to grow. As director of the USC Office of Special Community Affairs and advisor to President Hubbard in the area of community affairs, I found that the demands on the office necessitated additional staff. Mrs. Mary Kurishima and Ms. Janice Hsia were employed as office manager and secretary. At midyear the office created a new program on the campus. A letter went out to a number of African-American alumni requesting their interest and participation in the development of a support organization for black students needing financial assistance. The response to the letter was overwhelming. Within a month we had created and legalized the Ebonics Support Group. Through the medium of its annual financial drives, Ebonics has made scholarships available to scores of USC students. Before he retired from the presidency of the university, Dr. James Zumberge contributed $100,000 to the Ebonics fund. The group has grown stronger through the years and now administers grants to students in need of financial aid from the earnings of an endowed fund of approximately $300,000.

My extended ministry during 1976 included serving as chairman of the Board of Trustees of Morehouse College and board memberships in the Golden State Mutual Life Insurance Company, the Los Angeles County OIC, the Bank of Finance–Los Angeles Branch, the NAACP, the Los Angeles Council of Churches, the Morehouse School of Religion, and the Southern Christian Leadership Conference.

•

The name of the first month in the year, comes from Janus, one of the most ancient of Latin divinities. Janus was the spirit of the doorway invoked at the entrance and exit. In time, Janus came to be revered as the divinity presiding over all beginnings. The first hour, the first day, and the first month of the year were all sacred to Janus. He was always the first to be invoked in prayer. The image of Janus was that of a double-headed creature that looked in both directions at the same time.

It may be that we reached some new dimensions of faith in 1977. As we viewed the world about us, we were pleased to see major attempts to establish peace. Though we saw a continued traffic of deadly drugs, runaway inflation, high unemployment, and bizarre and wanton killings, we were still able to see some gleam of hope for a better world. Like Janus, we looked at 1977 with much apprehension, but we looked to 1978 with hope.

At the beginning of the year, I presided at an Ecumenical Convocation at Ebenezer Baptist Church in Atlanta, which was a birthday observance for Martin Luther King Jr. In late January, I presided over the midwinter meeting of the Progressive National Baptist Convention in Memphis. During the month of February, I presided at the 110th Anniversary Dinner of Morehouse College in Atlanta. In late February, I was honored as "Man of the Year" by the Zeta Phi Beta Sorority.

In late March and early April, I addressed the Progressive National Baptist Convention Eastern regional meeting and the Southwestern regional meeting. On May 1, I had conferred on me an honorary doctor of divinity degree (D.D.) by Morehouse School of Religion, part of the Interdenominational Theological Center in Atlanta. On May 15, I delivered the commencement address and received an honorary L.H.D. degree from Shaw College in Detroit, a satellite of Shaw University in Raleigh, North Carolina.

The August session of the Progressive National Baptist Convention was held in Atlanta. Under the leadership of Rev. Howard Creecy, chairman of the entertainment committee, unusual efforts were put forth to accommodate pleasantly the many needs and desires of the convention messengers.

As we met in Atlanta, we recognized that our host city, under the leadership of one of America's most enlightened mayors, Maynard Jackson, was by all odds the commercial, industrial, manufacturing, and transportation center of the South. We were also cognizant that in the areas of justice, government, education, social service, and religion there was a racial balance unparalleled in the country. No other city in America has given birth to and nurtured as many institutions of higher education for African-Americans as Atlanta. African-Americans would be poorer educationally had it not been for the creative educational enterprises of Atlanta University, Clarke College, the Interdenominational Theological Center, Morehouse College, Morris Brown College, Morehouse School of Medicine, and Spelman College.

The Sixteenth Annual Session of the PNBC was highlighted by cool and calm deliberations, great music under the leadership of Dr. Fredick D. Hall, Dr. Wendell Whalum, and, from Second Baptist Church, Lillie Hill Jones. Among the resolutions passed was the creation of the One Percent Plan, which called for all churches in the convention to contribute 1 percent of their annual operating budgets to the unified program of the convention.

My presidential address, delivered before an audience of about four thousand persons, was entitled, "Walking the Edge of the New," based upon 2 Corinthians 5:13–21 and Revelation 21:1 (see below p. 169).

At Second Baptist, our Fall Forum for 1977 featured Jesse Jackson, president, Operation Push; Howard Miller, Los Angeles School Board president; Congresswoman Yvonne Brathwaite Burke; and the Honorable Andrew Young, United States ambassador to the United Nations.

Second Baptist closed the year with its annual Christmas Eve Candlelight Service. For our Healing and Hunger program, benevolences, Christian education, and national and international mission, we gave $81,204.

•

My extended ministry as senior pastor of Second Baptist Church during 1978 included many activities in various areas. I was deep in my fifth year as advisor to the president of the University of Southern California in the area of community affairs and director of the Office of Special Community Affairs. I was completing my second year as president of the Progressive National Baptist Convention. My first year of service as a member of the board of National Public Radio was completed. My membership on the boards of the Golden State Mutual Life Insurance Company, the Bank of Finance, the Los Angeles Council of Churches, the Morehouse School of Religion, the Atlanta University Center, and the SCLC continued. In mid-February, I addressed the Morehouse Alumni banquet and participated in the dedication of the Martin Luther King Chapel and Auditorium and Hugh M. Gloster Hall at Morehouse.

Dr. D. E. King, chairman of the Board of Directors of the Nannie Helen Burroughs School in Washington, D.C., approached me with the suggestion that the Progressive National Baptist Convention consider ownership of the school and its properties. The school at that time had a debt of a half million dollars plus, which was due on the recently built administration building. On April 20, we held our first meeting in Washington for the purpose of planning the transfer of the school to the convention.

From April 26 to May 2, I traveled with Dr. Joseph H. Beatty, the director of PNBC's foreign mission work in Haiti. We spent six days visiting schools, preaching in churches, and baptizing candidates in the Grande River. I was shocked when I learned that Haitian school teachers' salaries were $18 per month. When we returned, I recommended that the salaries be doubled. The board of the Foreign Mission Bureau approved my recommendation, much to the delight of the teachers.

Following my trip to Haiti, Second Baptist Church raised the funds and built a school in the remote Haitian mountain village of Ranquitte. The church later established a library in the school. A group of members of Second Baptist and I participated in the dedication of the school and library, named in memory of Deacon Steve Rivers.

Second Baptist served as the host church for the organization and development of one of the best gatherings ever witnessed by the PNBC. From December 1977 to the end of August 1978, our church was a veritable beehive of activity. Our entertainment committee registered 5,057 delegates and visitors as we met in the Los Angeles Shrine Auditorium. The persons chairing the ten committees were Rev. Gerald Adams, Musical; Frank Christine Jr., Finance; Cleo Caldwell, Welcome Program; Ola Mae Dailey, Souvenir Journal; Fannie B. Harris, Hospitality; R. O. Harris, Pulpit Invitations; William Gartrell, Transportation; Jeannetta, Registration; Edna Moten, Housing; Lorene Wilhite, Booths.

There were many highlights in the Seventeenth Annual Session of the convention. Among these were the excellent accommodations afforded by the University of Southern California and the transfer of the Nannie Helen Burroughs School property to the convention. (This property, valued at several millions of dollars, was deeded to the convention for $500,000, plus the establishment of the $200,000 Nannie Helen Burroughs Scholarship program.) The transfer took place as Dr. D. E. King presented the deeds to me as president of the convention. A final highlight of the Seventeenth Annual Session was the series of four lectures delivered in the Ministers Seminar by Dr. Howard Thurman. Dr. Thurman, one of our country's leading theologians, was dean of Marsh Chapel and professor of Spiritual Resources and Disciplines at Boston University as well as dean of the chapel at Howard University. Dr. Thurman was an author and lecturer and teacher on a number of campuses, including Morehouse, and was cofounder of the Fellowship Church in San Francisco, reputed to be the first fully multiethnic congregation in the United States. He was widely thought of as a pastor to pastors and conducted special spiritual retreats for religious leaders, some of which I was privileged to attend. At the end of his PNBC lectures, Dr. Thurman stated to me that the PNBC was the only black Baptist national convention that had ever invited him to speak.

As the year closed, our Religion and Life Forum Series was a success. The speakers were California State Assemblywoman Maxine Waters, California Lt. Governor Mervyn Dymally, and Dr. Francis Kornegay, a board member of Golden State Mutual Insurance Company, which he is credited for expanding in Detroit. Dr. Kornegay also led in the development of health maintenance organizations.

We kept our commitment to the world at home and abroad. We were not unmindful of the problems of runaway inflation, hurting unemployment, senseless killings, the alcohol-drug syndromes, and Jim Jones and Guyana. We were mindful of the peace overtures to China, which seemed to point the way for normal relations between our country and almost a fourth of the people of the world.

An occasion of joy near the end of the year was the pleasure of being a guest of President and Mrs. Jimmy Carter at a White House dinner. Since Jeannetta was unable to attend, I escorted her sister, Blanche Webb, a Washington, D.C., resident.

•

As I faced 1979, my tenure as senior pastor of Second Baptist had reached fifteen years and three months. Nineteen seventy-nine was a year of high peaks and low valleys. In the church we started the year with a workshop on "Caring and Sharing." We came face to face with our strengths and weaknesses as a church family, we bared our souls to each other, and we ended up with a clearer vision of what it means to love one another. As we examined our African origins, explored means to love one another, and looked at cultural roots in the context of Christian faith, we found new levels of understanding and more positive ways to relate. But as we looked at ourselves, we could not overlook the scenes of life in our city, nation, and world: high unemployment, poor schools, bad police-community relations, and inadequate housing.

In the late spring, I sent a letter to 376 pastors of various denominations, inviting them to a planning meeting at Second Baptist Church; 131 pastors responded. The purpose of the meeting was to create a religious interracial and ecumenical movement to confront some of the social evils that were corrupting the community and city. The result of this coming together was the organization of a movement called the Gathering.

Our concerns were focused on affordable housing for low- and moderate-income families, affirmative action in employment, voter registration, improved public schools, and better police-community relations.

Almost simultaneously with the organization of the Gathering, Eulia Love, an African-American mother from South Central Los Angeles, was killed by the police. There was a dispute between Ms. Love and a utility company. She challenged the company representative with a butcher knife, and the police were called. She was asked to drop the knife, but she refused, and the police opened fire and killed her.

The death of Eulia Love at the hands of the police threw the community into turmoil. At this point, the Gathering, under the leadership of Rev. James Lawson and Rev. Milton Merriweather, took the police to task for what we were convinced was a senseless slaying of a citizen. For weeks we met with Chief of Police Darryl Gates and the Police Commission, which resulted in some changes in the police manual, the elimination of "choke hold," and clarification of when and how to exercise fatal firepower.

The Gathering activities covered a span of about five years. The group's first major celebration took place in the Shrine Auditorium on December 30, 1980, in the form of "A Festival of Faith–Spiritual Mobilization." Twelve denominations made presentations before an audience of about three thousand persons. During its life, the Gathering was favored with a $26,000 grant from the Lily Endowment to assist in our community organization efforts.

The year 1979 also marked the birth date of the Black Agenda, another group that resulted from the letter that I sent to the pastors. The Black Agenda's purpose was to focus solely on our African-American communities and to create some type of movement to better the community. During the years of its existence, the Black Agenda has held community-wide forums on economic development and housing, and has held successful annual luncheons with nationally recognized speakers. Dr. Maulana Ron Karenga and I have worked closely together in planning these events. Dr. Karenga is nationally known for having developed KWANZAA as an African-American cultural celebration, observed annually in December. Following is the challenge that the group adopted to express its goals.

Our Challenge. Make no mistake, the fundamental problem facing the black community today is lack of economic clout. We simply don't own or control the resources in our own community. To this extent, we are only guests in our own house.

Crime, unemployment, inadequate housing, homelessness and rampant drug trafficking are all byproducts of our fundamental problems of economic deficiency. As someone once remarked, "No one can save us, but us." If we accept this as a given, then let us stop the talking and bemoaning and be about the serious business of taking back economic control of our community.

Reality and Challenge. African-Americans of Los Angeles and our country face a challenge in the decade ahead to build and maintain strong, unified, proud and productive communities. The logic of this assumption is expressed in the social and political wisdom that the poverty and powerlessness in a community in the midst of abundant wealth and power are a reflection of the quality of social justice in the larger society, and the lethargy and division in the black community. The time for the correction of this problem is far spent.

The solution of any problem calls for a first step. The Black Agenda of greater Los Angeles was born in the critical time of history. It came into existence to call African-American life to closer cooperation and togetherness. We are challenged as never before to delineate clearly our concerns to diligently pool together our economic, educational, and social endeavors; and to form a black network that is sensitive, responsive, and caring.

The Los Angeles Black Agenda has determined that some collective body must step forward to carefully pull together all of the talented community resources amid a spirit of togetherness and cooperation.

The Black Agenda believes that we can no longer afford the luxury of spending the majority of our money outside of the black community. This is economic suicide! We can no longer be mere guests in our own house.

Let Us Be More Specific. Other ethnic groups have, and are, pooling their resources in order to own and operate businesses in their and our communities. The African-American community should and *can* come together to control more of the businesses which cater to African-Americans. After our initial success with the creation of profitable family housing, marketing studies will be undertaken which will enable us to select those businesses which the Black Agenda will pursue. The pooling of our resources will enable us to gain more control over our economic destiny.

The Los Angeles Black Agenda has determined that it is imperative to form a union of economic, human and other resources. To this extent, the organization's Economic Development Committee has identified possible economic development projects in which to direct our resources, i.e., investments and development of products and services consumed within our community.

The Black Agenda's challenge has not been fulfilled, but the group continues to work toward the economic development of our communities.

Nationally, during 1979, we saw the dollar shrinking, gasoline prices rising, and auto sales sagging. Internationally, Israel and Egypt moved closer to peace. Ireland cooled off somewhat, Zimbabwe moved toward peace, and the Shah of Iran escaped. As the year ended, the U.S.A. and the U.S.S.R. moved away from detente. *Time* magazine chose the Ayatollah Khomeini as the Man of the Year, while many wondered why the choice was not Pope John Paul II, or Mother Teresa as the Woman of the Year.

Nineteen hundred seventy-nine gave us shocks and shouts, jitters and joys, and some consolation. But in our church life, all of these and other paradoxical pairings left us a better and more loving church. They also left us more able to work together toward a redeemed world and a renewed society.

As the year ended, I was guest lecturer at Fuller Theological Seminary, gave the benediction at a luncheon honoring Archbishop Iakovis of the Greek Orthodox Church of North and South America, was a delegate to the General Board meeting of the National Council of Churches, U.S.A., and received the Community Service Award from the Los Angeles County Human Relations Commission.

•

In late January 1980, I journeyed to Brevard and Asheville, North Carolina, to join with a fellow minister in a celebration of our fifty years in the Christian ministry. Rev. H. B. Ferguson and I were licensed to preach in 1930 by Bethel Baptist Church in Brevard, pastored by the venerable Rev. A. H. Wilson. Both of us began pastoring churches in the Asheville area after finishing high school and college.

A new interreligious fellowship was created in 1980, beginning on February 22, when I was honored by Wilshire Boulevard Temple and Rabbi Edgar Magnin. Hundreds of Second Baptist members and friends attended a worship service at the Temple, and I delivered the sermon "The Family of God" (see below p. 183). The service was followed by a reception at which Mayor Tom Bradley presided.

On March 9, Rabbi Magnin and members of the Wilshire Boulevard Temple worshiped with Second Baptist. The rabbi preached and was honored in a reception at which I presented him with a silver plate. The covenant relationship between Second Baptist and Wilshire Boulevard Temple has continued through the years.

In 1980, a year of changes, the yoke of white English domination was lifted from the central African country of Rhodesia, so the country reclaimed its ancestral name Zimbabwe, and political control shifted to native Africans. The Shah of Iran died, which created a new shift to the far right in the leadership of the country. Ronald Reagan was elected president of the United States, the first movie actor to occupy the leadership position of the world's most powerful democracy.

On March 16, a tribute dinner was given in my honor at the Century Plaza Hotel. This event marked my fiftieth year in the Christian ministry and netted $35,000 that was equally divided between Second Baptist community programs and the USC Ebonics Support Group.

Between June 22, 1980, and the end of the year, there were several highlights in the life of Second Baptist. Our NAACP Day was favored with a powerful sermon by Dr. Benjamin Hooks, national director of the NAACP, and fourteen memberships were received for the local branch as a result of the untiring work of Second Baptist members Kathryn Anderson, Jesse Holmes, and others. In mid-August, Dr. Benjamin E. Mays preached at our morning worship service and addressed the Love Feast and Twilight Vesper Service that Jeannetta and I hosted at our home each year. Our Women's Day speakers in the fall were Mrs. Coretta Scott King, and Jini, who had announced her call into ministry in 1978.

A program called S.E.L.F. (Services for Everyday Living for Families), directed by Thomas Sippio, was created at Second Baptist and funded by a $10,000 grant from the proceeds of the tribute dinner that was given for me in March.

In November, the Reverend Doctor Ella P. Mitchell was named minister of Christian education, becoming the first female staff minister at Second Baptist. We closed the year by giving $103,744 for benevolences, missions, and Christian education.

•

Except for many dynamic worship services and unusual inspirational programs, 1981 was an average year. We did, however, reach a high peak of unity and cooperation when Second Baptist established a retreat center in Lake Elsinore and financed its purchase by low interest loans from fifty-three families and individuals in the church. Within two years the loans in the amount of $200,000 were liquidated. The center, named Kilgore Hill, has from its inception hosted numerous large and small retreats sponsored by Second Baptist Church and other churches and organizations.

Another highlight of the year was a tour to the Haitian Baptist Mission by twenty-two Second Baptist members and friends. During our five-day stay in Haiti, we visited several churches and mission stations and approved a plot of ground for developing the Vincent Hughes Memorial Playground, named for the teenage son of our members Catherine and Ronald Hughes, who tragically died in an automobile accident. But one of our main purposes for the Haitian trip was thwarted by heavy rains and mud slides. We were unable to reach Ranquitte to dedicate the school building and to hang the portrait of Deacon Steve Rivers, for whom the school library was named. Those who made the trip were Charlie Mae Bell, Shirley Bell, Miller Bell, Armanda Escobedo, Bernice Flowers, Edith Featherstone, Patsie Grant, Catherine Hughes, Ronald Hughes, Helen Henderson, Annie Kilgore, Herman Kilgore, Jessie Marrero, Delores Nehemiah, Ernestine Palmer, Emma Perry, Rosentene Purnell, Pearl Price, Audrey Quarles, Nona Rice, Ruth Rivers, Saxton Spencer, Mr. and Mrs. Delmar Taylor, Jeannetta, and I.

•

We began 1982 with two major events. From January through March, 211 persons met on Wednesday evenings in an in-depth study of the Bible which emphasized the origin, structure, authors, types of literature, translations, canonization, and many other pertinent features involved in the making of the Bible. This Bible study program proved to be exceedingly helpful for Sunday school teachers and for many others. A spin-off of the study of the Bible was a church group analysis retreat held at Kilgore Hill. This retreat helped greatly in shoring up and improving the operation of the various church groups.

During 1982, three members of Second Baptist were elected to denominational offices: Shirley Bell, treasurer of the Progressive Baptist State Convention; Vernon Dunlap, president of the Laymen's Department, Progressive National Baptist Convention Southwest Region; and Doris Perkins, vice president of the Women's Auxiliary, Progressive National Baptist Convention.

Second Baptist established a prison ministry in 1983, and brother Albert Robinson, a former prisoner, was selected as director. The church also licensed him and another young person, Pamela Davis, for gospel ministry.

On October 26, I gave a birthday party for Jeannetta, which was made unforgettable by the more than four hundred persons who attended and gave joyful recognition to her for nineteen years as an active church member and leader, as well as her fourteen years as director of Second Baptist Children's Center. Under her leadership the center, with an enrollment of approximately one hundred children, became an award-winning preschool recognized as exemplary by the state of California. This fine tribute to my lovely wife was held on her ?? birthday. (Even though God blessed us in 1996 with the celebration of our sixtieth wedding anniversary, Jeannetta still does not tell her age.)

My other field of labor, the Office of Special Community Affairs, continued to grow. The Ebonics Support Group continued to raise funds and give assistance to African-American students, and our influence among the campus community helped greatly to strengthen the relationship between the university and the community.

My visits out of the city were many, and I logged 65,690 miles in 1982. I was guest preacher at Shiloh Baptist Church, Greensboro, North Carolina; Wheeler Avenue Baptist Church, Houston, Texas; Metropolitan Baptist Church, Washington, D.C.; and Second Baptist Church, Riverside, California.

In my wider parish activities, I participated in a National Council of Churches clergy educators meeting in Washington, D.C., addressed a drug awareness conference in Montgomery, Alabama,

and attended the board meeting of the Congress of National Black
Churches in New York.

In 1982, for the first year since my pastorate began we failed to
meet our budget at Second Baptist Church. But of the total gifts
of $485,440 that we raised, we gave for benevolences and mission
programs $87,559.

•

In 1983, Second Baptist Church started its precentennial celebrations
on Sunday, February 27. Three hundred plus members participated
in a dinner and planning session to outline and approve seven
precentennial programs and projects:

1. Liquidation of mortgage on Elsinore Retreat Center —
    $111,440

2. Earthquake security building construction — $75,000

3. New communication system — $27,750

4. Organ repair — $30,000

5. Haitian mission projects — $9,500

6. New dining room tables and chairs — $4,417

7. Initial funding for Upper Central Friendship House — $8,000

Projects 1, 3, 6, and 7, were completed by the end of the year.

The church established two new programs for community ministry
in 1983. PRePP (People Resource Participation Program), directed
by Eugene Kenourgios, was designed to work with individuals and
groups, aid families in problem solving, tutoring, and conflict resolution, and offer various kinds of referral services. UCFH (Upper
Central Friendship House) was created to feed the hungry, clothe
and shelter the needy, and evangelize. The idea for Friendship House
was generated at a young adult spiritual retreat at our Elsinore center. After the retreat, the program blossomed under the leadership
of Bernard Brown, who became its first board president, and Sher-
ryl MacDonald, who coordinated the Saturday free lunch program
there. A year later, Jini joined retired Deacon Wilbur Williams, who
was distributing groceries for the program and offering counseling
to many indigent persons, and became the ministry's first full-time
director. Under the leadership of the young people, Friendship House

established an aggressive ministry involving a grocery distribution program three times a week to families and others in need, a drop-in hot lunch program six days a week, emergency and transitional shelter for families and single men, social service referrals, and the daily presentation of the gospel. Of the thousands of persons who benefitted from this ministry, several became members of Second Baptist Church.

In addition to her duties as director of Friendship House, my daughter, a professional journalist before becoming a minister, maintained a monthly newsletter to report the activities of this outreach ministry to its board directors and the church, and to recognize the more than fifty persons, many of whom were retired members of Second Baptist, whose volunteer services made the ceaseless work of Friendship House possible. Jini also represented the church and Friendship House in the broader Los Angeles community by serving as cochairperson of the Emergency Food Council of Southern California, sponsored by the Southern California Ecumenical Council. She remained director of Friendship House until the end of 1987, securing several grants for the program to expand its mission to serve as host and enabler to indigent persons who were in need of physical bread and spiritual nourishment. In addition to Friendship House, Second Baptist now operates Harmony House, which provides shelter to women and children.

During 1983, the Second Baptist family sent Hermine Johnigan, Ernestine Palmer, Ruth Rivers, and me to Ranquitte, Haiti, for the dedication of our school building and the Steve Rivers Library. We also experienced two inspirational concerts, rendered by the Glee Clubs of Morehouse and Spelman Colleges. Our annual Forum Series, entitled "The Black Family Crisis and Hope," was addressed by Dr. Deotis Roberts, a Christian scholar and an architect of black theology, Attorney Marion Wright Edelman, head of the Children's Defense Fund, and Dr. Dolly Adams, educator and community activist. The annual revival featured the unique preaching of Dr. D. E. King, and we closed the year with a Twentieth Anniversary recognition of the service that my wife and I had given the church.

•

The Second Baptist Church family started 1984 on a high note. On the eve of our hundredth anniversary, our major precentennial event was the presentation of concert singer Leona Mitchell at the Los Angeles Music Center. This well-attended and inspirational event was joyfully received by the audience and netted $24,000 from gross receipts of $42,100.

Beginning in the early part of the year, we provided opportunities for Bible study and group prayer. Jini initiated a Prayer Warriors group and a grief recovery support group. The Prayer Warriors, led by Nora Freeman Cole, met each Tuesday afternoon. The grief support group, led by Jini, met as needed to assist persons and families in making adjustments after the loss of loved ones. My family and I experienced such a loss when my brother Lamar passed on February 4. Lamar was the second oldest brother in the family. His funeral was held at Meridian Hill Baptist Church in Washington, D.C., and I delivered the eulogy.

On April 12, I represented Morehouse College as a delegate to the inaugural of Dr. David P. Gardner as president of the University of California system.

Our centennial celebrations began in the month of May, with a sermon delivered by Second Baptist Church Pastor Emeritus Dr. J. Raymond Henderson. This worship service was the launching event of a stream of subsequent ones in the celebration of our hundred years of service. But we also started in the month of May a dusty, dirty, and at times disturbing task of renovating our church building for seismic protection. The cost went far beyond the original estimation of $125,000 to $352,000, and the inconvenience for more than twelve months seriously affected our daily operations.

In the late spring, I was guest speaker in a convocation series at Ottawa University. In mid-June, I participated in a "Children Having Children" conference, sponsored by the Children's Defense Fund, held at Spelman College, and I delivered the address for Men's Day at Mt. Zion Baptist Church in Seattle, pastored by Dr. Samuel B. McKinney.

During 1984, there were many opportunities for service outside of Second Baptist. I addressed the Gandhi Colloquium as guest lecturer at Claremont School of Theology and was scholar theologian for the Department of Education of American Baptist Churches, lecturing at Shaw University in Raleigh, North Carolina, and William Jewell College in Liberty, Missouri. My topic was "In Search for Freedom and Wholeness" (2 Kings 7:1).

Councilman Gilbert Lindsay opened the way for the construction of the fifty-two-unit Second Baptist Community House, and the Los Angeles Community Redevelopment Agency extended a loan of $880,000 for land purchase.

In 1984 the Olympics were held in Los Angeles. As part of the overall entertainment for this major event, Mayor Bradley and the City of Los Angeles held a festival. I was appointed to the festival committee by Mayor Bradley, and our committee contacted the internationally famous festival director Peter Sellars, who accepted our invitation to be the festival's director. Due to its huge initial success, the Los Angeles Festival has been held every two years since that first one. Participation in this very popular event has consistently been representative of all of the racial groups in the city.

In August, I was appointed by Mayor Bradley to serve as a commissioner on the Community Redevelopment Agency Board (CRA). I was a commissioner until 1993, serving as treasurer for one three-year term. The CRA, the Airport Commission, the Water and Power Commission, and the Port Commission are the four largest agencies in the city of Los Angeles. The CRA, with a staff of more than three hundred full-time workers and an annual budget of more than $350 million, is responsible for many areas of development in the city. During my nine years as a commissioner, areas that were greatly revitalized in Los Angeles included the Skid Row downtown area and the downtown big business area. In the predominantly African-American community the $100 million Crenshaw-Baldwin Hills Shopping Center was built. In Watts, we rebuilt the old train station, refurbished the Watts Towers, and created a crescent development from the train station to the tower, a walkway of about a quarter of a mile. The agency was also responsible for building housing developments in many sections of the city.

In 1993, Jim Wood, chairman of the CRA, planned a special luncheon for member Frank Kuwahara and me in celebration of our eightieth birthdays. More than five hundred persons attended this luncheon at the downtown Hilton Hotel.

In early August of 1984, two events took place that brought joy and happiness. On August 4, in the sanctuary of Friendship Baptist Church, New York, Jini and I performed the marriage ceremony of her sister, Lynn Elda, and Dr. Abel Hendy III, a pharmacist and dentist. On August 12, I was guest speaker at the fiftieth pastoral anniversary banquet of my friend Rev. Dr. Howard Mitchell in Ahoskie, North Carolina.

During 1984, two men passed away who had in differing ways deeply affected my own life and ministry: Dr. Benjamin E. Mays, and Dr. Martin Luther King Sr. On March 31, I attended the funeral service of Dr. Mays, held at the Martin Luther King Jr. International Chapel at Morehouse. Even though I was a student at Morehouse College before Dr. Mays's presidency there, he and I had a close relationship in religious and ecumenical movements. His concern for proper thinking and serious moral and religious commitment was completely impeccable. The Morehouse students who listened to his Tuesday lectures were deeply motivated by his challenges for goodness and excellence in all endeavors.

On November 15, Dr. King was funeralized at Ebenezer Baptist Church in Atlanta. As one of the mourners at his service, I reflected seriously on our relationship, which spanned fifty-three years. He had affectionately called me "Kill" and was kind and encouraging from the time I met him in the fall of 1931 until his passing. The first church that I attended when I became a student at Morehouse College was Ebenezer Baptist, where he pastored. Because I was a licensed preacher, Dr. King gave me opportunities to teach Sunday school class and occasionally to deliver a sermon. From the beginning of our relationship until his passing, he proved to be a strong big brother and friend.

As we closed the church year of 1984, Second Baptist gave recognition to Jeannetta for twenty years (1964–84) of committed service and involvement. She served as the first director of the PIC (Program, Interpretation, Communications) office; as the editor of *Second Baptist Informer;* as associate superintendent of Sunday church school; as chair of the Ninetieth Church Anniversary celebration, the $10,000 Morehouse College Fund, and the Elsinore Kilgore Hill Retreat Center Commission; as Women's Day speaker on two occasions; as full-time director of the Second Baptist Child Development Center for fourteen years and four months; as member of the General Board, Executive Committee; and as coordinator of church bulletin boards.

•

It is not easy to chronicle the events of a special kind of year that comes only once in a century and, thus, only once in most persons' lifetimes. Second Baptist Church celebrated its centennial year in 1985. We had looked forward to our hundredth anniversary with great anticipation, and our hopes were truly fulfilled. Our beloved pastor emeritus, Dr. J. Raymond Henderson, had launched our precentennial events with a powerful and challenging sermon on Sunday, May 20, 1984, and for the rest of 1984, there had been many precentennial events. Outstanding among these were the Sixth Annual Interdenominational Festival of Sacred Music, under the direction of Second Baptist's incomparable minister of music, Dr. J. Harrison Wilson. The well-attended concert, held September 23, featured choirs from Grant A.M.E. Church, the Los Angeles Christian Center, and Second Baptist Church. Another unforgettable precentennial event was the Recognition and Appreciation Luncheon honoring the Second Baptist Church and Child Care Center staffs, held at the Proud Bird Restaurant on October 27. Sixty-one persons were honored, and a special booklet was published listing their names, positions of service, and contributions.

Following this tremendous build-up, 1985 began with highest expectations. On January 6, we carried out a traditional Emancipation Day black community celebration, and our speaker, the Reverend C. T. Vivian of Atlanta, vividly reminded us that the job of complete emancipation is not yet finished. That experience gave us much thought for action.

On February 22, a truly classy affair — our Centennial Dinner at the Century Plaza Hotel — was held. One thousand persons subscribed, and 969 were present for the dinner. Dr. James H. Zumberge was the dinner chairman, Ossie Davis and Scoey Mitchlll served as toastmasters, and Johnny L. Cochran Sr. and Diane Brown coordinated the dinner. Guests came from both southern and northern California, Atlanta, New York, Detroit, and Winslow, Arizona. All in all, it was an evening of inspiration, joy, and happiness. Dr. J. Raymond Henderson and 105-year-old Mrs. Catherine Jones were honored.

During the month of February, eight of the sons of Second Baptist, all pastors now, preached for the eight regular worship services: Gerald Adams, Louis Brown, William Campbell, Ellis Keck, Paul Martin, David Morris, Val Sauer, and Percy Williams. Between February and May 15, many musical and inspirational programs were held. Our spring revival in April carried us to a high peak evangelistically and inspirationally. Dr. Charles Adams, pastor of Hartford Avenue Baptist Church in Detroit, was at his best night after night.

The climax of our centennial celebrations was reached in the Ecumenical and Interreligious Convocation on May 15. Many members took a holiday that day, and about a thousand persons attended the convocation service, which began with a march of several dozen clergy persons from our Velva Henderson Christian Education Building across the street from the church to the church sanctuary. Dr. Otis Moss Jr. delivered a dynamic convocation sermon. Following the worship service, a grand community reception was held under a huge tent in the street, which had been blocked off for the occasion. That day will never be erased from our memories.

Along with all the spiritual and inspirational events in our centennial year, we also completed the renovation work on our church building, installed a new sound system, finished the renovation of our organ, moved forward the ministries of Friendship House and PRePP, and with the aid of the Los Angeles Community Redevelopment Agency, purchased all the land but one lot between our church property and Central Avenue on the north side of Twenty-Fourth Street.

Nineteen hundred eighty-five was not without seasons of grief. A pall of sadness was experienced by the Second Baptist family and the Los Angeles religious community at the death of my predecessor, Dr. J. Raymond Henderson, on July 15. His memorial service, held on July 20, was attended by clergy, city and county officials, and hundreds of Second Baptist members and friends. I served as officiant for the service, and Dr. Floyd Massey gave the eulogy.

Sunday, July 28, was an unusual day in Second Baptist. At the 11:00 a.m. worship service, we were hosts to more than a hundred members of the Ralph David Abernathy family, in town for their reunion. Dr. Abernathy preached that morning, and after service, the church hosted dinner for the Abernathy family.

That evening, a triple ordination ceremony took place: Hilly Hicks, Oscar Owens Jr., and Jini, all ministerial interns at Second Baptist, were elevated to the position of ordained ministers. Dr. J. Alfred Smith Sr. gave the charge to the ordinands. Jini had been licensed to preach in 1982, at the church that Dr. Smith pastors, Allen Temple Baptist, in Oakland, where she held active membership for thirteen years and where I had been privileged to install Dr. Smith as pastor in 1971. She was the first woman to be ordained in the history of Second Baptist Church, and, coincidentally, her ordination took place on the hundredth birth date anniversary of her paternal grandmother, Mrs. Eugenia Kilgore, my mother, and during the centennial year of Second Baptist Church. Shortly before her ordination, Jini had graduated in May, magna cum laude, from the American Baptist Seminary of the West in Berkeley, with an M.Div. degree.

My wider parish ministries that took me beyond my pastoral duties at Second Baptist led me in many directions in 1985. I continued my part-time work as director of the Office of Special Community Affairs at USC. By 1985, we were making steady progress in developing an endowment for the Ebonics Support Group. Other commitments that I fulfilled were the inaugural Martin Luther King Jr. lecture at the Claremont School of Theology in January; the keynote address at the Ministers Institute at Bishop College in Dallas, in April, and an address for the International Conference on Drug Abuse, held in Atlanta, also in April.

Mayor Bradley appointed me to the Board of Trustees of the Los Angeles Festival on May 16. On May 19, I delivered the baccalaureate sermon at Morehouse and was back in Atlanta on July 20 to participate in the funeral service for Mrs. Beulah Gloster, beloved wife of my friend Dr. Hugh Gloster, then president of Morehouse. Later the same year, I joined with the Kilgore family in our reunion in Atlanta. Our family received from Rev. Abernathy and West Hunter Street Baptist Church courtesies comparable to those extended by Second Baptist Church during the Abernathy reunion in Los Angeles.

The month of November was one of joy and sadness. I delivered the sermon for the forty-ninth anniversary of Friendship Baptist Church in Harlem, where I pastored for sixteen years, and I received the ABEL (Association for Black Law Enforcement) Achievement Award at the Dorothy Chandler Pavilion in Los Angeles. On November 14, I visited my brother, Rev. Harold Kilgore, who was critically ill in Baltimore. He died on November 20. Harold's active ministry was that of assistant to Rev. I. Logan Kearse, pastor of Cornerstone Church of Christ in Baltimore. On November 25, I participated in Harold's funeral service.

In October, I became part of a statewide commission to explore the problem of drug and alcohol abuse in California public schools. California Attorney General John Van de Kamp created a statewide commission, comprised of twenty-six persons who represented medical societies, school health care programs, public education, police and sheriff departments, clergy, educators, and others. The commission was well balanced by gender and race, and I was chosen to be the chair.

In December, Dr. Elliott J. Mason Sr., retired pastor of Trinity Baptist Church in Los Angeles, and I united in matrimony our daughter Jini and Clifford Moore, an artist and licensed preacher who had grown up with our daughters in Friendship Church in New York. They were married in our home in the presence of a few family members and friends. This marriage was short-lived, however, since a few years later Clifford was stricken with pancreatic cancer and died.

During our centennial year, we experienced many powerful and dynamic worship services, and our evangelistic emphasis was continued and to some extent strengthened. This was also the year that I retired as senior pastor of the church, in December 1985. In spite of a ripple here and there, based upon a misunderstanding of the mandate given to the new pastor search committee, our level of Christian fellowship remained constant. Our love and loyalty lifted us above any serious difficulty and division. We kept in prayer, and the level of love and caring among us was high.

We were saddened during the hundredth year by the passing of thirty-six members. Many of these were true and faithful servants of the Lord and were greatly missed. As the Lord took back to Himself the faithful souls that passed during our centennial year, He sent seventy-two new members to us.

In my final message in an annual report to the church, I expressed my profound thanks and appreciation to all families and members who had shown love, respect, concern, and cooperation for what Jeannetta and I had tried to do in Christian ministry for twenty-two years and two months. All that transpired had not been perfect, nor at times good. But at times all was fair, at other times good, at other times better, and, thank God, on occasion best.

I left my position as senior pastor of Second Baptist Church with a deep feeling of nostalgia, but with a high feeling of joy. Where I had wronged or hurt, I asked for forgiveness; where I had failed, I asked for understanding; where I had helped or enabled, I sought no reward; where I had inspired or uplifted, I said, Give God the praise; and where I had advocated a quality of life that is more excellent, I implored all to follow that trend.

As I was bringing to a close my pastoral ministry in Second Baptist, I expressed my appreciation to the staff members for their cooperation and help. These included Gerald Adams, clerk; Celia Bell, photographer; Shirley Bell, pastor's administrative assistant; Melinda Bennett, secretary; Bernard Brown, photographer; Jeanne Coleman, general secretary; William H. Dailey, photographer; Fred L. Daniels, choir director; William H. Henderson, photographer; Richard L. Horton, associate pastor; my wife, Jeannetta, bulletin board coordinator/recording secretary; my daughter Jini, minister of evangelism and spiritual disciplines; Richard Jones, media assistant; Thelma Taylor, business manager, and J. Harrison Wilson, minister of music. Shirley Bell, my administrative assistant, has continued to work with me on a part-time basis during the years of my retirement.

•

After my retirement as senior pastor of Second Baptist Church, the church experienced a split. Some 150 members left Second Baptist to form Eternal Promise Baptist Church, under the leadership of my former associate pastor, Richard Horton. Before this split occurred, the New Pastor Search Committee had extended a call to Dr. Otis Moss, pastor of Olivet Institutional Baptist Church in Cleveland, Ohio. Dr. Moss had accepted the call, but shortly afterward changed his mind, which raised the issue of an interim pastor until a new pastor could be called.

Some members of the church wanted Associate Pastor Richard Horton to be both the new pastor and the interim pastor; others did not. Among the underlying issues driving these choices was the type of pastor and mission the members envisioned for Second Baptist Church. At the extreme ends of the discussion, some members argued for a church and pastor that primarily took care of its own while others appreciated the far-reaching local, national, and international witness Second Baptist Church — known to many Angelenos as the "Mother" black Baptist church — had maintained for decades, long before I became its pastor. Issues such as these were worthy of discussion, and our church was offered assistance in carrying out this discussion by the late Dr. Emory Campbell, then executive minister of the Los Angeles Baptist City Mission Society. Unfortunately, there was not much desire on the part of some for the constructive discussion of underlying issues. The conversation, instead, focused on personalities, with Pastor Horton symbolizing one faction and the search committee and its attempts to find another pastor representing the other.

This eventually led to a church split, with the Horton faction pulling out in 1987. As the mother church of all the black Baptist congregations in Los Angeles, Second Baptist had directly given birth to several strong congregations, but this was the first time in its 102-year history (1885–1987) that a new congregation had formed due to such an acrimonious church split. All of us who loved the church were hurt by this episode in its rich and positive life. In due time, however, the wounds began to heal. I was subsequently invited on more than one occasion to preach at Eternal Promise, and Pastor Horton and I have remained colleagues and friends.

Second Baptist Church and I continue to be deeply grateful to key church leaders who rose to the occasion during this turbulent time in the church's life and planned and conducted vibrant and meaningful worship services that helped keep the church body encouraged. Among these persons were chairman of the Deacon Board Judge Albert Matthews and two young people who were just beginning their ministries when the split occurred, Rev. Oscar O. Owens Jr., and my daughter Jini, as well as then minister of music Dr. J. Harrison Wilson and his assistant James Calhoun and the faithful choir members. These persons, faithfully, dependably, and lovingly, along with the dedicated church staff members named above and hundreds of members and friends, prayed hard as they carried out the day-to-day ministries and led the worship services and programs of the church during the twenty-two months that Second Baptist was without a pastor until Dr. William Saxe Epps came in the fall of 1987. I express gratitude to God that Second Baptist Church was able to stand firmly on the solid rock of Jesus Christ during the tempestuous storm.

Chapter 6

Retirement Years
1986–1992

My retirement has been gradual. Though I retired from the pastorate and the day-to-day operations of a busy and involved servant church in a bustling urban center, I continued my work with USC for several years afterward, as well as many of my board memberships. After my retirement, Jeannetta and I began building a retirement home in Pisgah Forest, North Carolina, a small community adjacent to my hometown, scenic Brevard, which sits in a valley surrounded by the Great Smoky and Blue Ridge mountain ranges. In the late 1970s or early 1980s, television's *60 Minutes* identified Brevard as the ideal retirement location in the United States. To its credit, Brevard and the area boast the breathtakingly beautiful Pisgah National Forest, which with its surging waterfall and many nature trails and scenic spots attracts thousands of tourists annually. Brevard also has an internationally acclaimed music camp plus many other summer camp sites, an amphitheater, and a small private college. Nearby, the Cherokee Indian Reservation annually presents a play in its amphitheater, "Unto These Hills," which portrays the history of the Cherokee Nation and the tragic "trail of tears," when the Cherokees and other Native Americans were taken from their homes and forced to walk to their new location in Oklahoma. With these attractions and others, much of the community has now been geared to the needs and enjoyments of retirees, and Jeannetta and I have spent our summer months there since 1987.

During these summers, I have enjoyed planting and tending a large vegetable garden, ably assisted by my brother, Thaddeus, and preaching in the local churches. Jeannetta stocks up on good literature for summer reading and has organized thousands of family photographs. She has continued her personal ministry of sending

115

timely magazine, journal, and newspaper articles to our children and grandchildren and corresponding with persons who need a word of encouragement. Naturally, Jeannetta's words are encouraging, but a large part of that correspondence ministry is the beautiful penmanship that she developed as a youth and that God has blessed her hand to still steadily execute. At our summer home, Jeannetta and I have spent time with my brothers and their families who live in Brevard and Asheville, and we've entertained many local and vacationing family members and friends.

The retirement years have been full, with many speaking engagements for me and other memorable events. Following is a list of just a few of them.

1988: In February, Second Baptist Church held the first Pastor Emeritus Day, honoring my years of service. Thereafter, every third Sunday in February has been observed as Pastor Emeritus Day. In June, my brother-in-law, Robert Webb, was buried in Washington, D.C. As the year ended, the Claremont School of Theology, with funds from Second Baptist Church, established a $10,000 scholarship in my name. This endowment has grown to approximately $13,000.

1991: During April, I was pleased to return to my hometown, Brevard, North Carolina, to conduct the Institute on Ministry and Evangelism with both Bethel and Bethel "A" Baptist Churches. The institute, held at Jeannetta's and my retirement home in Pisgah Forest, North Carolina, took the form of an ashram during the last two days. In November, I joined Progressive National Baptist Convention leaders in Cincinnati in celebrating the thirtieth anniversary of the PNBC.

1992: On February 20, which also happened to be my birthday, Jeannetta and I had the honor of cutting the ribbon during the dedication ceremony for Morehouse College's new campus center, named in my honor. This event took place during the college's 125th anniversary celebration, and many of my family members were present. In August, I delivered the eulogy for my brother Wells Kilgore at Tunsil Funeral Home in Camden, New Jersey, and I delivered the eulogy for my brother Frank Kilgore at Bethel Baptist Church in Brevard in December.

Conclusion

No book is perfect, and no book ever says all the things that its author would like to say. Each one would like to give credit to all the people with whom he or she has lived and worked, but this kind of credit has no ending.

In this memoir, I have tried to tell the story of the life and acts of one person and his relationship to hundreds of other persons and to scores of organizations and movements. I realize that there are some persons and some movements that my path has crossed that have not been mentioned in this book. I apologize for these omissions.

If, when you read this book, you find anything that will add to the quality of your daily living, I will think that my writing has not been in vain.

I extend my thanks and appreciation to my daughter, Rev. Jini Kilgore Ross, for her assistance in making this book possible.

Epilogue

On February 4, 1998, my father, Thomas Kilgore Jr., passed away at Good Samaritan Hospital in Los Angeles. Joyous services of thanksgiving and celebration were held for him at Second Baptist Church in Los Angeles on February 9, and at his home church (where he preached his trial sermon in 1930), Bethel Baptist, in Brevard, North Carolina, on February 11. His body was laid to rest in nearby Pisgah Forest, North Carolina.

My father met his death as faithfully and courageously as he had lived his life. With a sense of peace, readiness, and trust in God, he prepared the family for his passing by sharing with our mother, and she, in turn with us, that his time was coming soon. One of his last acts on behalf of the family was to send our mother to us at Christmastime, where we were all gathered in Texas. Daddy was supposed to be with us, but he was prevented from coming when he fell and broke his hip on Sunday, December 21. Though he had hip replacement surgery the very next day, he insisted that our mother come for Christmas because he wanted her to enjoy the holiday with us children, grandchildren, and great-grandchildren that he and she had planned for months. He also wanted her to have a chance to see New Vision Baptist Church, which my husband and I planted, for they had not yet had the opportunity to visit. There would be days and weeks ahead for her to spend visiting him in the hospital. But not Christmas. The trip was his gift to her. He was unselfish that way.

Daddy had another reason for sending mother to Texas. He wanted her to bring us and our families (all of whom live outside of California) copies of *The African American Devotional Bible* that he had bought for our Christmas presents and checks in curiously varying amounts that he had written for each family. He did not specify the reason for the checks, but we vowed to save these monetary gifts. About a week after his passing, we all realized that he had

118

given us enough for airfares for ourselves, our spouses, and our children to Los Angeles and North Carolina, and back to our respective homes. For Daddy, living was giving, right up to the end.

JKR

Photographs

Family pet, "Duke."

Jeannetta and I at a Black Agenda luncheon.

At Jeannetta's and my twenty-fifth wedding anniversary, my boyhood friend, Bill Downs, officiated, and my brother Herman, Jeannetta's sister Blanche Webb, and Herman's wife, Annie (far right), were attendants. (A. Hansen Studio)

In 1984, I proudly gave away my daughter, Lynn Elda, in marriage at Friendship Baptist Church in New York.

One of the proudest moments in my life was attending the graduation ceremonies of our eldest grandchild, Robin, at Spelman College in 1993.

Many members of the extended family joined Jeannetta and me for our fiftieth wedding anniversary in 1986. Back row (l-r): Abel Hendy III, Malissa Kilgore Briley (seated), Gerald Briley, Blanche Webb, Robert Webb, Fisseha Egziabher, Tommy Mae Kilgore, Dolores Williams, Annie Kilgore, Clifford Moore, Herman Kilgore. Middle row (l-r): Lynn Kilgore Hendy, Jeannetta and me, Jini Kilgore Moore, Ella Mae Kilgore Adams. Front row (l-r): Niambi Robinson, Okera Robinson, Robin Raschard.

A few members of the family came together for a casual at-home cebebration of Jeannetta's and my sixtieth wedding anniversary in 1996. (L-r): Jeannetta and I; daughter Jini and her husband Earl; daughter Lynn Elda and her husband Abel; granddaughter Niambi, her husband, Charles, and their two sons, Justen and Joshua; grandchildren Robin and Okera; and sister Malissa and her husband, Gerald.

Jeannetta and I
on our sixtieth
wedding anniversary,
December 28, 1996.

The grandchildren and great-grandchildren visted Jeanetta and me
to help us celebrate our sixtieth wedding anniversary in 1996.

Jeannetta and I during my pastorate
at Friendship Baptist Church in
Winston-Salem (1939–47).

Our daughters during the early days
of my pastorate in New York: 1949.
(A. Hansen Studio)

The late Cora Langston Hurley (center) was one of our "daughters." She came to New York from North Carolina to live with us to attend college, graduated, and stayed in our home until she married. Her sons Sean (l) and Noel are shown here, along with a granddaughter.

Our "sons" who came from Ethiopia in the '70s to attend school are pictured here with Jini: the late Yohannes Melaku (l) and the two who lived with Jeanetta and me, Girma Selassie (2d from l) and Fisseha Egziabher (r).

Since Mama's death in 1968, the Kilgore clan has held a reunion every two years. In 1976, we met in Los Angeles. (Edward W. Pearson)

My Morehouse College graduation picture, 1935.

I was born in this house in Woodruff, South Carolina, in 1913.

THE WASHINGTON AFRO-AMERICAN, AUGUST 11, 1959

FOR THE FIRST TIME in 24 years Mrs. Eugenia Kilgore of Brevard, N. C. (seated center at front) had all her 12 children at home at the same time. The occasion was the celebration of her 74th birthday. Rockefeller Kilgore of Brevard, Lamar Kilgore of Washington, D. C., Waymon Kilgore of Asheville, N. C. and Frank Kilgore of Brevard; standing, left to right: Thaddeus Kilgore of Baltimore, Md.; Mrs. Malissa Stiger of Hawthorne, Calif. the Thomas Kilgore Jr., of East Elmhurst, L. I., N. Y., Wells Kilgore of Camden, N. J., the Rev. Harold Kilgore of Baltimore, Mrs. Ella Maye Adams of Chicopee Falls, Mass., Herman Kilgore of Washington and Mrs.

All of Mama's twelve children came home to Brevard to celebrate her seventy-fourth birthday, July 28, 1959. Back row (l-r): Thaddeus, Malissa, Thomas, Wells, Harold, Ella Mae, Herman, Mamie. Front row (l-r): Rockerfeller, Lamar, Mama, Waymon, Frank.

The first seven children born to my father and mother, Thomas and Eugenia Kilgore, were all boys. That's me seated on Papa's lap and my brother Harold on Mama's lap. Standing are (l-r) Wells, Frank, Lamar, Waymon, and Rockerfeller.

My grandmother,
Ella Langston-Miles,
1952.

Mama (r) with her sister and brother, Aunt Daisy and Uncle Herbert.

I was licensed to preach at the age of seventeen at Bethel Baptist Church
in Brevard, North Carolina, on January 30, 1930.

After I finished college, I was ordained by Bethel Baptist Church in Brevard, North Carolina, on August 15, 1935.

Friendship Baptist Church in Winston-Salem, my second pastorate, from 1939 to 1947.

Friendship Baptist Church in Harlem, New York, my third pastorate, from 1947 to 1963. (A. Hansen Studio)

Second Baptist Church in Los Angeles, my fifth pastorate, from 1963 to 1985. (Harry H. Adams)

The late Mr. A. Hansen was a widely acclaimed New York photographer, who chronicled life in Harlem for many years. A retrospective of his work, shown at Harlem's renowned Schomberg Library, attracted widespread attention, and one of his photos of Jeannetta and me and the girls was included in the exhibit. He snapped this photo of me in the beginning years of my pastorate at Friendship Baptist Church in New York (ca. 1948). (A. Hansen Studio)

The early years at Second Baptist Church, during worship (l-r): Rev. U. S. Donaldson, Trustee Charles Anderson, me, Jeannetta, and Deacon Board Chairman Vernon Dunlap. (Cliff Hall)

Second Baptist Trustee Bill Elkins (l), Jeannetta, me, and Deacon Board Chairman Judge Albert D. Matthews at the dedication of the Kilgore Hill Christian Retreat Center in Lake Elsinore, California.

Griffith Gardens, Second Baptist's modern and convenient thirty-nine unit apartment complex for senior citizens and small families, located directly beside the church, was completed and dedicated in 1973, and named after Dr. and Mrs. Thomas L. Griffith, the fifth pastor and his wife, who served from 1921 to 1940. (Harry H. Adams)

In 1970, members of the "Around the World Tour" group, mostly from Second Baptist, posed for this picture. It was our first trip together. While we were in Ethiopia, we met some students who wanted to come to the United States to study. The group sponsored six of them, two of whom lived with Jeannetta and me and became "sons" to us, Fisseha Egziabher and Girma Selassie.

Members of the Second Baptist Church "Around the World Tour" group met with Prime Minister Indira Gandhi of India (seated) in 1970. (Copyright: Photo Division, Ministry of I. & B., Government of India)

I moderated a television program in New York during the early sixties called "Inside Black." During this panel discussion Dr. King and the other panelists were in a lighthearted mood: (l-r) newsmen Robert Teague, WNBC-TV; Leon Lewis, WWRL radio; Steve Duncan, World-Telegram & Sun.

The Southern Christian Leadership Conference West (SCLC) was opened in Los Angeles in 1964, with the official ribbon-cutting ceremony. Pictured with Dr. King and me are Rev. Mansfield Collins (l) and Rev. Wyatt Tee Walker (glasses).

During one of Dr. King's speaking engagements at Second Baptist Church (1964), he signed his new book, *Strength to Love*. My niece Barbara Adams Carney is pictured at left. (Harry H. Adams)

At Morehouse College, singing the alma mater, "Dear Old Morehouse," historian Dr. Lerone Bennett, a Morehouse alumnus, is on my right, and former Morehouse president Dr. LeRoy Keith is on my left.

My good friend Dr. Hugh M. Gloster, president emeritus of Morehouse College. (Arthur "Bud" Smith)

I was thrilled to congratulate actor Louis Gossett Jr., who was on the Morehouse campus in 1992 to receive the college's "Candle in the Dark" award for Arts and Entertainment, during the celebration of Morehouse's 125th anniversary.

Father George Clements, the Chicago priest who adopted a son and began the "One Church One Child" adoption movement, was a recipient of Morehouse's "Candle in the Dark" award for Religion during the celebration of the college's 125th anniversary in 1992.

I was deeply humbled and honored by the naming of Morehouse's new campus center the Thomas Kilgore Jr. Campus Center. The dedication and ribbon-cutting ceremony coincidentally occurred on my birthday, February 20, 1992, during Morehouse's 125th anniversary celebration. My daughters are standing in front of the building.

Jeannetta and I were on hand to
share a special moment with film
producer Spike Lee when he received the NAACP Image Award.

Rev. Jesse Jackson has been a frequent
visitor to Los Angeles. On a recent
occasion, he spoke at Bovard
Auditorium on the University of
Southern California campus.

At a Black Agenda Awards luncheon (l-r): Bishop H. H. Brookins,
L.A. City Councilman Mark Ridley-Thomas, Black Agenda President
Dr. Roy Petitt, Councilwoman Rita Walters, Subira Kisano, Herbert
Troup, and Tulivu Jadi.

In my office chatting with my adminstrative assistant Mrs. Shirley Bell and University of Southern California President Dr. Samuel Sample.

Fellow Los Angeles Community Redevelopment Agency Commissioner Frank Kuwahara and I were feted by the other commissioners at a special luncheon on our eightieth birthdays.

Los Angeles Supervisor Kenneth Hahn (l) and I greeted Dr. H. Claude Hudson, known as "Mr. NAACP" for his pioneering civil rights work in Southern California.

My friend Dr. Martin Luther King Sr., known affectionately as "Daddy King."

Jeannetta and I shared a blissful moment during the seventies with Los Angeles Mayor Tom Bradley, Mrs. Coretta Scott King, and Dr. Benjamin Elijah Mays, former president of Morehouse College.

The University of Southern California developed strong community ties through its Office of Community Affairs. Officials from Anheuser-Busch, Inc. are shown here in this eighties photo with a scholarship check for the USC Ebonics Support Group, a group of African-American students and alumni. (L-r): Ed Lara, president, Westside Distributors: John T. Stevens, Special Field Markets manager; and Bill Brooks, area manager.

I was honored by the citizens of Los Angeles for fifty years in ministry at Los Angeles' Century Plaza Hotel in 1980. Shown on the dais are (l-r) toastmaster actor Ossie Davis and USC President and Mrs. James Zumberge.

One year the women of Second Baptist Church chose as their speakers for the church's two morning services Mrs. Coretta Scott King and our daughter, Jini, who had announced her call to ministry.

Part II

Sermons, Speeches, and Writings

The Next Phase
in American Emancipation

Emancipation Address
Forsythe County Emancipation Celebration
County Courthouse, Winston-Salem, North Carolina
January 1, 1958

Ninety-five years ago, this country, under Abraham Lincoln, found enough moral courage to tackle head-on the powerful institution of chattel slavery. And though the Emancipation Proclamation escalated a bloody civil war, the end result was the abolition of slavery as the basis of the South's economy and the freedom of some 4 million Negroes. The stand of Abraham Lincoln took deep insight, strong moral courage, breadth of economic know-how, and undaunted spiritual fortitude. The work of men like Frederick Douglass, William Lloyd Garrison, and others demanded the kind of spirit that went against the tide, and nothing less than the ideals and practices of an Abraham Lincoln, a William Lloyd Garrison, and a Frederick Douglass will free our great country today from a mental and spiritual slavery that in the long run could be more devastating than the chattel slavery of 1619–1863.

We stand at the doorway today of another great emancipation. The choice of America is to go in and be free or stay out and be reduced to a third-rate power or maybe to ashes. The emancipation this time is not the freedom of a segment of the population from chattel slavery, but rather the freedom of bigoted minds from hidebound traditions and the freedom of warped spirits from the destructive power of hate and prejudice. It is the freedom of Negroes, Chinese-Americans, Italian-Americans, Mexican-Americans, Catholic Americans, Jewish Americans, Protestant Americans — yes, *all* Americans — to have equal access to that which is the basic concept of our way of life, "That all men are created equal, and that they are endowed with certain inalienable rights, among these are life, liberty and the pursuit of happiness."

Our struggle for a free country is not an isolated struggle. We work in cooperation with the satellite countries of Eastern Europe, the semicolonial areas of Africa, and the emerging nationalistic development in Asia. We are in our fight for freedom — a part of the worldwide symphony which is composed of peoples of many colors, races, religions, and cultures. We are blending the instruments of our voices and our actions for freedom with those of all of God's children who have felt the pangs of poverty, hunger, and disinheritance. And though we have not developed a perfect orchestration in the symphony for freedom, and though there are major discords and disharmonies in South Africa, Hungary, the Middle East, Indonesia, and Little Rock, there is a faith abroad in the world that is saying FREEDOM OR DEATH, and *faith* is destined to triumph over all discord, bigotry, and prejudice.

Assuming, then, that we are a part of a worldwide movement for freedom for all peoples, what is America's role? What is white America's role? What is Negro America's role? How will we achieve our 1958, 1959, 1960 emancipation?

We are now ninety-five years from Lincoln's Emancipation Proclamation. Great strides have been made. None can deny this. The American scene is far more emancipated today than it was in the early part of the seventeenth century when the slave trade began to flourish. We are far more liberated that we were in 1720, when Americans were buying slaves in increasing numbers. There is a vast difference in the lot of the Negro — and that of the white man — in 1957 than their lots in 1793, when the cotton gin, invented by slaves and perfected by Eli Whitney, ironically caused a deeper entrenchment of the slave system.

We are far better off today than in 1821, when many thought the solution to the problems in America was to send the Negroes back to Africa, and thus the establishing of the American Colonization Society and the Republic of Liberia. By this time even the slaves knew that their home was in America and not in Africa, for only a few went back to Africa.

Our condition economically, socially, culturally, and religiously is far better now than in the mid-1850s. Church bodies then were voting to split; now they are voting to unite and integrate. Farms and the crude industries then were wholly dominated by whites; now the Negro owns thousands of farms and millions work in industry. Yes, we are far better off.

Secretary of Labor Mitchell, in his article "The Negro Moves Up," in the December 1957 issue of *Reader's Digest*, suggests that we have made great strides toward freedom in the past score of years.

From 1940 to 1957:

- Negroes employed in private households dropped 83 percent

- Negroes employed in private farm labor dropped 44 percent

- Negro wages increased five times but are still only one-half that of the average white wage-earner

- Since 1942, life expectancy for Negroes increased eight years

- One-third of Negroes in America own homes

- Negroes' purchasing power increased to $17.5 million

- Twelve states, representing 33 percent of the U.S. States population, have laws that prohibit discrimination in employment

- Civil Service jobs for Negroes in Washington, D.C., increased from 3 percent in 1930 to 24 percent in 1957, with 16.6 percent holding jobs on a supervisory level

Yes, we have made great strides; we have come a long way. Look at Asa Spaulding with thirty savings and loan associations worth $60 million, fourteen banks worth $40 million, and two hundred insurance companies with 5 million policyholders. Look at S. B. Fuller with five thousand salesmen, one-fifth of whom are white. Look at John Johnson with *Ebony* and *Jet* magazines and other publications and a readership of 2 million persons. Look at Martin King: religion in action. Yes, we have made great strides; we have come a long way.

But wait, let us not become lost in astronomical statistics of progress and fail to look at the other side of the picture. To look at it properly we must ask a few questions.

Why is the State Department so busy sending so many Negro artists and entertainers through Europe, Asia, and Africa? Could this have anything to do with an effort to counteract Russia's propaganda, or could it have more to do with counteracting American hypocrisy? One wonders whether Marian Anderson can sing charmingly and beautifully enough in India, Vietnam, and Burma to wipe out the ugly image of a Negro reporter being kicked by an angry mob in Little Rock. One wonders further if Louis Armstrong can play his trumpet loud enough and excite those "cats" in Europe and Asia intensely enough to cause them to forget that Dorothy Counts was spat at, jeered, and ridiculed in Charlotte until her spirit was broken. It is hard to erase these images from the minds of people who want freedom.

In 1956–57, five states, Virginia, Georgia, Tennessee, Mississippi, and Texas, passed laws penalizing and fining anyone outside of the state who financed or gave legal assistance to state residents specifically engaged in a law suit. These laws are aimed at the NAACP.

In 1957, a school was bombed in Nashville, mobs had to be quelled by troops in Little Rock, a minister was beaten by a mob in Birmingham, and a Negro child's spirit was crucified in Charlotte. How free are we?

I am not able to say *how* free we are, but I know, and all of America knows, that our democracy is sick. We are afraid. We are guilty. Why did Sputnik I and Sputnik II hit us with such devastating shock? Was it because we have lagged behind scientifically? No. It was because we have lagged behind morally. Our false image has been broken. We see our inadequacies. To quote Lerner, we are disenchanted. We can be liberated if we want to be. How?

Since I am talking to an audience that is predominantly Negro, let us begin with us. The Negro must keep improving his lot, not to prove that we are worthy of democracy but because we are the heart of American democracy. There can be no democracy *without us*. So regardless of the ruggedness of the path, we must keep tramping.

We must keep tramping socially. We must keep tramping economically. We are spending $56 million annually on numbers games and liquor. Instead, let us spend our money on credit unions and co-ops, banks and businesses. We must keep tramping educationally as we press for freedom and full integration of our nation's schools. We must keep tramping for full citizenship, supporting the Southern voting rights drive. We must keep tramping religiously, for as Langston Hughes's character Jesse B. Simple says, perhaps we need to grow "backwards" and become like innocent children again, and like a child declare, "We're all brothers — everybody, white and black — not just during Brotherhood Week, but every week." To which Simple says he would testify, "Amen!"*

---

*George Braziller, ed., "Simple Stakes a Claim," *The Langston Hughes Reader* (New York: George Braziller, 1958).

Confrontation and Reconciliation

TOWARD A RELEVANT BLACK CHURCH

Ministers' Breakfast, Sixtieth Annual NAACP Convention
Roof Garden, Heidelberg Hotel, Jackson, Mississippi
July 1, 1969

Mr. Chairman, and Fellow Human Beings: I use this brief salutation with the hope that it will be safe. It is no longer proper to refer to race. It is hard to know when to use "Negro," "colored," "Afro-American," "black," or "brother," and because of such drastic changes in dress habits and hair styles, it becomes increasingly more difficult to say, "Ladies and Gentlemen." So, I say, "Folks, I am glad to be here."

I presided at this breakfast ten years ago in New York and, at that time, mused to myself about the ungodliness of asking someone to speak so early in the day. Little did I think that I would be the victim in such a short decade. In seriousness, however, I am grateful to the committee for granting me the opportunity to say some words in this hour of the convention and in this moment of history.

I was not told how long to speak, and I do not know how well I have prepared (you will have to judge this later), but when someone asked Woodrow Wilson how long he took to prepare a ten-minute speech, he said, "Two weeks." "How long for an hour speech?" "One week." How long for a two-hour speech?" "I am ready now," he replied. So, here I am!

When we assess the tenor of our times, poets' words come to our minds. Much of our frustration today is summed up in Gwendolyn Brooks's poem, "We Real Cool"

> We real cool. We
> Left school. We
> Lurk late. We
> Strike straight. We

150

Sing sin. We
Thin gin. We
Use pot. We
Jazz June. We
Die soon.

When we look intently at our society today, we are faced with maddening confrontations, deep-seated frustrations, self-appropriated grandeur, and destructive anarchy. Campuses have been turned upside down, many streets are unsafe, and many home ties no longer hold. Confrontation is the name of the game; nonnegotiable is the password for "takeover." Our country is divided on war and peace. Anyone who sees the kind of society that we have handed to sensitive, unfettered, and free-thinking youth and expects them to act and react "normally" is either a fool or a knave. The time has come for us to redefine our goals. Our priorities must be put in order. Our values are inverted, and we must get them straight. We cannot keep on killing and being killed in Vietnam and expect a nonviolent society at home: some 34,329 young Americans dead, 209,045 wounded, and $100 billion spent. This is too great a price to pay for a war that no one can justify. Tragically, the Vietnamese have paid a price in lives and casualties much greater than ours. We cannot keep on expanding an economy to the point that our GNP is almost a trillion dollars while at the same time winking at dire poverty in our rural areas and city ghettos and barrios. We cannot continue to miseducate thousands of black, brown, red, and white children, leaving them ill-fitted to function in a highly complex society.

We dare not expect to evade facing up to our problems of self-education, economics, politics, and religion by trying to land on the moon or on Mars. We can never justify spending $30 billion to go to the moon when there are 40 million earthlings who live below the poverty level. Our number one problem is to redefine our goals and move our nation from confrontation to reconciliation. The number one prime movers for this task are the nation's churches and preachers. There never was a time when the nation needed prophets, priests, ministers, watchmen, and servants in the pulpits as in this present confrontational age. The challenge is ours. Black American preachers and churches must lead in cultivating the field. May I be so bold as to say that we must take leadership in at least five areas if our country is to survive as a sane social order.

First, we must preach, advocate, and work for peace. The voices for peace are too subdued. Our Lord said: "Blessed are the peacemakers." Did you read *Life* magazine last week? Did those more than two hundred faces of the flower of youth in America speak to you? They did to me. We should cry from every pulpit, "Come out of Vietnam." I dare anyone to give me a valid moral, military, economic, or political reason for us to keep our men fighting in Vietnam. I have yet to find a justifiable reason for our being there. The Communist scare and the domino theory are just not valid, and we should stop being dupes. As pastors, we must counsel with young men who are of draft age and give them guidance. I know many of these young men who feel that they have no right to die in Vietnam. We cannot ignore the conscience of our youth.

The black church should mount a mighty crusade to end the war and confront the military-business-industrial complex with God's Word and our moral force. We just cannot talk about reconciliation at home and continue in a senseless war in Vietnam.

Second, a new style of politics must be developed. The preacher has a unique role to play in politics. Unfortunately, it has been a bad role in too many instances. We stand at that point in history where we must do at least four things:

- Involve our churches in community voter registration campaigns, checking on electors to see that they vote.

- Study issues and candidates, and lead people to vote intelligently.

- Stop taking political payoffs, and put money in decent campaigns. In Los Angeles, a group of preachers called the Concerned Clergy supported Hubert Humphrey in 1968. They vowed not to accept money from politicians, but raised their own instead. Money was offered in hundred-dollar bills to the preachers; fifty thousand more votes were needed. They gave the money back.

- Say, "To hell!" with political parties unless they are just, operate with integrity, and, as far as possible, are void of racism. We cannot afford to be a slave to any political party.

In short, we need a politics of honesty, integrity, fiscal soundness, and concern for people. There is no such animal now. We must create him.

Third, bold and creative ventures in economic survival must be developed. James Forman walked down the aisle of Riverside Church a few Sundays ago and created more dialogue in our American churches than we have had in a long time. It is highly possible that the National Black Economic Development Conference is the judgment of God on the injustices of our economic order. A long time ago, another strange creature in religious circles walked into the city and into worship places and said, "Let justice run down as waters, and righteousness as a mighty stream" (Amos 5:24). A few centuries later, another young prophet and lay preacher walked into the Jerusalem Temple, overturned tables, broke up a cultic practice, and said that the Lord's house, which should be a house of prayer, had been turned into a den of thieves (Matt. 21:12–13).

There is something radically wrong with our economic order when we have gross unemployment, while we spend $30 billion to put a man on the moon. I am no economist, but I know that the rich and super-rich are so manipulating our economy that they perpetuate poverty. In the State of Mississippi, wealthy farmers and farm combines draw welfare checks from the federal government that total hundreds of times more than all the poor in Mississippi receive from welfare.

Black churches and preachers must lead in setting up bread basket movements, co-ops, shopping centers, investment clubs, and schools for entrepreneurs.

We must do our share to lift the economic yoke from our people even if we are helping to impose that yoke. We must be enablers and not exploiters.

Fourth, we must conduct new experiments in education. Education is in trouble in our country. At the higher levels, we have computerized the learning process to the extent that we are turning out robots instead of truly educated men and women. Where we have not computerized it, we have depersonalized it. The delicate and precious teacher-student relationship has gone in most of our colleges and universities. Students are numbers now, not personalities. Herein is the root cause of our present student rebellion. Add to this the hand of big business, government, and the military establishment in our education process, and you have a monster against whom somebody had better rebel!

Black studies is another cry of today, a cry that has come so late. Had we been fair in our country in education, the role of blacks in making our nation would have been put into perspective long ago. But black studies must remain true to its purpose. It must be studies for all people. It must take place in an arena of democracy. Black studies must not mean black separation. I am all for certain kinds of interim separations in order to get "our thing" together, but I am no more for all-black education than I have been for all-white education. I am for quality education and equal opportunity for all our citizens.

Our real trouble in education is not at the college and graduate level, but at the kindergarten and elementary school level. We are sunk educationally if we cannot vastly increase our number of dedicated teachers, multiply many fold our administrators who care, and elect school boards who are living in the twentieth century. We cannot continue to run irrelevant educational mills, sadly lacking in creativity and educational experimentation, and expect to prepare young people to function in our complex society. Once again, the home, church, and school must get together and do a job of education for this day.

Fifth, and finally, we must relate religion to life. Some are saying that God is dead and that the church is drying up. This is not so. I know that we have tried to institutionalize God. On occasion, we have tried to defend Him. The fact is we can do neither. He is too big to be caught up in any institution, and if He needs our defense, then we don't need Him. God has not failed, but our theology has. We have been masters at splitting life into segments instead of looking at it as a whole. We have constantly made young people and others choose between the church and life. We have frowned upon dancing when we have not been willing to walk picket lines.

Will Durant has said that we must solve our problems or we will dissolve, but Jesus said, "I have come that you may have life and have it more abundantly" (John 10:10). We must speak to the conscience of our nation; we must speak to the power structures of our nation; we must speak to the establishments, and we must speak to the church. The tragedy of this hour is that the stirrings are not coming from the preachers but from the hippies, the students, and the black radical militants. As they cause social foment and unrest, we must not dare to condemn, for it could be because our voices are so mute that God is speaking through them. You and I should pray that God will not have to make a run around the church and the preacher in order to get redemption. Let us also pray that we may not shrink from confrontations, whether they be between old and young, black and white, or radical and conservative. Let us pray that our confrontations are creative and reconciling as we seek to create a relevant black church.

Toward a Soul-Full Community

Baccalaureate Address, Bovard Auditorium,
University of Southern California
June 7, 1972

In May 1972 the Associated Press published an article entitled, "The Merry Month of Mayhem." Ironically, May is usually looked upon as the time of year for merriment, rejoicing, and rebirth. But this May matured into a grim catalogue of violence and tragedy. As if the daily kill and savagery in Vietnam and the complacently accepted homicides in this and other countries were not enough, during twenty-seven days in the "merry" month of May, priceless art desecration, killings, and wanton recklessness took place in eight countries, with heavy concentration in this country.

On Memorial Day weekend, we used our highways and streets in a macabre way to add 565 more persons to the list to be memorialized next year. A self-appointed assassin came close to achieving his goal as he shot down a presidential candidate. A crazed gunman killed five persons and seriously injured eight more before killing himself in a shopping center in a southeastern state. A deranged man, using a twelve-pound sledgehammer, damaged Michelangelo's *Pietà* sculpture in St. Peter's Basilica in Vatican City. Three terrorists opened fire on travelers in Tel Aviv's International Airport, killing twenty-six persons and wounding seventy-seven. Bombings, highway mayhem, death, and destruction. What goes here?

Maybe these sparks of violence that are flying freely in so many parts of the world are no more than the anticipated reflections of a society on the move, a society in the process of change. There is danger, however, in the possibility that these sparks reflect a widespread malaise, a chronic sickness that, if not checked, could lead to the destruction of much that we hold dear.

Every commencement should be a time of reassessing and a time of values inventorying. Each group of graduates lives under a

156

binding injunction to scrutinize society and its institutions carefully and to raise serious questions about its role as an agent of creative change. To do less than this is to forfeit one's right to claim his part in an educational discipline.

Serious commitments to the use of knowledge, skills, expertise, and native wisdom will be needed in the days ahead if we are to survive and function as a community of human beings. War can no longer be accepted as a means of settling national or international problems. The price is too high in lives, in property destruction, and in money. Since World War I, over 25 million men and women have died in the armed forces; one-half that many civilians have perished in wars. The cost of killing a person during a war has risen from seventy-five cents in Caesar's wars to $375,000 for every Viet Cong killed by United States troops. There is no way to calculate the legacy of human suffering, societal disruption, and moral and spiritual decay caused by war. For ten years now, we have been engaged in an unwinnable, inglorious, counterproductive, and immorally wasteful conflict in Southeast Asia. Our president [of the United States], who braved criticism and held summit meetings in Peking and Moscow, should expand his agenda to include Hanoi. Shall we continue to stand on national pride and move closer to the brink of international genocide?

As we prosecute wars with the latest technological equipment, we find ourselves becoming victims of our technology on another front. At this present time, the United Nations is holding a conference on the human environment in Stockholm, Sweden. Hopefully, there will come out of this meeting a World Heritage Trust that will include treaties to protect the oceans from further pollution, treaties to protect endangered species from further decimation, a global monitoring system and information exchanges, an international environment fund, and an international environment staff. Let us hope that this will be the beginning of a comprehensive response to what is, in fact, a planet-wide environmental crisis. Let us hope and pray that our children will be able to drink purer water, to breathe cleaner air, and to eat purer food.

In the early days of the Stockholm conference, a serious breach threatens its effectiveness. The question of environmental protection, as opposed to economic development, has been injected. A polarity between north and south and between rich and poor countries has developed. The European and American nations are concerned about development. Under no circumstance must the environmental concerns become a new escape for the rich nations to shun their responsibility to the poor. The poor countries can dissipate waste while the rich countries increase their flow of capital to fund environmental projects. This could promote a growing awareness of the unity of man.

If we stopped wars tomorrow and cleaned up the environment the day after tomorrow, and if we *ipso facto* developed some kind of international economic parity, we would still be the victims of a terrible sickness that we must overcome. This sickness is the malaise of racism. America is a racist society. Racism is reflected in every system and in every institution. We have preached brotherhood, but we have not lived it; we have talked community, but we have not developed it. Start where you please: politics, economics, education, employment, housing patterns, and religion. All, in one way or another, show the ugly head of racism. It is not divinely decreed that over three-fifths of the black and brown children in the Los Angeles school system should read and achieve between zero and 20 percent, when the national average is 51 percent. Why are our prison populations in great states like New York and California composed of 70–85 percent blacks and other minority groups? Why is the unemployment rate among young blacks and Chicanos in Los Angeles twice that of the white community? The "whys" could go on *ad infinitum*. The root cause lies in a racist society. The very fact that we, in a land that is called "the land of the free and the home of the brave," have to use categories like "majority" and "minority" is evidence of this sickness in our society.

What is our hope?

Sensing the perils of perversity that afflict our society, we must constantly employ all possible models we have to perfect change. There is a dimension in life that is available to all of us, but we have done certain things in our society that have cut us away from that dimension. Therefore, we find ourselves in a kind of estrangement, where we find it easier to kill our fellow man, easier to cheat him, easier not to speak to him, easier to set up categories of mankind, and easier to be involved in what Rod MacLeish calls "a crisis of legitimacy." The erosion of the precept "thou shalt not kill" is so all-prevailing and so much a part of our national life that it became relatively easy for weak, warped, and twisted minds to assassinate Medgar Evers, John Kennedy, Martin Luther King Jr., and Robert Kennedy, and to shoot George Wallace. This is a dangerous crisis to be in. If it is permitted to run its course, it simply means that our days as a free society are numbered.

In the New Testament, a question is raised: "What shall it profit a man if he shall gain the whole world and lose his own soul; or what shall a man give in exchange for his soul?" (Mark 8:36–37, KJV) If we have lost our national soul, or if we are on the verge of doing so, we must, for the sake of survival, look for it and find it.

We can develop a society, a community with soul, if we want to. Compassion is not dead; kindness is not passé; concern is not outmoded; and happiness and joy are still possible. In a kind of pseudo-sophistication, we try to be impervious to these natural human traits, but if they are not expressed, they lie dormant in all of us.

Howard Thurman, in his book *Search for Common Ground,* picks up the thread of our need for community and says that the principle of community is written into the laws of the physical universe. If man really wants to know what community is, he does not have to wait for some lofty revelation to come into the existential from the transcendental. All he needs to do is go to nature, because the basis for community is found in the living structures. In some strange way, it is written into the universe that life feeds life. Understanding and being involved in this life-giving process give soul to our society.

When we talk about a community with soul, we are talking about more than the "American way of life," more than free enterprise, more than money and materials, and more than the accumulation of knowledge. We are talking about something as simple as "soul food," "soul music," a "soul handshake," and at the same time, something as profound as the overriding concepts, causes, and concerns that pull us together as we contribute from the depths of our inner humanity. We are talking about a community experiencing life and death together, a community celebrating, worshiping, and dancing together. We are talking about a community that realizes that it cannot feed long upon itself; a community that knows that it can flourish only when its boundaries are giving way to the coming of others from beyond it; a community where unknown and undiscovered brothers will say, "We have sought and we have found our own identity."

The community of soul will be the arena where men of all races and classes can function freely and relate to each other. In it, hearts and nervous systems are committed to a feeling of belonging, and spirits are no longer isolated and afraid. In it, there will be no fear of brothers, and self-shame will have died. This kind of community can go forth and save the land of our birth from the plague that first drove us into separate enclaves and behind closed walls. In this community, we will understand why we were born. Man, all men, belong to each other. He who shuts himself away diminishes himself.

New life is possible for all who want it. We are tired of war, for it no longer produces heroes, victories, or even patriotic songs. It only produces death, destruction, and awful waste. We are concerned about pollution, for in its wake are sickness, disease, and death. We are tired of poverty, because it breeds misery, malnutrition, and all manner of social evils. We are fed up with injustice, because it denies the equality of human beings. We are sick of racism, because it denies the essential worth of human beings and sets race against race in an indeterminable conflict. We want life; therefore, we must follow every lead that means life.

Ideals and reality must replace our idols and illusions. Hope and assurance must replace our many false securities. The French Protestant theologian Jacques Ellul speaks eloquently and prophetically of the categorical wrongness of our idols of war, of money, of state, and of technology in his book *The Judgment of Jonah:*

> These idols can indeed give a great deal to man. They can solve his problems. They can grant him happiness and power, and even virtue and good. But they cannot give him the very thing he needs — mercy. For these idols have no heart. No relationship of love can be set up with them, only relations of possession. The man who loves money, or the state, is not loved by them; he is owned by them. This is why the fundamental problem of man cannot be solved by these powers. For man has definitive need of only one thing: to be loved, which also means to be pardoned and lifted above himself. None of these idols can do this for him. But man does not know this, or hear it, until he has learned the emptiness of idols, until he has been

disillusioned, until in truth he finds himself naked and without mercy, until he begs in an empty world for mercy which cannot come to him from the world.

And this is where God comes in. The God who is really God. Not the watchmaker god, who set the planets in their courses; not the errand-boy god, who is waiting to do our bidding at the cajoling of the right kind of prayer; not the benevolent godfather god waiting to give us pie-in-the-sky; not the god of the gaps, invoked to account for anything the scientists haven't figured out.

These are concepts of a god that never lived. The real God gives soul and meaning to existence. This happens in many ways and in many forms. It is not necessarily a "religious" phenomenon. God moves in a welfare system that restores clients to honor, dignity, and responsibility; or in an economic system that recognizes the basic needs of all people in the society; or in a foreign policy that deals not in prejudices and stereotypes, but in terms of a world-wide human community; or in a church whose work and worship reflect the Spirit of God releasing the captives, opening the eyes of the blind, feeding the hungry and clothing the naked; or in a great university that sends forth graduates in many disciplines who are committed to unending service in liberating mankind.

History has recorded many models of societies that found liberation through soul force. Harvey Cox, in his book *Feast of Fools*, calls the American church to question for losing its spirit of joy and its spark of spontaneity. He deplores the fact that organized religion celebrates so seldom. What Cox sees as a problem in the church is also a problem in our society. In the midst of all of our problems, we have tremendous blessings. We must use these blessings to *solve* our problems and to liberate our fellow man. We must move with *soul* to develop community and with spirit to give life to it. So let us not be afraid to look backwards from whence we came and to look to the future singing:

> Lift ev'ry voice and sing,
> 'Til earth and heaven ring,
> Ring with the harmonies of Liberty;
> Let our rejoicing rise
> High as the list'ning skies
> Let it resound loud as the rolling sea.

Sing a song full of the faith that the dark past
   has taught us;
Sing a song full of the hope that the present
   has brought us;
Facing the rising sun of our new day begun,
Let us march on 'til victory is won.*

---

*James Weldon Johnson, "Negro National Anthem." Composed by Hall Johnson.

Fellowship beyond Frontiers

*Thirteenth Baptist World Congress
of the Baptist World Alliance
Stockholm, July 12, 1975*

We are indebted to the Greek New Testament for the word *koinonia*. It literally means, "fellowship in love and concern." In its broader connotation, it expresses an enterprise in which we learn from one another, pray for one another, support one another, and share with one another. This mutual sharing reaches its zenith in the sharing of the word and the sharing of the elements of the Lord's Supper. Whatever roots of any significant depth we may have in Christian faith, whatever foundations we may claim, we must ever be aware that it is with all of God's people that we are to establish the deeper roots and the firmer foundations.

The common task of the worshiping and serving community is to establish deeper roots and firmer foundations. For it is from this position that we move from our limited self-interest to universal concern. Only when we are grounded properly in the faith delivered to us by the saints can we move with a sense of awareness to develop a universal network of concerned Christians. We need to grasp more firmly with all of God's people the breadth, length, height, and depth of the love of Christ, and to know it as best we can (Eph. 3:18–19).

Many are abandoning all religious belief and trying other ways to find reality. There are still some atheists and agnostics around trying their Victorian rationalism in the solution of all life's problems. Still others are trying frantically to rationalize religion itself. Like the Greeks of old, they want to make it a *gnosis* (knowledge); like the avant-garde of today, they want a religious science. But it is hard to know what "knowing" means. Newtonian physics declared that everything works rationally and predictably and that science simply confirms what common sense already knows. Alexander Pope expressed the confidence of the age of reason when he said:

> Nature and nature's laws lay hid in night:
> God said: Let Newton be and all was light.

Two centuries later, Father Ronald Knox replied:

> It did not last; the devil howling Ho!
> Let Einstein be, restored the status quo.

The ambiguity of existence so often blurs the lines between different kinds of knowing. So the dogmatism about the certainty of science as compared to the speculation of religion has literally vanished. Men and women of faith believe in the power and progress of knowledge and science, but beyond that they stake their lives on the power of Almighty God in His creative and redemptive process. He and He alone determines the course of history, the mental capacity of the scientist, and the life span of the sparrow. He and He alone is worthy of our complete allegiance and faith.

To understand the dimensions of our *koinonia* and to find practical Christian ways to develop fellowship beyond frontiers, we must understand the nature of the world we live in, the diversity of its lands, peoples, religions, and customs, and we must with a great degree of clarity identify the present-day frontiers. Moreover, technology in both travel and communications has for all intents and purposes done away with former geographical frontiers. Geographically, the world is a community. We can literally eat our three meals a day (those who enjoy this luxury) on any three different continents of our choice. Therefore, when we think in terms of frontiers, we must identify areas in which we have not identified with one another, then take into consideration our social, racial, ethnic, and psychological strange lands as well as those who live in geographical locations other than ours. In some instances, these strange geographical new lands are across town, and in others they are across the world.

When we talk about fellowship beyond frontiers, we are really talking about exploring different lands, meeting other peoples, developing a new race consciousness, understanding other cultures and religions, and discovering other dimensions of an old mystery that has given life and vitality to our faith. We are talking about a venture that transcends all selfish economic interest, all limited and conscripted social customs, all bigoted, culture-dominated religious patterns, and all arrogant, intellectual, and educational exclusions. We are talking about a community in which the Arab and the Jew will view a common destiny, in which East and West will understand their mutual dependence, in which king and peasant will know a common brotherhood, in which rich and poor can see together the need for justice and equity, and in which the lips of prince and pauper can drink from a common communion cup.

As we attempt to fellowship beyond frontiers, the changes and ambiguities of our globe must be reckoned with. The dynamics of the developing nationalistic movements in Asia, Africa, Latin America, and other parts of the world must be viewed in proper perspective. The powerful technological development of the Western nations and others must be carefully analyzed in the light of a proper balance between awesome scientific and technical knowhow and our moral, ethical, and spiritual convictions. We cannot talk with any authority or credibility about fellowship beyond frontiers as long as some nations spend millions of dollars trying to reduce from overeating while millions in other nations are starving. There is no dichotomy in our Lord's teachings or in His commands. His gospel is never self-contradictory. "In him we live, and move, and have our being" (Acts 17:28, KJV). Under His judgment are our politics, economics, social orders, cultures, educational systems, and religious practices. He is no less concerned with the salvation of societies and human structures than He is with the salvation of individuals. All are under His judgment.

If those of us who are Christians and Baptists from all parts of the world would develop a widening fellowship of believers, would keep our witness from corroding, would certify creatively our credentials as witnesses and make some difference in a difficult world, we must concentrate on some definite approaches to the task. We must find new and better ways than the ones of the past. We will have to discover and understand as fully as possible the words of our Lord, "Ye shall know the truth, and the truth shall make you free" (John 8:32, KJV), and "I must work the works of him that sent me while it is day: the night cometh, when no man can work" (John 9:4, KJV).

The frontier of a highly developed technological and materialistic world must be crossed and challenged. We must try harder than ever to coordinate our scientific and technical knowledge with moral wisdom. The Christian witness has to be made boldly as we face the problems of scientific powers and moral quandary. In my own country we are struggling with the question of legal abortion. The global picture of abortion is alarming. The population council reports that as many as 10 million abortions are performed in just one country each year. Other nations present statistics just as alarming.

Global decisions will have to be made so we can determine whether we will continue to begin life and destroy it, or whether we can and will use our scientific know-how to stop chronic starvation and unconscionable misery with massive emergency aid, agricultural assistance, long-range development, and education. Do we have the moral courage on a world basis to move away from the anonymity of "do your own thing," and construct new forms of supportive community life? I hope we have not lost the capacity to care. I hope that the church and secular society can in some way receive a sense of their responsibility to bear one another's burdens.

The arrogance of privilege based upon material wealth, accidents of history, color, and race must be counteracted by development of a kind of two-way frontiersmanship carried on by developed and underdeveloped nations. The great powers of our world have developed arsenals that have the capability to destroy the whole population of the world sixteen times. This is an awesome thought. This power has produced arrogance. This arrogant frontier has to be crossed. The message of the Lord is badly needed in this area. These powers and principalities have to be "wrestled" with. The world can no longer live with great pockets of wealth and great pockets of poverty and misery. "The earth is the LORD's, and the fulness thereof" (Ps. 24:1, KJV). The imbalance caused by the concentration of wealth and power in certain nations, certain races, and certain powerful cartels and international monopolies has to be dealt with in the light of our Christian responsibility.

We can no longer permit the so-called developing countries to continue to deteriorate. In the 1960s the per capita income of developed countries increased by $650, while in the developing countries the increase was only by about $40. The share of world trade of the developing countries in exports declined from 21.3 percent in 1960 to 17.6 percent in 1970.

If we would do much more than just broaden the dialogue about new frontiers to cross, we must be instruments in creating international movements and programs that promote justice, fair play, and equity in economics, education, and social services. Churches and denominations must not be satisfied with developing sophisticated mutual admiration societies and powerful bureaucratic structures. We must be models of simple but profound Christian living. We cannot conform to prevailing cultural and materialistic patterns. We must move to transform societies.

In the process of working for renewal and change there must be a developed appreciation for different worship and liturgical patterns. The spiritual motivations of various ethnic groups, nations, and races must be respected by those of other groups, nations, and races.

Developed and underdeveloped nations need to bring closer their understanding of development. Both must cross frontiers. If we who claim allegiance to Jesus Christ would cross these frontiers, we must know that development and social change are set in motion not only by the autonomous processes of science and technology, but also are subject to the convictions and aspirations of men and women. So within this dynamic and complex process, Christian responsibility is to seek to develop social and positive institutions and processes that embody and enhance human dignity, and then give the glory and honor to God (Ps. 115:1).

We recognize that each of us belongs simultaneously to different communities, religions, nations, and cultures, but at the same time we are in communities of common concern that cut across lines of indigenous religious practices, nations, and cultures. As we understand community in this sense, we realize that we all are concerned about our responsibility to other human beings and our responsibility to God. Knowing this, we move by faith, hope, and love across all kinds of frontiers to witness and fellowship.

With a new sense of mission and evangelism we must cross frontiers of all kinds. Following our Lord we will know that, "The spirit of the Lord is upon me, because he hath anointed me to preach the gospel to the poor; he hath sent me to heal the brokenhearted, to preach deliverance to the captives, and recovering of sight to the blind, to set at liberty them that are bruised, to preach the acceptable year of the Lord" (Luke 4:18–19, KJV). This is a daring position to take, but Jesus took it and faced the consequences. We too must take it.

If we move by the Spirit of God, we will have to cross frontiers into other Christian denominations. We will need to learn the truth of true ecumenism. We will need to practice a gospel that leads to cooperation with all Christians. We will have to go further than that. We will have to cross the frontier of other world religions. We cannot ignore the gifts that have come to mankind from religions that have stabilized great civilizations. We must in the name of Jesus Christ know and love those who are not of our fold.

Walking the Edge of the New

2 COR. 5:13–21, REV. 21:1

The President's Annual Address, Sixteenth Annual Session
Progressive National Baptist Convention
Atlanta Municipal Auditorium, August 11, 1977

Eleven months ago, you chose me as president of America's most exciting and challenging religious movement. I thank you for the honor bestowed. I have tried to worthily perform the duties implied.

We Have Come This Far — Let Us Go On by Faith. On a chilly November day in 1961, November 14 to be exact, twenty-two Baptist pastors and one lay woman, representing twenty-two Baptist churches and fourteen states, met at the Zion Baptist Church, Cincinnati, Ohio, Dr. L. V. Booth, pastor, and the Progressive National Baptist Convention was born. An offering of $239.90 was received, a gift of $181.36 was made for foreign mission, and churches reported $300. All together, thirty-three persons were there from the following states:*

Alabama	1	Michigan	3
California	3	Mississippi	1
Florida	3	New Jersey	2
Illinois	3	Ohio	8
Iowa	1	Virginia	2
Kentucky	1	West Virginia	1

Sixteen years later, we have added more than fourteen hundred churches and four hundred thousand plus constituents. In 1976, we gave to foreign mission $165,000, to Christian education $105,146,

---

*Some numbers are missing, including the delegation from New York.

and raised for all purposes $856,479. We also kept our commit-
ment to an aggressive evangelism program, and we forgot not our
mandate in the arena of civil rights and human freedom.

Our history is short, but it is rich and full. Our beginnings were
small but distinguished. Our present is full of change and is exciting.
Our future is bright and our hope is undiminished.

As we move into the future, let us never forget those who
launched this ship of faith. As we sail the rough and smooth waters
of the future, knowing full well that we will land safely, let us not
forget those who launched the boat. In the Progressive Hall of Fame
belong the names of:

L. V. Booth	J. C. Mitchell
W. H. Brinford	W. W. Parker
A. R. Brent	H. W. Patterson
T. M. Chambers Sr.	Louis Rawls
W. W. Glover	B. W. Robertson
J. F. Greene	L. S. Sorrell
J. R. Henderson	C. E. Wagner
Joseph Hill	Mrs. Thelma Walton
S. S. Hodges	J. A. Williams
I. V. Lavinge	J. B. Williams
A. L. Mason	J. F. Williams
H. D. McBride	

Like those pioneers, we can all distinguish ourselves and leave our
names written in the annals of PNBC. This kind of distinction comes
through faith undaunted, concern uncorrupted, support undiminished, sacrifice unblemished, and hope unlimited. Some of us have
walked this path; others of you will need to join us as we "Walk the
Edge of the New."

It has been no accident that we have grown from thirty-three persons participating to annual meetings that involve more than five
thousand persons. It took much hard work, much prayer, and unusual dedication to build a structure (though still in the making) that
is mission- and goal-centered and is void of the curse of personality
cult development. It has taken much grace and foresight to live by a
principle of trying to select the best leadership for a given time and
making the simple principle of nonautomatic succession work. No

pains have been spared in developing a convention with a theme centered in the Progressive concept "Fellowship — Progress — Peace." Now we add "service." No small amount of teaching and evangelical zeal have gone into bringing in hundreds of new churches and thousands of new constituents. An unusual stewardship of financial resources among black Baptists is budding in PNBC. It has been by strong teaching and some serious sacrificing that we have increased our annual income from $721.26 in 1961 to more than $800,000 in 1976. With God's help and your cooperation, we have come a long way in sixteen short years.

But we have a long way to go, and the hour is at hand! We must walk together the edge of the new.

I hope by now that we have developed a high level of trust among ourselves. I believe that we have entered into a state of *koinonia.* Even though we recognize the value and privilege of free speech, I hope that in our deliberations we will use restraint, because I believe we have passed the stage of wanting to talk for rhetorical demonstration or to register our presence in the meeting. The leadership of the convention will continue to provide adequate time and proper procedures for on-the-point discussion.

If we are going to walk the edge of the new and discover riches that we have never dreamed of, we will have to form an orderly procession. Certainly I do not mean army-type regimentation. This is abhorrent to free Baptists. But I do mean taking care of business on time and within reasonable time frames. We are duty bound to be good stewards of the resources that our churches give us to attend the convention. They give us time away from our regular duties, and they give us money to take care of our Christian needs. It is not fair, and it may be extortion, to accept church financing to come to the convention, and then spend a significant portion of your time outside of the sessions. My brothers and sisters, if your church sends you here as a delegate, it is not fair for you to use your money and time for a semivacation. We need you in each session — on time and for the whole time!

As we continue to develop our constitution, we will muster all wisdom that is at our disposal to make it a working instrument. We will follow it as closely as possible in the total area of convention operations. We all know by this time that PNBC is more than an annual religious gathering. It is a year-round operating convention.

Immediately following this annual session, boards and committees and staff will begin all the detail work for another year's journey.

During the past year, many board and committee members have traveled miles and spent days in hotels at their own expense taking care of convention business. Some of the new experience and new procedures you have seen here represent hours of free labor of many of your brothers and sisters. I challenge you to provide the resources so that the effective and creative work of the convention can be carried on, and not at the expense of the persons who do it. To walk the edge of the new costs, I am confident that you will share.

In speaking of sharing, I call to your attention our need for every pastor and church to carry a fair share of the load. We have projected a million-dollar-plus budget for 1978. We are placing in the field two full-time associate secretaries who will work among you as stewardship developers. And we are asking each church to accept a definite responsibility for convention support that is fair and just to all. We are further asking the four regions to take responsibility for promoting the raising of certain percentages of the budget. We are asking a lot, but not too much! Progress carries its price, and PNBC has no bargain basement. All of our commodities are top quality, manufactured in heaven, and carry the trademark of the Cross. These goods demand top price. This price cannot be paid by a church that sends a "representation fee" of $50 as its sole annual gift to the convention, and then spends $1,500 to send five delegates to make decisions on how to spend that $50. This is poor economics and an inverted use of church resources. We can pay the price if we develop the habit of the Monthly Support Plan. Every church could send to the headquarters a gift monthly if every church tried. Certainly if you can't do it each month, at least it should be done quarterly.

The future is bright and the path before us beckons us. Are we willing to walk the edge of the new?

As we move into our seventeenth year as a convention, we face many opportunities and challenges. To relevantly minister to ourselves and to our society's needs, we must get ourselves in proper spiritual condition. We may perfect our structure to perform like a smoothly working machine, and we may raise more than our budget calls for, but if we lose our spiritual balance and composure, we can neither deal properly with ourselves nor our society.

Let us resolve from this hour to open ourselves as completely as possible to the inward working of the Holy Spirit and develop across this convention churches that are on fire for God in an unashamed evangelical thrust. Let us resolve to make every worship service a "mighty happening." Let us pray so earnestly and so regularly for our churches, for all of our constituents, and for the convention as a whole, that spiritual vibrations can be felt from Boston to Los Angeles, and from Miami to Detroit. There is plenty of power if we exercise the faith of a mustard seed.

God has given to us gifts of song, smiles, fervent prayers, and mourning voices. Don't deny expression to these beautiful gifts. We sang and prayed and schemed and planned our way out of slavery. Surely we can use these same natural gifts backed up by our educational attainment and economic advancement to literally bring about miracles in this convention.

Brother preachers, preach. Each of you is unique. Use your gifts to the glory of God, the advancement of His church, and the salvation of sinners. Don't play with preaching. It is no joke. It is serious business. Preach the way God has given you talent to preach. If you read a manuscript, read it with the accuracy, power, and dignity of an Ossie Davis. If you are a "whooper," build the "whoop" on some solid theological information, then sweeten it to our edification and to the glory of God. If you are a moaner, say something, and then put the doves to shame. If you are an orator, make Demosthenes drop his head. If you are dialogical, make it so plain that the wayfaring man will understand. If you preach someone else's sermons, then be sure you make preparations before you preach them. Take a good dictionary and learn all the unfamiliar words and pronounce them correctly. Get some good commentaries and check out the theological content of the sermon. As far as possible, make it yours. But don't forget to find some way to give the author of the sermon credit. The richness of the imagination of most black preachers should make it easy to do this without reflecting on any shortcomings of yours. Brother preachers, preach!

Another challenge before us is to teach and train. We must do this effectively at the local church level, at the association level, the state and regional levels, and at the national level. Specifically, at the national level we must walk the edge of the new in the area of Christian education. The day for massive yearly congresses for Sunday school teachers and students, B.T.U., and youth leaders is gone. This was good when it was started, but is not good now. The time, the money, and the teaching energy expended in this now archaic system are far too costly for the results received. Seventy-five percent of all the work now done in our annual national congress could be done more effectively at the local, state, or regional level. I propose that we begin in 1978 to plan an entirely new format for the convention's educational program. I have definite and positive ideas and concepts, and I am certain than many of you have the same, which I will submit to the Board of Education and Publication, with the request that the board present the first draft to the Board of Directors no later than January 1978.

Our ministries in Africa and Haiti must be continued and strengthened. The Foreign Mission Bureau is doing a good job with unusual assistance from other convention agencies. I hope during 1977–78 to plan a president's tour to our mission fields and to work with the Foreign Mission Bureau on some much needed expansion in these areas. The gospel enjoins us to preach, teach, and heal. The resources are available if we exercise the faith.

The Home Mission program of our convention is on the move. For a while some said it was a "proper program." There is now strong evidence that this board and secretary of that part of our work are making new ventures in evangelism, stewardship, and church planning.

The Publishing Board continues to serve well our churches and our constituency. But far too few of us are using our literature. The quality of our literature deserves the attention and use of many more of our churches. We are encouraged that the book publishing division of our Publishing Board is presenting to us some excellent books written by Progressive authors.

Our Pension Board will be formally organized during the next convention year. This board needs the support of many more pastors and lay workers. Those who are a part of the program know the blessings of it.

I hope you are for FOR (Fund of Renewal). Five years ago, a dream of this president began to take shape. American Baptists and Progressive Baptists teamed up to conduct a fund drive for $12 million. The going has been hard, but we have had some success. To date, approximately $6 million have been committed. Some of our Progressive churches have pledged and paid pledges of multiple thousands. If you have not participated, it isn't too late. The institutions and community projects which we have funded and will fund further will call you blessed.

Our inside challenges must be met so that we may be about our Father's business in our Father's world. There are many issues that Progressives must address. Our resolutions passed here this week and released to the world will be our voice on these. I want to simply mention a few issues here that demand our attention and comment briefly on them.

Education. American youth are growing up early. Preadolescents are asserting their rights. At age twelve or thirteen, many girls are street walkers. Preteenagers are smoking tobacco and pot, skipping classes, and staying out late at night. There is an undertone of heavy violence. In many cities about 50 percent of the homicides are committed by youth ages fourteen to twenty-four. America's youth, and all too many black youth, are angry, bored, misguided, and confused. We must walk this edge and do something about it.

Churches could set up:

1. Tutoring classes

2. Antipregnancy classes

3. Antialcohol and drug groups

4. Classes in manners and personal pride

5. Opportunities for jobs

6. Study halls

7. Negro history classes

8. Classes in ethics and morals

9. Educational trips to parks, civic centers, and other places of interest

10. Classes in preparation for accepting Christ.

There will be a new day for youth when the church, the home, and the school learn to work together again.

Jobs. According to the Gibson Report, 14 percent of the 9.4 million blacks age sixteen and over in the civilian labor force in March

1976 were unemployed; 66 percent of all employed blacks are blue-collar or service workers and 32 percent white-collar workers. In 1976, 31 percent, or about 7.5 million, blacks of all ages were below the poverty level. The median income in 1976 for white males, age fourteen and over, was $9,300 and for black males, age fourteen and over, $5,560. This convention must join with other progressive forces in this country to see that the Carter administration, business and industry, and the local governments throughout the nation mount an aggressive attack on these gross inequities.

Cities. The cities are dying, but they will rise again. We must continue to gain political, economic, and educational power in our great cities. Behind these power blocks must be the spiritual power of the church. All power must be constantly checked with conscience. You and I are the conscience of our cities. White flight has reached its peak. It has been caught in the energy crunch. Whites will be coming back to our cities, but they will be coming back to cities that were abandoned to blacks. We have them now; let's keep them and rule them well by using the talents and expertise of all people, black, brown, red, and white. And let us prove to the world that cities can be beautiful, liveable, and redemptive. The day is now ripe for a powerful coalition of black church leaders, black political leaders, and black business and professional and labor leaders. Let us use this day and build a better America.

Gays. Homosexuality is out in the open. What do we do? Do we all line up behind Anita Bryant, or do we go the way of Nancy Krody? Anita says, "Put them out and save the children." Nancy says that we must deal with the contradiction in a life where the same person is a woman, a lesbian, a feminist, and a Christian. What do you say?

I have trouble with Anita because I think her drive to save the children is one-sided. I have no patience with homosexuals or heterosexuals who prey on defenseless children. But I do have trouble when homosexuals are made the scapegoat for destroying our children, when more than two hundred thousand children are mauled and beaten and permanently scarred and many killed each year by parents, guardians, and others in charge of raising children. I have trouble when Nancy says that love between two persons of the same sex must be given the same credence and respect as love between two persons of opposite sexes. I believe that there is a

God-given natural order where sexes are concerned, and that implicit in that natural order is procreation. Where this is impossible in the love relationship, a divine and sacred element is missing.

I will not be the judge on the matter of two consenting adults expressing themselves sexually in private in whatever manner they please. Suffice it to be said that promiscuity in the area of sex, whether by homosexuals or heterosexuals, is a curse to any society and a shame before God.

What do we advocate then, moderation in homosexuality and heterosexuality? No! We advocate sex where it belongs: in the bedroom of a married man and woman.

My knowledge is too limited to know why there are homosexuals or how and where they should have sexual expression. But I do know that they are children of God. I do know that homosexuals are human beings with minds, hearts, spirits, and feelings like all other persons. I do know that God loves homosexuals. So when it comes to opportunities and employment, I say draw no line. The worlds of literature, music, art, education, and religion would be far poorer if these people that Anita Bryant wants restrained had been locked out of society.

President Carter and Ambassador Young. In the Carter administration, now only seven months old, the chief executive and his ambassador to the United Nations have made the most headlines. It is interesting that both are vowed, born-again Christians. A brief assessment of their influence on American and international life is in place.

Governor Meldrim Thomson Jr. of New Hampshire has started a movement to unseat ambassador Young. The Ambassador is accused of supporting communist butchers and terrorists. Two hundred thousand letters have gone out attacking Mr. Young, and "Andrew Young Must Go" action kits are being distributed. This vitriolic attack is but the latest attempt on the part of many apparently misguided, miseducated, misinformed, and mischievous persons to discredit a fine public servant.

Andy Young has gambled, and he is winning, in international and domestic circles. He has dared to throw the dice of truth on the global table, and they have rolled right each time. The gamblers in international lies don't understand and can't appreciate this new game.

Jealous bigots and overanxious newspersons point to the ambassador as a flamboyant, shoot-from-the-hip, radical character. But those of us who know him know that he is careful, cautious, and moderate, while at the same time sharp, incisive, extremely intelligent, and compassionate. He has taken a post that has been, at best, ambiguous. Well-known persons have held the post with great prestige and little power. Our black ambassador has shown that the post is pretty much what you make it. He has used the visibility of the office to dramatize the change in our foreign policy toward the "third world," and particularly Africa. He has also used the post to give the American people a course of continuing education on racism. We need both of these things. This convention must stand behind Ambassador Young as he dares to tell the truth, even though it hurts. We must not expect him to solve all the problems of black people. We simply want him to continue to be a good United States ambassador to the United Nations.

President Carter shows signs of being able to handle the power and influence of the presidency effectively and for the best interest of all of the American people. For some of us he is moving too slowly on the domestic scene. For others his accommodation to giant industries in massive sales of arms and war hardware to rich Arab nations and others causes wonder about his commitment to the intrinsic worth of human life. Some shudder when the thought arises that he may give his okay on the development of the neutron bomb. Still others say that he is too slow on his commitment to the suffering cities, his promises on housing and jobs, and a new day for laborers and farmers.

All of us know that a minimum wage of less than $3.50 an hour is unfair for any working person. We know that too many millions in this country are living in substandard houses and on the fringe of existence. We know that systemic racism still runs through the fabric of all American life. And we know that blacks and other minorities are the last hired and the first fired. Mr. Carter says that he needs time. Well, let's buy that, in part. Seven months is a short time to undo a mess of ten years duration. The Vietnam war, the Nixon years, Watergate, and Gerald Ford can't be overcome overnight. Their legacies left long streams of benign neglect.

We must be patient, but we must be persistent. We must be articulate, but we must be righteously angry. We must be forgiving, but we must be forceful. We must be merciful, but we must give mandates. And we must be understanding, but we must be urgent.

As the president talks of balancing the national budget by the beginning of his second term, we must talk about the possibility of a second term for him only if there is a balancing of the accounts long overdue for poor blacks, whites, and others in America. A balanced budget must not take precedence over a decent house for every citizen, an adequate national medical program, a welfare system that makes for independence and not continued cycles of dependence, cities that are liveable, and countrysides that are clean. We can have a great nation if we want it. But all must pay the price.

Our president believes in the Bible. I would hope that he would invite to his Sunday school class the seven members of the Supreme Court who recently ruled that workers whose employment rights were first legislatively recognized in Title VII of the 1964 Civil Rights Act may still be rendered last by *bona fide* seniority systems which perpetrated the effect of discrimination before July 2, 1965, when the title went into effect. We are tired of the cry of "reverse discrimination." I wish the President would use for his lesson for the Justices Matthew 20:1–16. Maybe he could get over to them and to the rest of the country that those who have enjoyed the benefits of long-term employment should not feel cheated when justice in the vineyard demands that all should be taken care of, even the least and the last.

Our Mandate and Our Hope. Our task is to participate to the extent of our capacity in convincing and convicting an alienated, materialistic, and pleasure-loving society that God lives, and that Jesus Christ is Lord and Savior. As we worship and evangelize, missionize and educate, renew and reform, and build and expand, we must never forget the true path that we must walk. It is as old as the faith, and as new as tomorrow's dawn. It is risky and it is dangerous. It is uphill and perilous. It demands hard work and sacrifice, but there is no other way.

The moment of truth is here. History has run full circle, and time is running out. Government cannot and will not save us. Big business is interested in profits first and people next. Education sharpens and prepares us but does not wholly free us. Pleasures make us feel good but leave us with hangovers. There is only one hope. The way of the Cross. This is the business that we major in.

Like Him whom we follow, we must walk the edge of the new. Let the Holy Spirit unleash the latent powers we have on a dying society in need of enablement, renewal, power, and hope. This path will be hard, but it will make us strong; risky, but it will make us alert; cutting, but the blood shed will be redemptive; dangerous, but there is no fearlessness where there is no danger; sacrificial, but without sacrifice there is no life.

Black Christians in America are on the spot. With all of our problems, we are the most fortunate black people in the world. Our blessings far exceed those of our brothers and sisters in other countries. It stands to reason, then, that we have a divine mandate to unify for a saving action. We must build models of Christian unity, educational excellence, political know-how, and economic strength. At the heart of each of these efforts must be the Model: Jesus Christ. He is our Model.

Our Model refused the way of war and greed, exploitation and preference. He walked away from luxury and easy living. He shunned acclaim and exaltation. He chose, rather, to be a servant, a servant obedient unto the Cross. He chose to walk the narrow edge of service and sacrifice. He flinched not in the face of risk, danger, denial, and death. He walked the edge of the new and paid His price.

We who profess to follow Jesus have a mandate. Progressive Baptists are called upon in this hour to give America a new type of collective leadership. Ours must be a prophetic voice. We are God's church, His voice in the wilderness. Let not that voice be muted, and let us not lose sight of our mission.

America needs a new land. Out present land is worn, cluttered, polluted, and distorted. We need a land that is truly the land of the free and the home of the brave. So we Progressives must be a new breed of pioneers, plowing new grounds, digging new ditches, walking new edges, laying out new rows, and planting seeds that have never failed to produce. We can give America a new land if we walk the edge of the new.

The world needs a new race. We are divided by nationality, economic status, educational attainment, religious differences, ethnic exclusiveness, social status, and skin pigmentation. The mandate of the church is to proclaim and live the message that all people are God's children, and that all of us are on the way to common destinies: to heaven if we meet the requirements of a servant of God, and to hell if we don't. Nothing else matters. There is only one race: the human race. Our job is to help it find its divinity.

We need a new language. It may be spoken in many tongues and dialects, but it must be the same in substance. We need a language of peace, brotherhood, kindness, understanding, hope, and love. It must pervade homes, schools, jobs, government offices, and churches. It must supplant strident, cutting words that so often leave deep wounds. It can be spoken in a smile, a handshake, a nod of the head. It must always speak of new life.

Finally, we must walk the edge of the new and recapture an old mystery. It is as old as the hills and as eternal as God. It is the mystery that gives us faith when we are discouraged, hope when we are despondent, and love when we feel left alone.

We hear much these days about liberation theology, thanks to James Cone, Gustavo Gutiérrez, and others. And though we recognize that the pervasive emphasis of a given theology stems from the relationship of the theological theme to the experience of the theologian, we must admit that the theology of liberation came forth in due season.

Look at churches generally in this country and you will see much blandness and sterility. There is much confusion, and church life in American needs to be shaken to the roots. But there is a gleam of hope. The theological voices from South America and from black North America are saying that our experiences have forced us to find deeper meaning in faith and religion. They are also saying that the church is never what it seems to be at any one place or time, and that it is always the bearer of the source of its own transformation to its own renewal. It ever carries under the surface powerful explosive material. Herein lies its mystery.

The church can walk the edge of the new because the Head of the church walked it triumphantly before us. God in Jesus Christ has revealed Himself to us, and in the Holy Spirit is working through us, making us and all things new.

It's an old mystery, but it still has power. That mystery sent Abraham looking for a city; changed a cheating, scheming Jacob; captivated Moses at a burning bush; took Joshua across the swollen Jordan; made David a man after God's own heart; overshadowed Isaiah in the temple; sent Amos from the wilds of Tekoa to the teeming city to prophesy; saved Daniel from the hungry lions; delivered the Hebrew witnesses from the fiery furnace; sent John the Baptist preaching in the wilderness; delivered Paul and Silas from the Philippian jail; made Martin Luther King Jr. immortal. And the old mystery — ever new — saved you and me. That is why Paul said, "Therefore if any man [any convention] be in Christ, he is a new creature: old things are passed away; behold, all things are become new.... Now then we are ambassadors for Christ" (2 Cor. 5:17, 20, KJV). That's why John said, "And I saw a new heaven and a new earth: for the first heaven and the first earth were passed away; and there was no more sea" (Rev. 21:1, KJV).

The old mystery is ever new because some two thousand years ago God invaded history in a peculiar way. Bethlehem was shaken by the singing of angels. Wise men brought gifts to the King born in a stable. The Word became flesh and dwelt among men. New life became available for all who would receive it.

But the mystery reached its climax on a Sunday morning following a dark and dismal sabbath. He triumphed over denial, betrayal, ignominy, shame, and death. He descended into the regions of hell and chained permanently the dragons of destruction. He came back by the grave and took from death its sting and from the grave its victory. And as dawn broke on that Sunday morning, the old mystery became new forever.

> He arose from the dead!
> He arose from shame!
> He arose from disgrace!
> He arose over unconscious soldiers!
> He arose in spite of all the powers of hell!
> He arose!
> He arose from the dead!
> He arose in majesty!
> He arose in triumph!
> He arose in glory!
> He arose in power!

"All power in heaven and in earth is in my hands" (Matt. 28:18).
AMEN!

The Family of God

Wilshire Boulevard Temple
Los Angeles, February 22, 1980

As the family of God, we are pilgrims in process — we have some assurance of our destiny, but none of us knows what we will finally attain. The foundation of our existence is our common Father, God, and He has revealed Himself to us in the historical process, and in various religious forms, practices, and mystical experiences. Our responsibility as pilgrims in process, and as the family of God, is to keep trying to know our brothers and sisters whose sustained approach to the reality and verity of life has led us all along different paths and involved us in different kinds of religious practices. So limited are all of us in our vision and scope of reality that we dare not stand in judgment of one another. Our role, then, instead of a judgmental one, is a cooperative and understanding one. Someone well said in a short poetic piece, these words:

> If I knew you, and you knew me.
> And each of us could clearly see
> By an inner light divine
> The secrets of your heart and mine,
> I am sure that we would differ less,
> And clasp our hands in friendliness,
> If I knew you, and you knew me.

We meet tonight as religious people — mostly Christians and Jews — yea, Jews and black Christians, two segments of God's family whose historical experiences have many parallels, but also whose historical experiences have been vastly different. However, the common parallels have had more meaning in our separate and mutual survivals than the different experiences.

Your Jewish ancestors knew slavery in Egypt and Babylon, pogroms and ghettos in Europe, and the Holocaust in Germany.

183

Our black ancestors knew slavery in North and South America, Western exploitation and colonialism in Africa, lynching in America, and genocide of the body and spirit through awesome exploitation, discrimination, and segregation. And Jews, like blacks, are still not free from oppression at home and abroad. This is all the more reason that we must walk and work closely together as children of the family of God.

I. We share a common religious heritage. A monotheism filled with ethical excellence, moral purity, and spiritual dynamics has kept us alive through many vexing historical changes. God, in so many marvelous manifestations, has been real in our lives. The faith of Abraham, the leadership of Moses, the heart of David, the courage of the eighth-century prophets, the event of Jesus, and the life of Martin Luther King have kept alive a belief and a faith that have sustained us. God is our common Father, and we are His children.

II. We all have been delivered by the hand of God, even though there is a proneness on the part of man to feel that he has achieved by himself. But when we look at our vast vulnerability, we are convinced that it is God who has brought us thus far. The ancient story of the deliverance of the Hebrews from Egyptian slavery, and of their forty years of meandering in the Sinai desert, has spoken loudly in biblical and secular history of the hand of God that is mighty to deliver.

The race-crazed Nazis, under the terrible influence of Hitler, tried to exterminate a race and a religion in furnaces and gas chambers, but the Holocaust, as terrible as it was, could not undo the work of the hand of God. The remnants of Israel in Germany and Eastern Europe have risen like the Phoenix from the ashes and built a great nation like Israel of old. They looked at their enemies and praised their God and said, "If I forget you, O Jerusalem, let my right hand wither! Let my tongue cleave to the roof of my mouth, if I do not remember you, if I do not set Jerusalem above my highest joy" (Ps. 137:5–6, RSV).

In the seventeenth, eighteenth, and nineteenth centuries, the powerful slave traders of American colonists, English imperialists, and Portuguese shipping interests literally raped West Africa of millions of its strongest inhabitants. The slave system in America, as a result of this unholy triumvirate, was one of the worst the world has ever known. Dire segregation, color discrimination, and barbaric dehumanization were the daily diet of millions of slaves. But these same slaves, drawing upon their African religious roots and their Africanization of the American Christian religion, literally sang, preached, prayed, shouted, and maneuvered their way out of slavery. They did this because they saw God not as a pious, heavenly Father, but as a Father who delivered His children from the fiery furnace of slavery.

We Jews and blacks have our present-day Red Seas and middle passages. And together we must worship, work, and fight to overcome. We must no longer be victims of the ravages of war. We can no longer accept poor education for our children, unemployment for our youth and others, and a vast disparity in economic income based on ethnicity or race. The same God that delivered the Jews from Egypt and the blacks from slavery can deliver us from our present-day Red Seas and middle passages.

III. We need a covenant community. The Jews survived in the terrible ordeal of Egypt and in the long forty-year trek to the Promised Land because they came to understand that their bread and water and their very existence depended upon God. Therefore, under the leadership of Moses and others, they made a covenant with God. And that covenant to this very day is a perpetual reminder that existence and progress are dependent upon an unfaltering faith in God and a community bound together by that common faith. Black Americans in slavery could not have survived had they not developed the invisible church. They paid little attention to the music sung in their masters' churches, but they listened attentively to the words of the Old and New Testaments that talked about deliverance and the love of God. They took these great biblical themes and created their own songs and built a religious faith that became a highway to freedom.

IV. We share a common hope for the future. We must dream dreams and cultivate hopes for a future that is filled with faith and fairness, a future that offers real fortune to all of God's children. The old fortune of unbridled material success for some and a poverty existence for others will not give us the future we need. The old fortunes of the arrogance of privilege and the denial of the needy lead to ruin and not good fortunes. But, as children of God, we are challenged to live and work and hope for a future where Christian and Jew, Muslim and Sikh, black and white, educated and uneducated, laborer and manager, child and adult, and men and women can find their place, fully realize the potential given by God, and be free to develop, expand, live happily, and make a contribution to life.

Listen to the words of Micah and Jesus:

> He hath shewed thee, O man, what is good; and what doth the LORD require of thee, but to do justly, and to love mercy, and to walk humbly with thy God? (Micah 6:8, KJV)

> I must work the works of him that sent me, while it is day: the night cometh, when no man can work. (John 9:4, KJV)

> And ye shall know the truth, and the truth shall make you free. (John 8:32, KJV)

The Christian Ministry —
The Risks and the Security
(Excerpt)

JER. 1:1–10; MATT. 10:16–23

Commencement Address
Colgate Rochester Divinity School, Bexley Hall,
Crozer Theological Seminary
May 7, 1983

No desire for reputation and status must ever be paramount in the hearts and minds of those who have answered the call to Christian ministry. A deliberate process of self-emptying and risk taking must take place. The biblical texts upon which this talk is built suggest that the proper response to our acceptance of the Christian vocation is to dare to be change agents for God, at whatever price that has to be paid.

Jeremiah, the most subjective of the Old Testament prophets, whose inner life was marked by strong tensions between his natural desires and inclinations and his deep sense of vocation, and who was by nature sensitive, reticent, and introspective, found himself in the terrible bind of wanting the good will of his fellow men on the one hand, and answering to the call of God on the other. This experience is not atypical of present-day prophets. Jeremiah's deep sense of commitment as a prophet and his loyalty to that commitment caused him to be hated and even persecuted. It kept him from marrying and left him at times a very lonely man.

In that important transitional period in Near Eastern history, it was not easy for a sensitive citizen like Jeremiah to watch his country lose its political independence, as the Assyrian Empire fell and the Babylonian Empire rose and made Judah a subject province.

Jeremiah prophesied during the reigns of Kings Josiah, Jehoiakim, and Zedekiah, up to the captivity of Judah in 587 B.C. God told him:

> I called you, sanctified you, and ordained you unto the nations. Be not afraid. You will go where I send you and you will speak what I tell you to the nations and kingdoms. You will root out, pull down, destroy, throw down and build and plant. (see Jer. 1:5–10, KJV)

The New Testament biblical text gives a picture of the nature of the work of the early disciples. The deep profundities of kingdom truth were not known by the disciples. "The kingdom is at hand" was a strange message. The ministry that so far had stopped at the lips must now be tested by encounter with a strange and alienated society. Who was Jesus referring to when He mentioned the "lost sheep of the house of Israel"? What did He mean when he said, "The kingdom of heaven is at hand"? Why would he instruct his disciples to labor without pay — "no gold nor silver" — or to go without bag, sandals, or staff, and with only one coat? What did He mean when He said they must be "wise as serpents and harmless as doves?" (see Matt. 10:6–16, KJV)

The kingdom mission as set forth in the Matthew account is a blessing and an obligation. "Freely ye have received, freely give" (Matt. 10:8, KJV). The blessing is a debt. We do not own the gift; we are trustees.

The kingdom mission is also a welcome and a rebuff. Some will receive it, and some will not. Don't be disturbed by those who rebuff you. The kingdom presupposes opposition and persecution. The road is rough and rocky all the way. You are lambs among wolves, but possess compassionate shrewdness. Therefore, meet persecution with trust at the time of crisis.

To Jeremiah was given the task of prophesying; to go, to speak, to tear down, to destroy, to build and to plant. The early disciples were commanded to travel frugally, to preach, heal, comfort — to go as lambs among wolves, and to be wise and harmless. What then are the mandates and commands to you and to me, who are practicing present-day Christian ministry?

Colgate Rochester Divinity School–Bexley Hall–Crozer Theological Seminary, you have two rather clearly defined distinctions that you deem to be basic in theological preparation for service. In your thinking and planning, you assert that you have transcended one-dimensionality in terms of denomination, race, gender, age, and socio-economic class, and that you are working hard to develop a diverse community in which the particular richness of the parts is affirmed in a dynamic unity and wholeness that gives meaning to what it is to be a Body of Christ. But as you pursue the commitment to multidimensionality, one basic aim of this creative approach and of theological training must be a constant and definite focus on your other distinction: training and inspiring leaders. We must be certain that the leadership in the Christian community, especially the pastoral leadership, in this crucial period in history, is thoroughly committed to a posture of "strong hands" and "conformed knees." I would like, therefore, to humbly suggest a few areas in which a daring, risky Christian ministry must be practiced if we are to maintain a balanced, ordered, and sane society.

Just as a valid theological outlook determines the direction of curricula and programs in the seminary, so must adequate theological interpretations set the pattern for effective ministry. This theological perspective should always be in the direction of making life more human and therefore more responsive to the love of God.

How Do We Go About This Task?

I. Constant reappraisals of the structured church with regard to the effectiveness of her mission. We must not be afraid to raise the question of the importance of institutional survival. What is our image in Africa, Asia, Latin America? Are American churches, black, white, and other too much a part, or victim, of a capitalist-dominated society? Can we move beyond institutional survival in our society to be instruments of change and a revolutionary movement for freedom, justice, and compassion? How structure-bound are we, physically and organizationally? Are we too caught up in morphological fundamentalism and theological conservatism to dream and work for a new day of liberty, peace, and love in the church?

I submit that we must take the risk in Christian ministry of plucking up, breaking down, destroying, and overthrowing many of the organizational structures in churches, church-related bodies, and ecumenical movements. In their places, we must build and plant.

On the local level we must:

- Establish thorough educational programs; emphasize the nature and mission of the church.

- Break with tradition. The seven last words of a dying church are "We never did it this way before."

- Eliminate outmoded organizations.

- Develop democratic governing procedures.

On the national level we must:

- Reassess the purposes and goals of annual meetings, and do more than meet, eat, and greet.

- Avoid a bureaucratic syndrome.

- Face controversial issues with aims of finding the best possible solution.

- Develop strong auxiliary units with enough independence to do creative work and enough grace to understand what it means to be a part of a team.

The mission of the church is a precious and priceless commodity, and adequate vehicles for its conveyance are extremely important.

II. Our ministry must be one of wholeness: the whole person, the whole society. We must risk a ministry of a new socially built humanity that is God-centered, Christ-inspired, and Holy Spirit–empowered. We can never forget that people need God, one another, bread, clothes, shelter, leisure, entertainment, recreation, cultural attractions, education, religion, jobs, and equal opportunity. Not some people. All people.

Humanity is one, and the quality of life is the name of the game. Freedom and liberation are its manifestations. So, in our ministry, we persevere to bring life to the ghettos and the board rooms, to the streets of Calcutta and the capital of Lagos, to the cathedral and the storefront, to the synod, the conference, and the national convention.

At this point we need to take pages from the textbook of Martin Luther King Jr.'s life. King's thought and theological categories were born in the matrix of the love and protection of a strong black family that for generations has espoused the ethic of freedom and justice. His college training at Morehouse, under Benjamin E. Mays, stressed the virtue of being a full man and a prepared man.

Too little has been said and written about the theology of King. This may be the only theological seminary, black or white, that has as a part of its core curriculum a major in the life and works of Martin Luther King Jr. or the theological legacy of King. The social activism and powerful and persuasive oratory of King, or even the dramatic social changes that were made under his leadership, will not withstand the erosive rigors of constant change unless they are undergirded by a clear perception of his theological position. The unfolding chapters of history must extol King, not bury him!

At the heart of King's theology was the emergence of the Beloved Community. In a peculiar way he was able to absorb varied theological and philosophical concepts and cull from them those elements that contributed to freedom, justice, and the dignity of human life, seasoning them with a King flavor that was made palatable for countless thousands.

African religion and culture played no little part in the development of King's thought and in the construction of his theological categories. And even though black theology was just reaching a high point in its expression when he was assassinated fifteen years ago, and even though he had some problem with the political connotations of "Black Power," he was nevertheless a living embodiment of both as his life unfolded. In spirit he knew that the hallmark of the African religious experience was its optimism and faith in the justice of the universe. He would hold little argument with John S. Mbiti when he says, "Faith is illustrated by resiliency of African religious life under extreme pressures and conditions." King's theology was more than what another scholar has defined as the "truth force of Gandhi, the social gospel of Rauschenbusch, the realism of Niebuhr, or the personalism of Brightman." King demonstrated a new theological ethic that should be at the core of our theological curriculum. His theology of liberation, affirming life as a whole, assessed the realities of existence and espoused a holistic gospel that challenged unholy structures of society as well as unholy persons. He understood the invisibility in white theological deliberations. He also knew, as late as the early 1960s, that this invisibility had not been challenged as it should have been.

King understood the radical difference in the economic, social, and political power of the communities from which our theologies arise. Whites, in their privileged position, minimized the social determination of theological knowledge by appealing to the Bible, divine revelation, or a common humanity. King maximized the social determination of theological knowledge by exposing the injustices, deprivations, and insults heaped on black people, and by challenging blacks to throw off the yokes of fear and intimidation and, under God, to liberate themselves. The following period of black theology belongs to the period of the black struggle for liberation that followed the early spring of the civil rights movement. The objectives were clear and the enthusiasm great. The thrust of King at the deepest level was that the risk of faith is the risk of obedience to what Jesus *did* and is still doing today; that it should challenge men and women in the power of their lives, for which He has set them free, to engage in the struggle for the liberation of any and all who are oppressed or enslaved and to risk everything (even life) to create a new humanity.

III. The risk of challenging powers and principalities. Jim Geier, a semiartist and furniture designer, constructed a three-inch square "dot chart" to illustrate the current levels of nuclear power in the United States and the Soviet Union. The chart is composed of 132 squares, all but nine of which are filled with dots, overall numbering in the hundreds, if not thousands. Three dots on the chart represent enough power to destroy 224 cities. What is your reaction?

Tom Roderick teaches in an alternative school in East Harlem. He tells his students, "Study hard to get a job when you grow up." "I'm not going to grow up," a fourth-grade boy replies. "There's going to be a nuclear war."

"Megatrends" point away from an industrial society to an information society, from a national economy to a world economy, from institutional help to self-help, from hierarchies to networking, from either-or to multiple options.

But any insensitivity that these new trends foster must be countered with such programs as the Children's Defense Fund, which urges us to remember our greatest resource: our children. And the church must support such programs.

Writing in *Christian Century,* February 8, 1983, Dr. J. Deotis Roberts said:

When the New Right began to make its case to bring religion into politics, liberal churches were ill prepared to offer meaningful alternatives. For almost a decade, American religion had turned inward and abandoned the social activism of the '60s. Many black churches had also retreated from activism in a search for spiritual roots. There had been a wholesale abandonment of the gospel of social justice. Those few church leaders and professors who dared to be active and prophetic were religious mavericks. Courses on social justice were pushed to the edge of the seminary curriculum.

By about 1978, when the spontaneous politicization of the religious right began, we were unequipped to counter its powerful thrust. Political action surfaced among usually quietistic conservative Protestants. Fundamentalists and Pentecostals who had been fed a diet of separation from the world and the expectation of the imminent Second Coming were now more preoccupied with political and economic power than with saving souls. Liberal Christians are still reeling from the shock waves of this new phenomenon. It seems clear now that for all their talk about rapture and "pie in the sky," these religious conservatives have invested their basic hope in the American establishment.

The Real King Legacy

Martin Luther King Jr. Interfaith Prayer Breakfast
Trinity Baptist Church, Los Angeles
January 12, 1983

At a national conference on Religion and Race in 1963, Martin Luther King Jr. said, "I am happy to say that the nonviolent movement in America has come not from secular forces, but from the heart of the Negro church.... The great principles of love and justice which stand at the center of the nonviolent movement are deeply rooted in the Judeo-Christian heritage."

Martin Luther King Jr.'s span of life on earth was thirty-nine years, two months, and one week. He was and is well known as a civil rights activist who used nonviolent methods to achieve social justice for blacks and others. Not so well known is the fact that his acts were rooted and grounded in Christian theology and ethics, and not in social theories. King possessed a deeply personal religious faith, and he had a firm belief in a personal God who was a God of love and who acted profoundly in history.

It is true that King studied many non-Christian methods of achieving his goals. He was an avid student of Gandhi and was influenced by his traditional Afro-American history and culture. But his intellectual categories were drawn from Christian theology and ethics.

King's thought was framed from many ideas, concepts, and the influence of great scholars. Foremost in the framing of his thought was the love and protection of his Christian family given during his childhood and formative years. His education at Morehouse College strongly stressed manly development and the quest for knowledge. It was also seasoned with strong ethical and religious principles. At Crozer Theological Seminary the above principles were more rigorously taught and imbedded.

194

King said, "I gained my major influences in philosophy, theology, and ethics from Morehouse and Crozer. And I am greatly indebted to them. They gave me the basic truths that I now believe...and the worldview that I have...the idea of the oneness of humanity and the dignity and worth of all human personality."

African religion and culture also played a part in the development of King's thought. In black theology we have been made aware of African philosophy and religion by experts. King knew that the hallmark of African religious experience was its optimism and faith in the justice of the universe.

Of no little influence was Mahatma Gandhi on the thought of Martin Luther King Jr. Gandhi's two major philosophical and religious concepts, *Satyagraha,* meaning "holding fast to truth-force," and *Ahimsa,* meaning "noninjury," excited King's imagination, and he included Gandhi's concept of active nonviolence and civil disobedience in his approach to solve social problems.

The social gospel concept advocated in the evangelical liberalism of Walter Rauschenbusch had a deep impression on King's thought. King said, "The Gospel at its best deals with the whole person, not only the soul, but also the body. It deals with spiritual well-being and with material well-being. A religion that expresses a concern for the souls of people and is not equally concerned with the slums that damn them and the social conditions that cripple them is a spiritually moribund religion."

Reinhold Niebuhr's concept of sin and power and his theology of Christian Realism also had a profound effect on King's thinking. He agreed with Niebuhr that human nature is best understood in dialectical and paradoxical terms, i.e., in constant tension between man's essential creative nature and his existential self-determined character. King understood the ever-present conflict between man's good and evil impulses.

The theology of personalism of Brightman, Bowne, and DeWolfe gave great strength to King's early concept of a personal God. Over two-thirds of the courses that he pursued in his Ph.D. work were biblical and systematic theology, and philosophy of religion. He believed that conscious personality is both the supreme value and the supreme reality in the universe, and that fundamentally it is essential to the understanding of reality. King firmly believed in a personal God and that we are made in His image.

It was on the basis of King's theological and ethical presuppositions that he performed his tasks rather than from the stance of an active civil rights leader for social justice. Therefore, the following major problems were addressed by King in the interest of the development of a just and ordered society:

1. There should be no segregation and discrimination.

2. Poverty should be wiped out.

3. Racism should be eradicated.

4. Colonialism in all forms should be stopped.

5. War should be outlawed.

All of these goals were consistent with King's concept for the development of the Beloved Community. He firmly believed that people could live together in peace if they tried hard enough. The fact that he believed in a God who is creative, orderly, all-powerful, and completely loving made him also believe that since we are made in the image of God, we can possess the same attributes.

Preaching in the Black Church

Originally Published in The Christian Ministry,* *March–April 1988*

Preaching's dominance in worship is more pronounced in the black American religious experience than in that of other ethnic groups. The uniqueness of black churches lies more in their preaching than in such other areas as nurturing or administration.

Since 1619, blacks have been a part of the American population. A few came to this country as free Africans; most came as slaves. But all came from religious backgrounds with centuries-old roots. It is hard to imagine the impact of the cultural shock experienced by Africans who were the victims of the American, British, Dutch, French, Portuguese, and Spanish slave trade. But this cultural shock was not strong enough to destroy the slaves' search for meaning. Even though the experience of captivity disrupted their ritual patterns and religious practices, the African spirit was strong enough to survive disruptions and changes and to forge a new religious synthesis with the New World's Christian teaching and preaching.

Black preaching has undergone many changes during the third and fourth quarters of the twentieth century, but it has remained true to some basic principles that characterized it from the beginning. It has been priestly and prophetic and weighted with a plea for liberation. The black religious concept that all life is sacred has influenced the black preacher to preach about, and to participate in, politics, civil rights movements, public education endeavors, affirmative action programs, antiracism campaigns, and antiwar protests. American society has forced black people to develop survival techniques that lead to liberation, and the black preacher has been the chief spokesperson for this cause.

Many black preachers have clung to their African heritage and cultural roots. Most use their gifts to the glory of God and to the advancement of the church. As in any church, some few permit themselves to be made rulers instead of servants. A small number preach as entertainers, while a handful border on being charlatans.

One of the innovative attributes of black preaching is style. Sermon delivery varies widely. Some pastors use manuscripts masterfully, while others are "whoopers" who build their "whoop" on solid biblical theology and then sweeten it to the delight of their hearers. Some black preachers are "mourners" who intone in a way to put the doves to shame. Others are great orators in a class with the Athenian orator Demosthenes. Others are dialogical and conversational, and many are powerfully poetic in their delivery.

In all the different homiletical and hermeneutical approaches and styles of black preaching, there is a major constant: the sermon is central in worship. The expectancy in black worship is not about the liturgy, the music, or the offering; it is about what the preacher is going to say and how he or she is going to say it. The congregation waits not only to hear but also waits to witness. The vibrancy of black worship is greatly enhanced by the call and the response between black preachers and their congregations.

Charles Adams, pastor of Hartford Avenue Baptist Church in Detroit, Michigan, preaches masterfully from a manuscript, articulating with precision. His skillful use of antithetical couplets to drive home a point is extremely effective, as the following example from a sermon on dynamic living illustrates: "Life at its highest living demands that we move from aberration to action, from blundering to building, from cowardice to courage, from dodging to doing, from envy to enjoyment, from fear to faith, from getting to giving, from hating to hoping, from indolence to industry and from lust to love." Adams's powerful preaching has been heard at many national meetings and has built the Hartford Avenue Church membership to more than six thousand people.

Otis Moss, pastor of Olivet Institutional Baptist Church in Cleveland, Ohio, is gifted with a good memory and a storehouse of poetic expressions. An older preacher, William Holmes Borders of Wheat Street Baptist Church in Atlanta, Georgia, likes to close his sermons with dramatic poems.

John Hurst Adams, a bishop of the African Methodist Episcopal Church (A.M.E.) and president of the Congress of National Black Churches, is a powerful preacher who is not a "whooper," "mourner," or poetic artist. He is a liberation theologian and a strong advocate of black empowerment. In his preaching he clearly delineates the necessity for a black power that comes from adequate education, including theological training, from economic self-sufficiency, strong family ties, political astuteness, and ardent discipleship.

Gardner C. Taylor, pastor of Concord Baptist Church of Christ in Brooklyn, is regarded by many as the dean of American preachers, especially black preachers. A classical exponent of the gospel, he has few peers when it comes to painting pictures and poeticizing on the great themes — throughout the Old and New Testaments — of the Christian faith. With an almost photographic memory and a gift for putting together words and phrases to drive home a point, Taylor grips his audience through his complete involvement in the Good News he is proclaiming. Among younger peers following Taylor's style of preaching are William Epps, pastor of Second Baptist Church, and Bishop Charles Blake, pastor of the Church of God in Christ, both in Los Angeles.

Black preaching has always contained a strong prophetic element. Church members continue to look to the preacher to interpret current social problems; to assess the viability of community and national movements; and to criticize, evaluate, and propose solutions to problems in the performances of politicians, educators, and labor and business leaders. Among the strong prophetic voices in black church pulpits today are Samuel B. McKinney of Mt. Zion Baptist Church in Seattle; Cecil "Chip" Murray, pastor of First A.M.E. Church in Los Angeles; William A. Jones, pastor of Bethany Baptist Church in Brooklyn; and Floyd Flake, pastor of Allen A.M.E. Church in Jamaica, New York, and a U.S. congressman. Some black preachers do not fit into any of the above categories. They fall, instead, into one of two groups: those who have followed white evangelical fundamentalists of the far right, and those who are preaching a gospel of prosperity and physical healing. The former appear to have no understanding of the traditional black fundamentalism that stresses the wholeness of life and expresses black people's innate yearning for liberation. The latter seem to forget that at the heart of the Christian religion is a cross, not material gain and the absence of suffering.

As I view black preaching today, I see and hear black sisters as well as brothers in the pulpit. But I am appalled by the lack of understanding of some of my black brothers, who cannot see that God calls women to preach. At a recent meeting of a black Baptist state convention, a man presented me with a list of eighteen reasons, all backed by Scripture passages, claiming to prove that women should not preach. If some of the hallmarks of black preaching have been its prophetic propensity, its liberation emphasis, and its focus on enhancing the quality of life, certainly one of its weaknesses today is its failure to acknowledge and support the prophetic witness of black female preachers. Those who have proclaimed Amos's cry, "Let justice roll down like waters, and righteousness like an ever-flowing stream" (5:24), have ignored the prophecy in Joel 2:28–29. Ever since Pentecost, when Peter proclaimed this prophecy to be fulfilled, it has been appropriate for women to preach.

As important as has been the blacks' need for a place they could call their own, and as tolerant and permissive as God has been in pitying our oppression, the raising up of women to preach is God's way of saying that blacks must come of age and let the church be the church. Its ultimate purpose is not to preserve the black man's image or ego, but to glorify God. If black men and women are to achieve freedom, they must do it together. We cannot subordinate women's ministry and also claim to be for the liberation of the oppressed.

The majority of contemporary black preachers have developed their own hermeneutic styles. Some are Bible storytellers, others have a great facility for allegorizing, while still others do careful exegesis of Scripture; and their theological orientation runs the gamut from traditional fundamentalism to revolutionary liberation theology. But given the variation of styles of interpretation and theological orientation, most black preachers relate their preaching to the contemporary problems and challenges of our society. They courageously condemn racism (at home or in South Africa), economic injustice, political neglect, and educational inequality.

It would, however, be wrong to presume that this preaching is negative. In his or her prophetic role, the black preacher analyzes and criticizes the evils of the day but does not stop there. The theme of hope is inherent in most black preachers' sermons. These pastors have no qualms about God's power to deliver. And drawing upon their experience, culture, and faith, they proclaim to waiting congregations a powerful message of hope.

Appendix A

Letters, Tributes, and Articles

LETTERS

Dr. James Zumberge
President, University of Southern California

February 21, 1988

Dear Tom,

I want to extend my warmest regards and best wishes on your seventy-fifth birthday. What a wonderful milestone in your life, dedicated all these years to your church, community, and for so many years, to USC. Al Rudisill has told me of your prophetic Baccalaureate sermon which prompted Jack Hubbard to ask for your counsel and guidance. Your contribution to USC is immeasurable: not just building bridges with the community, but your work for the Community Center, creating Ebonics, leading the D-2 project, advocacy on behalf of BSU, and a hundred little things which have made people's lives better and full because you care.

All of us acknowledge that the work which we are presently accomplishing in the community would not have been possible without the foundation you helped to put in place and the advice you continue to provide. Happy Birthday, Tom! We look forward to wishing you well on your centennial year in 2013!

With all good wishes and warmest personal regards, I am

Cordially yours,
Jim Zumberge

Dr. Kathleen C. Jacobs
Former Youth Member of
Friendship Baptist Church, New York

February 22,1988

Dear Dr. and Mrs. Kilgore:

This is a belated, but much deserved "Thank You" from one of your "young" people at Friendship Baptist Church in New York. I have seldom

203

had the time to sit down and properly thank you for what I am today. It did not impact upon me until I was asked to be the keynote speaker this year for Black History Month at Langley Air Force Base in Virginia.

In my speech preparation, I am alluding to the importance of black churches helping their youth attend college. I am pointing out the fact that my minister made sure when I was young that every young person in the church who wanted to attend college went to college. I do not see that commitment nationwide anymore.

It feels good that young Kathleen Caldwell, who grew up in Harlem, went on to earn five degrees including a master's in business administration and a doctorate in education, all because Dr. and Mrs. Kilgore cared. The two of you laid a foundation of dedication to education and the betterment of society that is still with me today. My life has been devoted to teaching at the graduate and undergraduate level as well as trying to help all young people I come in contact with.

Currently, I am a member of Calvary Baptist Church in Dover, Delaware, and am the Chairperson of a group "Champions in Christ." This group consists of teenagers whom I work with every other Saturday to keep them busy in the name of the Lord.

Again, thank both of you and pray for me February 27, 1988, as I speak.

Sincerely,
Kathleen C. Jacobs, Ph.D.

Peter Sellars
Chairman, Los Angeles Festival

February 18, 1993

Dear Tom,

I will never forget the day, my first day in Los Angeles as the newly appointed director of the Los Angeles Festival, when you and I first met. There had been the usual financial difficulties and there we were in the executive board room at the headquarters of a major corporation in downtown Los Angeles. A group of civic and business leaders sitting around a conference table. It was a depressing discussion. Very few persons present could see their way clearly to moving forward with the life of the Festival. People were exhausted, fatigued by the financial and logistical reality that confronted us, and dispirited by the malaise which we all know can so easily afflict this sprawling city. The vote was on the table to shut the Festival for good. It was a worthy project but just too much trouble, and finally, at the end of the day, people wanted to cross it off their list and go home. I will never forget the way your voice rose and swept across the board room with determination and sparkle. You spoke eloquently of the needs of the people of Los Angeles and indeed the peoples of Los Angeles. You spoke not to their physical needs, to food and to shelter (although it was clear that you had spent a great deal of your life in the effort to supply these necessities), but you spoke to the moral and spiritual needs of an undernourished population, of a hunger for recognition, for celebration, for a sense of pleasure, of mutuality, and of respect. Every person in that room was stirred. The vote was postponed. We took a break. You came up to me at the small refreshment table in the corner of the room and whispered in my ear with that particular animated conviction that I have since come to recognize as your trademark: "There *will* be a Festival!" How? With what money? With what support? Nobody knew the answers to those questions. But you knew that there would be a Festival.

As always your certainty carried the day. Five years later this fledgling organization is meeting a need locally, nationally, and internationally. It is a service organization devoted to spreading joy, visions of common humanity, and providing a platform for the strong statements that need to be made at this point in history. The arts exist to ease the transition from the sacred to the secular, as a call to conscience, and as a persistent reminder to behold and acknowledge the awe and wonder of God's creation. Late one December afternoon in downtown Los Angeles you knew that, and at a time when no one else could see the way forward, you raised high your light.

We are all in your debt, we are all learning from you, again and again, the richest lessons that this life has to offer. You are a light, Tom, a bright flame, not just in the lives of individuals but in the life of this city and this age. We are all pleased and proud and blessed that you have entered our lives, agitating on behalf of the Spirit, hoping when no one dares to hope.

Yours,
Peter Sellars

Dr. J. Thomas Bertrand
President, Brevard College

January 16, 1996

Dear Tom:

I don't want to wait until I send you a check in order to thank you for the superb contribution you made to our celebration of the King birthday. For the audience yesterday, you rescued Dr. King from the limitations of our partial perspectives and from the mythologizing that inevitably begins to obscure the real man.

You brought the real man back to us, put him in historical context, demonstrated his importance as a leader, strategizer, and theologian, as well as his warmth and his humor. Many of us will never forget the image you painted of the little Martin sitting on your knee on the family porch on Auburn Avenue and asking important questions about life even at that tender age. And I'll never forget the shining face of the boy who came up to you yesterday outside our cafeteria after your speech and shook your hands and said, "Did you really know Martin Luther King?" He will never forget the graciousness of your interest in him, in what he wanted to do with his life.

I am sorry Jeannetta couldn't come with you this time, but I'll hope to see her this summer.

I enclose a copy of my introductory remarks from yesterday — they came from my heart. Please forward your expenses to us for reimbursement.

Sincerely, yours,
J. Thomas Bertrand

William A. Lawson
Pastor, Wheeler Avenue Baptist Church, Houston

May 29,1997

Dear Dr. Kilgore,

This comes to thank you for your contribution to our thirty-fifth anniversary celebration. But it expresses gratitude to God that He has chosen to place you in the world at a time when you could influence folks like me. You are indeed a giant, Tom, shown not only by the immensity of your contributions to our generation, but also by your humility and your willingness to identify with the small and the ordinary.

I enclose the program of our anniversary worship service. At this writing, the worship service is in our future — but I think I can promise even now that it will have been a pinnacle in our church's history.

God bless Mrs. Kilgore and your continuing ministry.

Sincerely your friend,
William A. Lawson

TRIBUTES

Coretta Scott King

*Reflections at the Service of Thanksgiving and Celebration
for the life of Thomas Kilgore Jr.
Second Baptist Church, Los Angeles
February 9, 1998*

We gather today at this homegoing service to celebrate the life of Dr. Thomas Kilgore Jr., one of the most dedicated servants of God and humankind. I am deeply honored to have been asked by Mrs. Kilgore and her daughters to give reflections on her devoted husband and their beloved father, who was a very dear friend of mine and the entire King family.

I knew Dr. Kilgore more than forty years, but the relationship between the King Family, Daddy and Mama King, Martin Jr., Christine, and A.D., and the Kilgore family existed long before Martin and I were married. I valued greatly Tom's friendship because he was a true friend who was there for you not only when the sun was shining bright, but most especially when the storms of your life were raging. He was one of Martin Luther King Jr.'s strongest supporters, serving on the board of the SCLC throughout Martin's lifetime. But he stood with me after Martin's death as I struggled to build a living memorial to Martin's life and contributions. He served on the Advisory Board of the King Center, gave his advice as well as his resources, and raised funds to support the King Center.

He was my kind of person. He led by example. He didn't just preach sermons; he lived them. When I think of Thomas Kilgore, I think of the fact that he was, first of all, a preacher of the Gospel of Jesus Christ, one of America's greatest; a pastor par excellence; a dedicated civil and human rights and peace activist, and humanitarian.

To the family of Dr. Kilgore: He bequeathed to you a great legacy of love, faith, wisdom, integrity, courage, and a warm and loving spirit. As a matter of fact, he bequeathed those to all of us, as well. He will be sorely missed, but his spirit will always be with you to guide you. I can't know the depth of your grief and pain, but I can say that almost thirty years ago, I sat where you sit today in a similar service and said goodbye to my husband and the father of my children. Your husband and father was a good man who lived his life so well that he will never die. I can promise you that his spirit will be with you when you need it most. I commend you to the Almighty God, Who loves each of you so much. He will lift you from the depths of despair to the buoyancy of hope.

Finally, Thomas Kilgore was a faithful servant of God. Having labored in God's vineyard for more than eighty-four years, he is now at rest and at peace. It seems that I can hear the Almighty God saying to Tom, "Well done, good and faithful servant. You are faithful over a few things. I will make you ruler over many things. Enter into the joys of your Lord."

Family Members

Tributes from the Family Members Present
on the Occasion of Thomas Kilgore's Eightieth Birthday
February 20, 1993

Lynn Elda (daughter): I remember Daddy cooking dinner when Ma had an evening meeting. Usually it was all the leftovers in the refrigerator that went into one pot for a "stew." Abel and I also remember our wedding day and daddy's fervent recitation of the vows. Everyone felt his emotions that day.

Jini (daughter): It's Sunday morning. Radio Station KJLH is about to broadcast Second Baptist's live morning program. The organ introduction brings us into the service. We are ready to hear the melodious strains of the well-trained choir when suddenly — what is it — a frog? Who is that over the microphone? Embarrassing!!! It's Daddy with his no-singing self, all off tune, drowning out everybody — and on the air!

Robin (granddaughter): I remember Granddaddy taking his garden work just as seriously as he did his ministry. He even had a unique attire for it: maroon polyester short pants, yellow cotton T-shirt, white knee-hi socks, a gigantic straw hat to block out the sun, and navy canvas sneakers that were dated about 1400 B.C.!!!

Okera (grandson): I remember his sense of humor. He was speaking in front of a large crowd and his teeth flopped down on the podium as he spoke. Folks were shocked, but he made everyone laugh it off. Usually he is a perfectionist. I inherited neatness and counting from him.

Malissa (sister): I remember when my friend Eva passed. Thomas and I arrived at the church at the same time. He rushed over to me and frantically asked me, "Malissa, what am I going to say about Eva?" I answered, "I don't know, but whatever you say will be appropriate." His answer was, "What's appropriate?"

Earl (son-in-law): I remember the first time I met Dr. Kilgore after hearing about him as a preacher. I found more than just a man of God, but a loving husband, a compassionate father, and a caring humanitarian.

Jeannetta (wife): I remember how, in his younger years, he would always back up as he preached. I remember his polishing everyone's shoes Saturday nights in New York, and how he sweated the day Lynn Elda was born.

Okera Damani Robinson, Grandson

Grandson's Reflections
at the Service of Thanksgiving and Celebration
for the Life of Thomas Kilgore Jr.
Second Baptist Church, Los Angeles
February 9, 1998

This is the hardest speech I've ever given in three minutes. Let me start off by saying that I love my grandfather very much, and my grandfather has been to me the closest thing to Superman that anybody could imagine. He's been there when others weren't. He's had advice in every single situation that you could have been in. He knew a little something about everything.

Thomas Kilgore Jr. leaves with us a legacy of love. We find it almost impossible to feel his absence when his lessons, his honesty, his generosity, his commitment, his caring, his accomplishments, his zest for life, his reach and drive for excellence, his stories, his support, his power and influence, and especially his laugh and smile are present in our lives and in our hearts and minds every day. I want to try to express a few qualities about my grandfather that other people may not have picked up on being on the outside looking in. I want to try to express to you today how we looked at him and how we look at him and see him and how everything you've said applies to his family, too.

All of us who called him granddaddy, all of us who called him uncle, cousin, brother, mentor, and teacher, those of us who called him daddy, and one of us who has called him husband for the past sixty-one years, one month, and seven days, have some very special memories we would like to share. Last night I was busy gathering some thoughts from my family about what they thought of when they heard his name, and I gathered over 250 adjectives and qualities of my grandfather. For those of us who called him grandaddy and uncle, we know him as our invincible, vibrant Superman, a man always on the go but who was never too busy to spend time telling us stories about our history to instill a sense of pride and a sense of being and a sense of purpose in us. To us he is our black history. He broadened our horizons. If it were not for my grandfather, I would not personally know Coretta Scott King; I would not know Tom Bradley; I would not know a lot of people that I've been blessed to meet because of him.

He always taught us that when you go visit somebody, you should have something for them, that it is not polite to visit somebody without bringing something. I met Coretta Scott King in 1981. I was six years old, and I didn't have a gift for her, so my grandfather gave me a couple of dollars, and I went to the Martin Luther King gift shop and bought a four-pack of Now-or-Laters. I ate two to make sure my breath was all right, and I generously gave her the other two, and she said thank you. But those were the things I picked up from my grandfather.

He taught us what it meant to be excellent, yet humble and helpful. And with a stern voice, he taught us fear and respect. Fear, mostly. And respect. But also with a hearty laugh he taught us the meaning of clean humor. He taught me how to tie my tie, how to lace up my shoes, how to dress, how to plant corn and lemon trees and cabbage and greens, how to harvest, how to study and deal with peer pressure. He always had advice for every situation. Granddaddy, your grandchildren and nieces and nephews will always treasure the lessons of daily living that you not only taught but you lived as our shining example.

He only said things once. My grandfather was not a repetitive man or redundant man. If he said, "Okera, stop cheating when you're playing a game with your sister," either I listened or I suffered the consequences. And I only had to suffer the consequences of cheating in front of him one time when I got off the floor and I felt the sting on my cheek. But I love him for that.

For those of us who call him cousin and brother, he leaves a legacy of kindness, greatness, gentleness, loving, and giving. He was a strong disciplinarian for those younger than he, and to those who were his senior, he baffled them with his knowledge, intellectual gifts, wisdom, and spirit. Everybody looked up to him, even if they had to look down at him to do so. His siblings remember that he never gave up on anybody. My grandfather was the type of man who could see the good in anybody. He could look at a crack fiend and say, "But he only smoked half today what he smoked yesterday." He always found the good in people. He always trusted that you were going to deliver your best. When I would come home from school, knowing I made a C or a D, he could see it in my face, but he wouldn't ask me like he knew that I made a C or a D; he would ask me like he believed that I made an A, and then it was up to me to tell him the truth. I did.

An example his sister, my Aunt Malissa, one time told me, when she was telling me that he never gave up on anybody and he was a strong disciplinarian, was that he used to walk her to school every single day, and she went to school by herself for a year and four months before her younger sister was able to go, and she cried every single day. But every single day my grandfather asked her, "You're not going to cry again today, are you?" And she would say, "No." And once he let her hand go, she would cry again.

For those of us who call him father, he is remembered as being a can-do type of person, very detail oriented, committed to his word, a problem solver, very sensitive, a nature lover, a lover of God, a lover of people, and a lover of his family. He always had time. Though he did all those wonderful things everybody says, we never felt that he was a missing person in the house. We were always treasured by him. He always spent time with us to tell us our wrongs, our rights; he trained us, got us on the right path when we were off of it, and we respected him.

For my grandmother, his wife of sixty-one years..., I never saw them argue, not one time. I never heard my grandfather say a filthy word in my life. He always respected women, and he was a gentle man to the end.

I love you, Granddaddy.

ARTICLES

ABC President Thomas Kilgore Jr.
The Man, His Church, His Faith

by Jack Barker and Audrey Wennblom
Crusader (The American Baptist Magazine), June 1969

Dr. Thomas Kilgore Jr.'s election as president of the American Baptist Convention was no surprise to delegates in Seattle — partly because the press all over the country had been predicting it for months, but also because Dr. Kilgore has been an effectively energetic leader in convention life.

Nationally, Dr. Kilgore has served as chairman of the convention's Baptist Action for Racial Brotherhood (BARB) and as a member of the Board of Managers of the American Baptist Home Mission Societies (he was western vice president until his election as ABC president).

In Los Angeles, where Dr. Kilgore is pastor of Second Baptist Church, he has been treasurer of the Los Angeles Council of Churches and vice president of the California-Nevada Progressive National Baptist Convention. He is a trustee of Morehouse College in Atlanta (where he received the A.B. degree) and is also a graduate of Union Theological Seminary in New York. Three schools have honored him with doctorates.

But most of Dr. Kilgore's concern centers on Second Baptist — an urban church sitting on the edge of the Watts community. That strategic position is one reason why the mission of Second Baptist goes beyond mere churchly concerns to include:

• A Child Development Center. The first federally funded child care training center ever set up in the U.S. under Title IV is housed in the educational building of Second Baptist. The school ministers to nearly a hundred children, has a staff of twenty-one (its director is Mrs. Kilgore), and an annual budget of $123,000. County funds also help support it. The school runs all day long from 6:00 a.m. to 6:00 p.m., and serves two meals. Children who are in public school come before and after school. Teen Post activities, from 3:00 p.m. to 9:00 p.m., are for older youth and are also federally funded.

"While the center cannot give specific religious instruction, the fact that it is conducted under the auspices of the church does create a favorable conditioning towards the church on the part of those who participate," says Miss Mildred Arnold, director of Ministry to Children for the Southern California Baptist Convention.

• Pueblo Christian Action Center. The church took over a building on East 55th Street that was once a liquor store, had skilled workmen from the congregation do the renovations, and now all kinds of things are happening: citizenship classes, youth and adult clubs, counseling, community organization, health and welfare programs, movies, referrals, religious instruction, tutoring. The center is run in cooperation with the Los Angeles Baptist City Mission Society, the Southern California Baptist Convention, and the American Baptist Home Mission Societies.

• The Storehouse. Located on church property and run by a committee of the church, the storehouse gives away canned goods and clothing to thousands of local residents and newcomers to the city.

• Mutual Assistance Team Endeavors (MATE). Three Los Angeles groups — Negro pastors, the state convention staff, and the city society staff — met the day before Martin Luther King was assassinated to see what they could do about common problems in Los Angeles — white racism, poverty, inadequate education. A steering committee was selected and out of that came MATE. Second Baptist helps fund it; Pastor Kilgore is an ardent supporter, and Judge Albert Matthews, a member of Second, is chairman of the board. To launch the program, ten inner-city and suburban churches set up activities for children, youth, and adults — athletics, tutoring, trips, self-improvement programs, day care. MATE's objectives: to involve low-income community groups in meaningful activities, especially during the summer months.

The theme running through all these programs is the desire on the part of Second Baptist to identify totally with the Watts community, and this has meant a very positive involvement in the black revolution. It has tried to direct the energies of its own people and others into every worthwhile effort "to break the shackles...forced on Negroes in the twentieth century."

The Black Youth Congress, an organization made up of some nine hundred young people from nine states, has met at Second Baptist. Church facilities are used for the Black Board of Education, a community group interested in improving education in the ghettos of Los Angeles. Dr. Kilgore and the lay chairman of the Social Action Committee work with black student unions on college campuses, with the Black Congress, and with other militants in these groups' efforts to press their legitimate claims and demands.

Dr. Kilgore has made it clear that as president of the ABC he will work for a better coalition between black militants and black pastors. He classifies himself as a militant. For him this means pressing and pushing in a nonviolent framework. "You can't be a Christian," he says, "without being militant — a militant with love."

Dr. Kilgore has a history of nonviolent militancy. He led in the organization of voter registration and unionization of tobacco workers in Winston-Salem, North Carolina, in 1943; he supervised the New York City office of the Southern Christian Leadership Conference from 1959 to 1963; he served as a member of the Administrative Committee and one of the organizers of the March on Washington in 1963; and he was western regional director of the SCLC in 1963.

While Second Baptist is concerned about its outreach, what happens inside the church is just as significant. The twenty-two hundred members have a choice of one of two Sunday morning services and Sunday school (a breakfast is served in between the first service and Sunday school). They are involved in choirs, a drama club, youth, college and adult fellowships, and as senior citizens. There are art and hobby shows, music festivals, and much more. The yearly operating budget is $256,000.

Several times during the Seattle meetings Dr. Kilgore was asked what issues he thought would be pressing the convention during his year in office. He replied:

Reconciliation, among black and white, young and old. "I hope our convention will involve more young people. I have not written off the dissident, radical youth. I think they are saying something to us that we should hear. I would like to see much more involvement with them whether they are church young people or not."

Peace: "I hope the church will face up to the whole issue of peace and what the war in Vietnam means for young people growing up in our country."

Education: "We are in real trouble at the level of elementary and high school education, particularly in our big cities." Working with other denominations, renewal in the local church, and a strong emphasis on evangelism are other areas in which he hopes the convention will move.

Dr. Kilgore's outlook is summed up in a statement he made after he was introduced at the convention as the new president: "We need to be a nation knowing our full humanity but living as servants of God."

L.A. Minister Embodies American Dream

Los Angeles Times, May 2, 1971
by Dan L. Thrapp, Times Religion Editor

Thomas Kilgore Jr. rose from a tightly segregated South Carolina village birthplace to the presidency of one of America's great, largely white, Protestant denominations, and along the way he touched the nation's soul.

If there is an American dream, this black Baptist minister embodies it. But that does not mean he is satisfied with the country, that he does not see its glaring faults, that he is not determined it must improve.

It is just that he is convinced it can and will perfect itself and thereby, one day, extend the "dream" to millions who must now conceive it to be a nightmare.

A man who used to bounce an infant Martin Luther King Jr. upon his knee, Dr. Kilgore is a close mixture of the love preached by Christ and the militancy of a James Forman — without Forman's strident rhetoric and threat of force. Dr. Kilgore does not believe in violence.

But in some ways he admires Forman, who two years ago sent a shock wave through the nation's churches by his demand for millions — later billions — in "reparations" for the evils done to blacks by whites.

"What James Forman did was a blessing," he asserts. "I think he did more to make the churches think about their responsibilities than all the revivals we had in this country in any single year."

He acknowledges the distance America has come toward social justice, but sees clearly that the goal remains remote.

"We've come a long, long way," he said. "I've seen this; I was born in the South, under strict segregation. But we've still got a long way to go.

"I say this to my young black brothers and sisters who so often say that it's just not going to happen, that brotherhood will always elude us.

"I know that we still are victims of systemic racism, and I say 'systemic' because I do not believe that all white people, or all people in power, are racist, whether they're white or black. But we have systems shot through with it.

"As we see this eroding, however, as I look at the long haul — another score of years, or another generation — I can see a better America."

Not only will there be more social justice, but a more peaceful, more prosperous nation, he believes.

"I cannot conceive of our continuing in war, of continuing to have poverty, when we can send a man to the moon. I cannot conceive of our not reordering our priorities in such a way as to relieve suffering, bring more people into the mainstream.

"I don't ask that everyone have split-level houses and all that, because

I don't think this makes that much difference. But I do think everybody should have access to a decent living, and to the development of whatever talents God has given him.

"And I can see this in America. My whole faith and hope as a Christian makes me see this opening up in America."

Dr. Kilgore is pastor of the Second Baptist Church, Griffith Avenue at 24th Street, and recently completed a year as president of the 1.5-million-member American Baptist Convention.

He was born fifty-eight years go in Woodruff, S.C., then a community of 1,500 in Spartanburg County, a Piedmont area of rolling hills, cotton, and corn. He was one of twelve children, eleven of whom are still living.

He decided to become a preacher as a boy when he saw that ministers wore good clothes and "when they came to our house we had the best dinner we'd ever had!"

"Line" Hymns. "I began listening intently to the preachers on Sundays, and I learned the hymns," he recalled. "In my day, in the deep South, they used to 'line' hymns: I don't know whether you know what that means?

"Someone would read a stanza, or a half-stanza, and then the congregation would sing it. Well, as a very little boy I worked through that; the minister let me do it once when I was five years old. I'd got the feel of it."

"Lining" was done partly because the poverty-stricken congregations could not afford enough hymnals to go around, he said, and "in many, churches there were no instruments. Therefore the one who lined the hymns would also have to set the tune, and the people would catch on."

Young Kilgore had a nice tenor which, through the years has developed into what Mrs. Kilgore calls a monotone, he says laughingly.

Trial Sermon. An older minister encouraged him, and at seventeen he preached "what we call in Baptist parlance my 'trial sermon.'" It was a success.

He moved to New York for a sixteen-year pastorate in Harlem, but he was satisfied neither with his training nor his mastery of the ministry, and enrolled at Union Theological Seminary, then as now among the foremost "liberal" seminaries in America.

"Certainly the liberal tradition was heavy there," he reflected. "Many from our more conservative seminaries thought everybody from Union was going to hell."

But under Dr. Reinhold Niebuhr and Paul Tillich, towering figures of modern theology, Union had enhanced its reputation, and Dr. Kilgore came to know them both, although Tillich only slightly.

"I know Dr. Niebuhr very well, knew him then on a friendly basis," he recalled. "I had two classes with him, and had the privilege of sitting in his apartment many times. We worked together in New York on many social problems."

Niebuhr, with his strong emphasis upon social action, was a mighty influence in Dr. Kilgore's development.

"I think he has done one of the better jobs of combining the fervency, and the piety, of the Gospel with social action," said the minister, speaking of a root problem over which many churchmen, lay and clergy, differ even today.

"His whole approach along this line has been a very strong one, and this has been my tendency as I have pastored and worked in the church."

Somewhere Between. Dr. Kilgore would place himself "somewhere between a liberal and a conservative" as a churchman, with perhaps a touch of the "Neo-Orthodox."

"By that I mean that I believe in some of the fundamental things like the fall of man and so forth, but at the same time I believe that the Gospel must be relevant in the whole human milieu, that we've got to think of saving structures just as we think in terms of saving individuals."

He believes there is a goodly group in Second Baptist who would agree with him that "we've got to make the church relevant." He added, "Unless we become the 'servant church,' we are not really the church at all."

Second Baptist is a middle-class church that draws its membership from throughout the Los Angeles Basin.

Membership Grows. Under Dr. Kilgore's seven-and-a-half-year pastorate its membership has increased from 1,983 to 2,354 and the budget from $150,000 to $235,000 a year, while "we bring in another quarter of a million in grants to carry on some of our programs."

Thus his pastorate has been a substantial success in a time of generally declining church membership and giving.

"Our new interest in making the church relevant to the community has given us some new enthusiasm," he said. "Also, we have not lost our young people. We've involved young people on the governing boards of our church, they take an active part in worship, they have a breakfast program for community children every Saturday."

Dr. Kilgore conceded that within the neighboring community there are "many, many problems" concerning youth — dope addiction, petty thefts, and so on — "that we have to be very careful about."

Making an Impact. "But somehow or other I think we are beginning to make some impact with the kind of things our church is doing."

He paused as the Reverend Ellis M. Keck, associate minister at Second Baptist, appeared at the doorway.

"There is a young man in the office, who was just released from prison, and I wish you would see him," said Dr. Kilgore. "The last time I saw him was six years ago, and he had just been released from prison then, too."

"I get the message," said Mr. Keck, withdrawing.

For Dr. Kilgore, the presidency of the ABC was "one of the toughest jobs I've had...and one of the most rewarding."

During that year he traveled 72,000 miles, spoke 150 times, and still tried to carry on his pastorate.

Time of Polarization. "I came into the presidency at the time when we were at the height of the polarization in this country, polarization in several ways," he recalled. "The generation gap, the polarization between black and white, between conservatives — the evangelicals — and the social action people.

"I think that the contribution, which I feel some sense of reward for, is that we reduced that polarization. Many people who did not understand me, particularly the white constituency, thought I was a wild-eyed militant, tied up with those who would burn. But I let it be known I was a militant for righteousness and love and for nonviolence, and against poverty and against racism and against war.

"I think that kind of interpreting made a difference in our convention. I think we have a more wholesome convention than we had before I became president."

Dr. Kilgore gives much of the credit for improvement in feeling in the ABC to the success of the black caucus within it.

Good Understanding. "The caucus has helped the ABC to move in the right direction, and has been accepted as part of the convention much better than the caucuses in many of the great denominations. We have really not had to slug it out, or walk out of communion services, and things like that, which happened elsewhere, because there's been a good understanding on the part of the white power structure that we are a valid part of the ABC."

Dr. Kilgore was elected at a 1969 convention at Seattle the same day James Forman appeared and demanded $60 million of the ABC — "and you can imagine the trap I was in!"

He is frank in his comments upon such things as FBI Director J. Edgar Hoover's purported tapes of indiscretions by the late Dr. King, who had preached at Second Baptist at least seven times, the last just before he was assassinated in Memphis in 1968.

Dr. Kilgore said he had been with Dr. King on many occasions, stayed at the same hotels, "and so far as I know Dr. King's moral life was up to par.

"The other thing is that, if there were some indiscretions, and I'm inclined to believe there were not, I feel that any man who made the impact on the American society as a moral leader in so many areas should not be condemned if he made some mistakes."

A "Disservice." He added that it was a "disservice" to the nation for the existence of such tapes to be leaked.

Dr. Kilgore believes that Dr. King was the great American hero of this century, as Washington was of the eighteenth, and Lincoln and Frederick Douglass of the nineteenth.

"On a Madison Square Garden program some years ago I was sitting next to Mrs. Eleanor Roosevelt," he recalled. "It was the night we were paying a tribute to King. She said to me, 'I think when the history of the twentieth century is written, that this young man [Dr. King] will be *the* man of the twentieth century.' And I share that view."

Releasing Systems. While acknowledging the importance of ecological goals, as well as social justice, Dr. Kilgore believes the primary end of man should be "the best kind of relationship that can be developed between brothers and sisters of different races, different classes, different cultural backgrounds.

"All these systems that interrelate in man must be releasing systems, rather than stifling systems."

Dr. Kilgore, married and the father of two grown daughters, said one of his hobbies is cooking.

"I cooked my way through college," he grinned. "I like to bring in a bunch of preachers and friends and cook us up a big breakfast, and things of that sort. I can bake, too. For instance we are having a church dinner here next Sunday, and I baked three cakes for it! I like pound cake best, but I can do fancy work — coconut, chocolate, stuff like that."

He has one other hobby, he admits, under pressure.

"I must do heavy reading for my sermons, and to relax I do light reading, mysteries and so on. And I — I'm an avid reader of the funnies.

"If I'm away for a week I have my wife save all the papers, for the special columns and editorials, certainly — and for the funnies. I'm catching up on them now."

Appendix B

History of the
Second Baptist Church

"Servant Church" Opens Doors
to the Community

Los Angeles Sentinel, March 13, 1980
by Virgie W. Murray

The historic Second Baptist Church, 2412 Griffith Avenue, Dr. Thomas Kilgore Jr. senior pastor, often refers to itself as the "servant church." This is a good description of this community-oriented church.

Second Baptist opens its doors to many organizations in the community. Mass meetings, civil rights groups, and other types of meetings use its facilities. This building has been used many times before and continues to attract groups.

The church is celebrating its ninety-fifth anniversary this year. It was founded May 13, 1885. The only black church in Los Angeles in 1872 was the African Methodist Episcopal Church. The First Baptist Church, a white congregation, was founded in 1874.

The few blacks who were not Methodist wanted a Baptist church of their own. The Reverend S. C. Pierce, his wife, and another person, were the founders of Second Baptist. The Reverend Pierce was the first pastor, and they met in a little upper room, which was a stable room over a small hall on Requina Street.

Pastors. Second Baptist has had only seven pastors in its ninety-five years of existence. The Reverend Pierce served only two years, 1885–87; the Reverend C. H. Anderson, 1887–1907: the Reverend J. L. McCoy, 1908–15; the Reverend H. D. Proud, 1915–20; Dr. Thomas L. Griffith, 1921–40; Dr. J. Raymond Henderson, 1941–63; and Dr. Kilgore since October 20, 1963.

The small membership decided to purchase some lots and build a church before they extended the call to the Reverend Anderson. With a membership of twenty-two, they purchased lots on Maple, between Seventh and

Eighth Streets. A rough frame building was erected on the back of the lot by the men of the church.

The membership grew to 134 and soon outgrew the little church. The Reverend Anderson led the members in building a two-story brick church on the front lot of the Maple Street property. The cornerstone was laid in 1892.

There were many days of disagreement and division in the church. One group after another left the main body to form their own missions. Among the offspring of Second Baptist are Mt. Zion, Tabernacle, and New Hope Baptist Churches.

Within eighteen years the membership rose to five hundred, and two services were held each Sunday. The Sunday school had an overwhelming growth along with the BYPU and the membership, so the members decided to find a new site since there was no room for expansion. Lots at Fourteenth and Paloma Streets were purchased.

"Father." The Reverend Anderson was honored many times as the "Father of Negro Baptists." He was responsible for organizing the black Baptist churches in 1888 and connecting them with the Los Angeles Baptist Association, which was white. This group withdrew from the white association and formed an association with the black Baptists in the northern area, known as the Western Baptist Association.

During the pastorate of the Reverend McCoy, the mortgage was paid. Plans were made to begin the building of the new edifice, but the Reverend McCoy died suddenly and everything was at a standstill.

The Reverend Proud served the church during the World War I era. He was away from the church several months serving as missionary in South America for the National Baptist Convention, Inc., Foreign Mission Board. Deaconesses were selected to serve the church during his administration.

Edifice. Dr. Griffith served the church during the absence of the Reverend Proud and later became the pastor. After his fourth year as pastor, he led the members into building its present edifice at a cost of approximately $200,000 in the early '20s.

The lots on Fourteenth and Paloma were sold. Dr. and Mrs. Griffith walked around the vicinity of Adams, Griffith, Stanford, and San Pedro [to survey the land]. As a result, the lots at Twenty-Fourth and Griffith Avenue were secured. Groundbreaking was held October 12, 1924.

Paul R. Williams was the architect and Norman F. Marsh drew up the plans according to Dr. Griffith's specifications. On January 3, 1926, the new building was opened for worship, fully completed and furnished from kitchen to the classrooms, standing on 135 by 104 feet of ground.

Dedication. Dr. Adam Clayton Powell Sr., pastor of Abyssinian Baptist Church, New York, was the dedication speaker.

During dedication, Dr. Griffith stated, "Second Baptist Church is built to meet the needs of a growing city, such as Los Angeles, for years to come. It is built for departmental purposes. It is built to house large audiences for programs and public meetings."

The sanctuary with a balcony, will seat sixteen hundred people. The baptistry was described as "a crowning adornment of our beautiful building with a hand-painted River Jordan scene."

Dr. Griffith died June 27, 1940. A year later, Dr. Henderson became the sixth pastor. The social hall was renamed Griffith Memorial Hall in 1942.

Dr. Henderson initiated a drive, "$55 in '44," which raised $83,000, and the indebtedness was liquidated. The excess money was used to purchase the Children's Home Society buildings, which were on the southeast corner of Griffith Avenue, adjoining the church.

Center. These buildings and premises were remodeled at a cost of $30,000 and converted into a community center named the Henderson Community Center, in honor of Dr. Henderson. He presented his plans for the construction of a Christian education building in 1959. The mortgage on the six-unit apartment building was paid off in 1960.

On March 10, 1963, the Christian education building was dedicated and named the Velva Henderson Christian Education Building in honor of the (first) lady. It was paid in full at the time of its completion.

Dr. Henderson retired in 1963 and Dr. Kilgore, pastor of Friendship Baptist Church, New York, was selected to lead the church, beginning October 20, 1963.

Dr. Kilgore launched the church into "the Serving Years," opening the doors to the community for meetings, conferences, and special services.

During Dr. Kilgore's administration, Henderson Community Center was reopened in 1965; Griffith Memorial Hall was rebuilt at a cost of $106,502.30, and dedicated January 23, 1966; the pipe organ was completely rebuilt; the Children's Day Care Center was opened and dedicated with a grant of $97,200 under Title V of the Office of Economic Opportunity (OEO).

Highlights. Other highlights of Dr. Kilgore's ministry include the dedication and opening of the Pueblo del Rio Christian Action Center in 1968 and the thirty-nine-unit housing complex adjacent to the church edifice, Griffith Gardens, for senior citizens.

From early morning to late evening, Second Baptist bears little resemblance to a house built merely for worship. There is a lot of creative community involvement from the street into the church. It was declared a historic monument in 1968.

Dr. Kilgore, a native of Woodruff, S.C., is a graduate of Morehouse College, having earned an A.B. degree in 1935. Graduate study was done at Howard University, 1944–45; he earned a B.D. degree from Union Theological Seminary in 1957, and two honorary doctorates from Shaw

University and Morehouse. Since October 1963, he has received three additional doctorates from Morris College, Virginia Union University, and USC.

He pastored three churches in North Carolina prior to his New York City congregation.

President. Dr. Kilgore was elected the first black president of the American Baptist Churches, U.S.A., in 1970. He was also elected president of the Progressive National Baptist Convention, Inc., in 1976.

On the "back-to-church" movement, Dr. Kilgore said, "There are a lot of people returning to church. A lot of them are disturbed about the electronic church and the money they are taking in. There is no visible evidence they are having any effect on church attendance.

"I feel the young adults after the '60s and '70s are beginning to understand some of the things that went on, which were not as fulfilling. The church is the first love of the majority of black people," continued the senior pastor.

He added, "The educators of the '20s and '30s frowned upon gospel music. The new people are not doing that. A good thing for the church and community is the Institute of Sacred Music, which was organized to preserve great black music, spirituals, and gospel songs."

Institute. "The institute was organized not only for this church, but for other churches. That is why it is listed as the Institute of Sacred Music 'at Second Baptist Church' and not 'of Second Baptist.' It operates here, but it belongs to the community. It is a community institution," said Dr. Kilgore, president of the Gathering and USC's director of the Office of Special Community Affairs.

Jeannetta Kilgore, first lady, is the director of the Children's Day Care Center.

Yearly, substantial contributions are made to Home Mission, World Mission, NAACP, the SCLC, the Urban League/OIC, the Brotherhood Crusade, and a number of colleges, including Virginia Union University, Morehouse College, Bishop College, Shaw University, Morris College, American Baptist Theological Seminary, and the Nannie Helen Burroughs School.

Sons of Second Baptist Church are serving at several churches throughout the city and in other cities. Among her local sons are Dr. Paul M. Martin, pastor of Redeemer Presbyterian Church; the Reverend David Morris, pastor of Angeles Mesa Presbyterian Church; the Reverend Gerald D. Adams, pastor of the Greater True Friendship Baptist Church; and the Reverend William Campbell, pastor of the Baptist Church of the New Covenant.

Appendix C

The Progressive National Baptist Convention, Inc.: Major Developments, 1961–1980*

This survey of the Progressive National Baptist Convention, Inc. (PNBC), will include discussions of its history, major developments, issues and themes, and numerical and financial growth. The information is compiled from minutes of the annual convention sessions plus the reports of the general secretary from 1961 to 1980. In addition, I have interviewed Dr. Thomas Kilgore Jr., a past-president of the PNBC.

History

The Progressive National Baptist Convention, Inc., came into being at the Zion Baptist Church in Cincinnati, Ohio, November 14–15, 1961. The meeting was called by Zion's pastor, L. Venchael Booth, who, along with thirty-two others, representing twenty-two churches in fourteen states, made a bold move to pull out of the National Baptist Convention U.S.A., Inc., which had been in existence since 1915.[1]

The chief issues instigating the split were tenure of officers and democratic governance (see "The Origin of the Progressive National Baptist Convention," by Dr. J. Carl Mitchell, in the box on p. 226). Tensions mounted during the annual session of the NBC held in September of 1961 in Kansas City, Missouri. The contender for the presidency was Dr. Gardner C. Taylor. His was not only a contest to become president, but was a serious challenge to the issue of tenure. The incumbent, Dr. J. H. Jackson, viewed the presidency as a life-term office. Added to this was Jackson's ultra-conservatism, which was out of step with the progressive movement of many activist-oriented pastors that was sweeping the country.

There had been an uproar at the 1960 convention in Philadelphia.[2] Delegates had marched with Taylor placards singing "Lift Him Up," in open

---

*A graduate paper submitted to the American Baptist Seminary of the West/Southwest, 1984, by Jini Kilgore Ross.

National News Release, September 11, 1961

A Volunteer Committee for the Formation of a New National Baptist Convention announced this week through its chairman, Rev. L. V. Booth, Pastor of Zion Baptist Church, Cincinnati, Ohio, that a meeting will be held November 14 and 15, 1961, at Zion Baptist Church, 630 Glenwood Avenue, Cincinnati 29, Ohio.

The two-day session will be devoted to discussion on How to Build a Democratic Convention Dedicated to Christian Objectives.

The keynote speaker will be Dr. William H. Borders, pastor of Wheat Street Baptist Church, Atlanta, Georgia. Dr. Borders is one of the ten outstanding pastors expelled from the National Baptist Convention, Inc., following its notorious session at Louisville, Kentucky, in 1957, when President Joseph H. Jackson ruled tenure unconstitutional. There has been great dissatisfaction since.

All freedom-loving, independent and peace-loving Baptists are invited. Those who do not wish to form a new convention are requested not to attend.

Both men and women are invited. Persons who are interested in attending this meeting are urged to write in for reservations to Rev. L. V. Booth at the above address and indicate whether a hotel or home is desired. This movement is in no way connected with the past effort of "The Taylor Team." It is an entirely new movement under new leadership. Persons who are concerned with redeeming the Baptist initiative and restoring a democratic thrust are invited.

---

defiance of the status quo. They had decided to register separately at the Kansas City convention because they felt that the election would probably be "fixed." It had been rumored that Jackson's repeated victories were predicated upon ballot box stuffing.

Recalling the Kansas City convention of 1961, PNBC President Emory R. Searcy (1970; see the box on p. 227 for a list of past presidents of the PNBC) told the delegates in his annual address at the meeting that was held in the same city: "White Baptists have had their separations from time to time in history, but usually it is on theological grounds. Black Baptists' separation is usually on political grounds."[3]

In order to have one registration, Jackson promised to hold a fair election. The Taylor faction turned in their registration money, and the election was held. Approximately 4,000 votes were cast. Jackson won 2,500; Taylor 1,575.[4]

After his victory was claimed, Jackson proceeded to oust officers who

**The Call Letter, from L. Venchael Booth, Minister,
Zion Baptist Church, Cincinnati, Ohio**

September 22, 1961

Dear Brother Pastor:

Our National Baptist Convention has reached an all-time low in fellowship, peace, and Christian dignity. We have completely lost our freedom to worship, participate, and grow in the kingdom work as it is expressed in the Convention. We can no longer trust the integrity of its leadership.

The time has come for freedom-loving, independent, and peace-loving Christians to unite in a fellowship that they can trust. Why are we so afraid of building a new Convention? We act as though it is a terrible sin. Organizations exist to unite persons of similar interest in multiplied strength. There is nothing on earth to keep us from working toward worthy objectives and lofty goals.

It is to this sacred call that you are invited to attend a special meeting for the formation of a new Convention on November 14 and 15 at Zion Baptist Church, 630 Glenwood Avenue, Cincinnati, Ohio. Kindly respond quickly if possible.

Yours in Christian Fellowship,
L. Venchael Booth

were deemed to be troublemakers. Among those ousted were Dr. Martin Luther King Jr., vice president of the Progressive Baptist Congress of Christian Education, and Dr. C. C. Adams, head of the Foreign Missions Board.[5]

Dr. Searcy gave these reflections on the 1961 convention:

In this city [Kansas City, Missouri], the rallying cry was, "Fair Vote" in the election. There was a determined effort to keep those who were committed to support of Dr. Taylor out of the city auditorium. That was so wrong and unbrotherly, until it fell by its own weight. We told the city authorities that we were going into the auditorium and unless they have enough jails to put 2,000 preachers — then get ready for we were going in the auditorium. They backed down and said we were free to go in and would not be hindered.

A committee from the Taylor team (so-called), Dr. Harrison serving as chairman, proposed a conference with Dr. Jackson to talk things over with the view of handling our own affairs without any outside participation. I felt mighty little when a judge of this city had to appoint a monitor to conduct our election, when the other side turned down our proposal.[6]

The Origin of the Progressive National Baptist Convention

The Progressive National Baptist Convention is largely an outgrowth of dissatisfaction over "TENURE" and the office of Executive Secretary in the National Baptist Convention, Inc. The meeting which culminated in a new organization was called at Cincinnati, after several previous meetings had been held by outstanding ministers in the National Baptist Convention, Inc. over a period of years.

The first of these meetings was held in St. Louis, Mo., in the Washington Avenue Tabernacle Church, of which Dr. John E. Nance is pastor. At this meeting, several prominent ministers met for the purpose of bringing about a solution to the problems that were confronting our Convention at the time. We pledged ourselves to work within the framework of our Convention without any suggestion of withdrawing ourselves from the Convention. We only expressed ourselves as to how we felt about the existing conditions of the Convention. Expressions were made and published about this meeting which created much dissatisfaction in the Convention's official ranks. Instead of the meeting improving conditions, greater opposition became apparent.

The following meetings of the National Baptist Convention, Inc. were destined to widen the breach. In Denver, Colorado, we spent a whole session seeking to prevent the election of officers by vote of state delegations. The following year in 1957, when we convened at Louisville, Ky., a chair-throwing session brought great disgrace to our Baptist Family. The two succeeding sessions marked a repeat in Baptist confusion in both Philadelphia, Pa., and Kansas City. By this time, more than 50 percent of the convention had pledged itself to support Dr. Gardner C. Taylor, distinguished pastor from Brooklyn, N.Y., as President. Dr. Taylor was defeated after a decision which resulted to the advantage of his opponent, Dr. J. H. Jackson.

The Reverend L. V. Booth of Zion Baptist Church, Cincinnati, Ohio, left the convention at Kansas City determined to call a meeting and allow the opposition to make a clear choice between tyranny and freedom, and confusion and peace. Before many of the messengers had reached their homes, a letter went out calling for all interested in peace, fellowship, and progress to attend a meeting in November. This was followed by a second letter in October, urging fellow pastors to come to Cincinnati. His invitation met with opposition from some of the strongest pastors in the nation. Among these were men who were trusted, revered, and respected. Very few could see then the wisdom and divine inspiration and unselfishness of his call.

The Cincinnati meeting drew representatives from fourteen states with a total of thirty-three delegates. After a formal opening, it was decided that Dr. J. Raymond Henderson, of Los Angeles, California, would preside over the business session. Dr. Henderson requested that we withdraw from the sanctuary of Zion Baptist Church to its chapel, where only registered messengers would participate. This request was unanimously accepted. After serious deliberations, two spokesmen were allowed to close the discussion. Dr. Marvin T. Robinson, of Pasadena, California, spoke against organizing at the time, and Rev. L. V. Booth of Cincinnati, Ohio, spoke for organizing. When the vote was taken by ballot and counted the group to organize had won by "one" vote. Every member, every church and convention that registered in the Cincinnati meeting were committed to "tenure."

Dr. J. Carl Mitchell

Convention Officers and Sites: 1961–1980

Year	City	President	Executive Secretary
1961	Cincinnati	T. M. Chambers	
1962	Philadelphia	T. M. Chambers	
1963	Detroit	T. M. Chambers	
1964	Atlanta	T. M. Chambers	L. Venchael Booth
1965	Los Angeles	T. M. Chambers	L. Venchael Booth
1966	Memphis	T. M. Chambers	L. Venchael Booth
1967	Cincinnati	Gardner C. Taylor	L. Venchael Booth
1968	Washington, D.C.	Gardner C. Taylor	L. Venchael Booth
1969	Miami Beach	Emory R. Searcy	L. Venchael Booth
1970	Kansas City, Mo.	Sloan S. Hodges	K. L. Moore
1971	Houston	E. L. Harrison	Sloan S. Hodges
1972	Chicago	L. Venchael Booth	Sloan S. Hodges
1973	Jackson, Miss.	L. Venchael Booth	Sloan S. Hodges
1974	Cleveland	L. Venchael Booth	Sloan S. Hodges
1975	Atlantic City	Nelson H. Smith	Sloan S. Hodges
1976	Washington, D.C.	Nelson H. Smith	Sloan S. Hodges
1977	Atlanta	Thomas Kilgore, Jr.	Sloan S. Hodges
1978	Los Angeles	Thomas Kilgore, Jr.	Sloan S. Hodges
1979	New Orleans	William A. Jones	Sloan S. Hodges
1980	Chicago	William A. Jones	C. J. Malloy

At the beginning of each book of convention proceedings is a statement of "the progressive concept," written by Dr. Thomas Kilgore Jr. (see the box on the following page). Its theme words are "fellowship," "progress," and "peace," to which was added "service" in 1977. These words form the inner circle of the convention insignia, along with the Scripture reference upon which the PNBC was founded:

Let love be genuine; hate what is evil; hold fast to what is good; love one another with brotherly affection; outdo one another in showing honor. Never flag in zeal, be aglow with the Spirit, serve the Lord. Rejoice in your hope, be patient in tribulation, be constant in prayer. Contribute to the needs of the saints, practice hospitality.

Bless those who persecute you; bless and do not curse them. Rejoice with those who rejoice, weep with those who weep. Live in harmony with one another; do not be haughty, but associate with the lowly; never be conceited. Repay no one evil for evil, but take thought for what is noble in the sight of all. If possible, so far as it depends upon you, live peaceably with all. Beloved, never avenge yourselves, but leave it to the wrath of God; for it is written, "Vengeance is mine,

The Progressive Concept

Someone has said wisely that when God has a job to be done he always gives the contract to one of faith. The Progressive Concept is basically an idea and movement of faith. Faith, understood by only a few people, was deeply imbedded in the hearts of the less than fifty persons who gathered at Zion Baptist Church in Cincinnati, Ohio, in November 1961 and started the movement which is now the Progressive Baptist Convention.

The onward march of time, the historical forwardness, and the continuous renewal in time and history of God's revelations cause sensitive and alert souls to shake off the old forms and welcome new opportunities and new avenues of Christian service. The first motivation struck fire in 1961, was fanned in 1962, came to a blaze in 1963, began to burn seriously in 1964.

The early Christian church faced a hostile community but inside the church was a spirit that kept her alive and caused her to overcome all opposition. This spirit can be summed up in the word *fellowship*. It was more than common interest. It was more than mutual interest. It was more than "Hail fellow, glad to see you." It was more than a type of comradeship. It was koinonia — fellowship in love and concern. Those of us who follow the gleam of the Progressive Concept are happy to be free to participate in a true Christian fellowship. The wholesomeness of this interchange will continue to develop a convention that is at heart Christian.

Inherent in the Progressive Concept is *progress*. We are going somewhere in the Progressive National Convention. We are done with the "cult of personalities." We are through with "play prayers" and "circus sermons." True worship has meaning for us. Orderly sessions mark our business deliberations. Tenure in office is our way of life. And a unified budget determines our expenditures. We are on our way to developing a valid and responsible convention. *Progress* is our theme word.

Peace is inherent in the Progressive Concept. By peace we do not mean docile inarticulation. We do not mean everyone agrees with every other one. But we do mean that we dwell together as brothers and sisters, that we can differ without confusion, and that we can pool points of view and reach compromises based on principle. Our *peace* is no soft, flabby one, but rather a virile, positive, and creative force.

The Progressive Concept...*fellowship, progress, peace.* We will keep these before us and go forward. We welcome all Baptists who want to travel this road of valid responsibility.

Thomas Kilgore, Jr.

A Prayer Fellowship Hymn by L. Venchael Booth
*(to be sung to the tune "God of Grace and God of Glory,"
by Harry E. Fosdick)*

We have come from o'er the nation   Grant us grace amid oppression
Seeking fellowship and peace,   When the foe assails our way
We are truly God's creation—   Save us from unwise aggression—
And our love shall e'er increase.   May our footsteps never stray.
We shall stand firm and united—   Make us holy with Thy spirit—
As we spread from shore to shore,   As we walk this pilgrim's way,
As we spread from shore to shore.   As we walk this pilgrim's way.

We believe God's Holy Spirit   Help us yield our great Convention
Brought us safely o'er the way,   To Thy Holy Spirit's power.
Thru our God we shall inherit—   May no wicked intervention—
Grace and glory day by day,   Mar the beauty of this hour.
Gracious God our Holy Father—   Holy Spirit lead and guide us—
Lead us safely, gently on,   In the path of peace and love,
Lead us safely, gently on.   In the path of peace and love.

I will repay, says the Lord." No, "if your enemy is hungry, feed him; if he is thirsty, give him drink; for by so doing you will heap burning goals upon his head." Do not be overcome by evil, but overcome evil with good. (Rom. 12:9–21, RSV)

In his annual address in Jackson, Mississippi, in 1973, President L. Venchael Booth said:

> When the PNBC was born she was not destined to be just another convention. She was born with an ideal of love, brotherhood and freedom. She was born with a challenging Scripture lesson and a song. God gave us the Scripture — Romans 12:9–21, and God gave us a song. All who seek to lead in this Convention should take time to read the Scripture and practice it. It would be well to sing the song and explore the depths of its inspiration (see "A Prayer Fellowship Hymn" in the box above). These are not the idle wanderings of man — but they are the lofty revelations of God. Take a look at our symbol and study the words. They are fraught with meaning, deep meditation, and lofty aspiration. Read the Progressive concept contributed by Dr. Thomas Kilgore — and view its literary excellence and character content.... Study the eloquence and brilliance in insight in Dr. Gardner Taylor's warning that our Convention is the "last best hope of Negro Baptists."[7]

Major changes were made in the PNBC constitution in 1975. Primarily, more general language was adopted to free the convention from the requirement of specific structures detailed in the first constitution. The old constitution read:

Article II: Objectives
2. For reasons of efficiency and effectiveness, the Convention shall function through Auxiliaries, Departments, Boards, Commissions, and Committees hereinafter described:

(a) The main Body of the Convention itself in sessions;

(b) The Departments of Women's Work; Congress of Christian Education; Men's Work; Foreign Missions; Home Missions; Church Extension; Evangelism; Stewardship; Publication and Literature; and the Department of Human Relations for Liberty, Freedom and Righteousness, and other auxiliaries.

(c) The church Extension work shall be done through the Home Mission Board.

The new Constitution said:

Article II: Objectives
Section 2. In the pursuit of these objectives, the Convention may function through such auxiliaries or departments, boards, agencies, commissions, committees, or other designated structures, as it shall determine.[8]

Major Developments

Major developments within the PNBC are numerous. The discussion of them will not be arranged in order of importance, for all of these developments have evident and less evident degrees of importance. Among those discussed here, eleven have been singled out for special mention.

• A full-time general secretary was appointed in 1970. The Reverend Dr. Sloan S. Hodges served the PNBC as the first full-time general secretary (1970–80). He was succeeded by the Reverend C. J. Malloy. Rev. Hodges had been recording secretary from 1964 to 1967. He succeeded Rev. L. Venchael Booth, who served as part-time executive secretary from 1964 to 1969. This appointment was a major development in the life of the new convention, for it provided much-needed continuity.
• The Baptist Foreign Mission Bureau was incorporated in 1971. The PNBC enjoyed a relationship with the Baptist Foreign Mission Bureau, which was in existence before PNBC was established. Its founder, Dr. C. C. Adams, created the bureau and became a PNBC officer. In 1975, the

property was transferred from Philadelphia to the PNBC Washington headquarters.

Foreign missions for PNBC has meant financial support and the financial undergirding of people from the foreign posts who will go back into their own areas to work once they have received their education. "This is part of the philosophy," said Dr. Kilgore. "PNBC doesn't own any of the properties in Haiti. We bought them and gave them to the people. The churches that have been built belong to the people. They report to the convention."

Foreign mission programs are active in Haiti and Nigeria. Financial support is given to churches in Grenada and Nicaragua.

• The Nannie Helen Burroughs School was purchased in 1971. This is a private elementary school in Washington, D.C., and the present site of the PNBC Headquarters. The Burroughs school, now seventy-five years old, was originally a boarding school where Christian education was taught to girls who came to Washington to work. The PNBC has taken over the operations of the elementary school.

• The Martin Luther King Jr. Award was established in the '70s to be given annually to a person of outstanding accomplishment who most nearly espouses the principles of King.

• A retirement pension plan for ministers and church workers was established with the Franklin Insurance Company in the '70s.

• The Fund of Renewal, a joint $11.5 million project between the PNBC and the American Baptist Churches, was established in 1972 to fund social action programs in local churches.

• A formal association with the American Baptist Churches was inaugurated in 1970.

• The Progressive Publishing House was established, publishing the newsletter *Baptist Progress* and the *Worker* group devotional journal.[9]

• The adoption of a unified budget in 1970 caused President Searcy to rejoice in these words: "This is the first time this has been attempted in a Baptist — National Baptist — body since 'the morning stars sang together.'" A black Baptist body in the United States had never before operated with a unified budget.[10]

• A record among black Baptist conventions was set in mission giving. General Secretary Hodges reported in 1970: "In foreign missions, we have shown our dedication to fulfilling the Great Commission by our support of the Baptist Foreign Mission Bureau, U.S.A., Inc. Not only have our churches contributed to the Bureau, but the convention itself has given from its treasury sums of $7,000 and $5,000 at one time. This has never been done by any other national Baptist convention."[11]

• The meeting time for the annual convention was changed, beginning in 1977, from the week after the first Sunday in September to the week after the first Sunday in August.

This may not seem like a major development, but in 1895, when the National Baptist Convention of America was established, the meeting time was set to accommodate delegates who represented for the most part the rural economy of cotton picking.

"By the first week in September, crops had been laid and there was a lull in activity until the second week when the cotton picking began. Black schools did not start session until cotton picking started," said Dr. Kilgore. "We no longer live in that reality. Now schools start in early September, so the change was made to accommodate youth and public school instructors to enable them to attend the conference."

While this seems like an insignificant change, it is symbolic of the PNBC spirit. The PNBC fellowship is willing to assess itself in the light of its response to contemporary issues and needs and make necessary adjustments. The other National Baptist bodies still convene the week after the first Sunday in September.

Following is a list of other major developments in the life of the PNBC:

- Partnership established with Cook Publishing Company, 1964

- Women's Auxiliary established, 1962

- Congress of Christian Education established to execute training programs, 1962

- Board of Education set up to formulate the education program, make up curriculum and standards and work with the publishing house to assign writers, 1962

- Laymen's Department established, 1964

- Youth Department established, 1964

- Ushers Department established, 1964

- Home Missions Department established in the early '70s by $15,000 grant from Southern Baptists. Home Missions includes teaching and stewardship for church expansion and administration, plus support of five civil rights organizations: the NAACP, the National Urban League, the SCLC, PUSH (People United to Save Humanity), and the Martin Luther King Center for Nonviolent Social Change.

- Representatives and delegates from the PNBC have been appointed to attend the Baptist World Alliance, North American Baptist Fellowship, Baptist Joint Committee on Public Affairs, National Council of Churches, World Council of Churches, General Commission on Chaplains and Armed Forces Personnel, and Church Women United.[12]

- The Progressive Hymnal published, 1976

Issues and Themes in Presidents' Messages and in Resolutions

In 1970, when the national rallying cry among the new black militancy was "Black Power!" President Searcy had this to say on the subject of power:

> There will be an increased assault on the ramparts of the status-quo during the '70s. The citadels of power in education, government, trade, commerce, and organized religion and politics will be challenged in no uncertain terms. However, the challengers are the *outs* and the challenged are the *ins*. Reinhold Niebuhr said that "History has not yet proved that the *outs* would not be as vicious and unmerciful as the *ins*. . . ." It boils down to the nitty-gritty that the man who is mad with the establishment and yelling all over the place for change, is no guarantee that his ethics toward his fellowman will contain any more grace than those whom he opposes now. As long as he is down, he can have a soft heart toward others, but as soon as he gets up, that softness of heart can fly out of the window, and he becomes an insensitive, hard-hearted neighbor like the unmerciful steward in Matthew's Gospel (Matt. 18:21–35). It takes nothing short of the grace of God to hold a man in check when he comes in possession of power! Political hearts are no guarantee of merciful rule. Redeemed hearts are![13]

Men and women of the PNBC with prophetic and visionary leadership stirred the imaginations and steered the course of action in their sermons, which contained the kind of searching self-criticism that fosters growth.

As early as 1971, President Earl L. Harrison addressed the controversial issue of women preachers:

> The increasing number of women seeking ordination that they may occupy pulpits is greatly disturbing many of our pastors. I too have been steeped in traditional prejudice against the encroachment of skirts over our hitherto off-limit holy places. I offer no proof of woman's right to the pulpit, nor do I build any fences to deny her the privilege, but I believe in a "called-sent" ministry. I shall not therefore assume to dictate to God whom He shall choose to deliver His messages to mankind. I only hope that He does not see fit to replace me with a woman, nor an angel. I remember the loyalty of women to Christ. They were last at the cross, and first at the tomb.
>
> St. Paul wrote that women should hold their peace in the church and ask their husbands about what they wanted to know, but he confuses me by saying, "In Christ there is neither male nor female."
>
> Jesus told the complaining Pharisees on the Jerusalem road that if the women and children held their peace the rocks would take their places. Have we men let Christ down? Are we attempting to serve

God and mammon? His church and Uncle Sam at the same time: Christianity and politics? I predict that in her battle of freedom and equality with men, the woman will ultimately win. I am convinced that God does not need my approval of what He chooses to do.[14]

Dr. Booth, who would succeed Harrison as president, advised that the matter of women preachers be laid to rest as an issue of the PNBC:

To take a position for women preachers would cause great pain and frustration for those who hold strong feelings against them. So, to take a position against them would alienate and embitter those who accept them. Let us then seek the healing balm of time which brings all who seek light nearer to it. Clearly then, if we really will be honest, fair and just, the women preachers issue does not belong on the Agenda of the Progressive National Baptist Convention.[15]

Booth said the local churches would have to independently decide whether women preachers would or would not occupy their pulpits.

Before his death in 1971, which shortened his term in office, President Harrison spoke in a prophetic voice of Christian stewardship. The current in his thoughts flows through the central streams of expression in the PNBC. He was aware of the enticements of assimilation and middle-class American life:

We have engaged in building fine houses for worship, luxurious manses, high salaries, high-priced automobiles, honors and offices of power and trips around the world, while the academic colleges, hospitals and mission stations our fathers started have survived at a gradual dying rate, so that now they are useless.

Today we are challenged to build, to maintain and to sustain the Kingdom of God. We are not short of means. We have the goods. God has given them to us. We are short on management. We must preach; we must teach; we must give; we must sacrifice; we must work; we must pray for the coming of the Kingdom of God on earth and thus fulfill our stewardship.[16]

This central stream of concern was echoed in 1978 when President Kilgore addressed the Seventeenth Annual Session. He said:

We must bring into balance our skills and our consumer interests. We cannot continue to be among the lowest paid workers and at the same time consume at our present level. The median income for blacks is only 61.5% that of whites. But the ownership and consumption of blacks must cause us to reflect soberly. Here is the picture:

	BLACK OWNERSHIP AND CONSUMPTION	WHITE OWNERSHIP AND CONSUMPTION
Automobiles	62%	66%
Homes	56%	70%
$50–$70 a week for groceries	30%	25%
Clothing annually	36%	22%
Credit Cards	52%	52%
Drink beer regularly	50%	44%
Drink beer heavily	17%	14%
Drink Scotch Whiskey	33%	16%
Bought digital watches last year	3.8%	1.4%

We must change this picture. We can do much more together with our $90 billion. Almost every one of the "Top 100" black businesses could double, triple, and quadruple its business. And the present annual income of these businesses of $888.7 million could easily be over $3 billion. Remember, these businesses hire mostly black workers.[17]

Resolutions coming from the Congress of Christian Education in 1973 at the Twelfth Annual Session called for personal and national morality in the wake of the Watergate scandal; a stand against abortion, except when the mother's life is endangered; a stand against capital punishment; a stand for Christian witness in the areas of social justice.

In 1974, President Booth, continually focusing on stewardship, said, "The greatest resolution that can take place in the Black Church is to match her giving with her singing and her preaching."[18] He cautioned the church to "watch and pray" during the period of glorification of the black religious experience, "lest we enter into temptation."[19]

These quotes are in no way exhaustive of the eloquent, prophetic, dynamic, and challenging dictates of the PNBC from 1970 to 1980, but they reflect the thinking of a group willing to grapple with the issues of its day. A list of the concerns of the Resolutions Committee (1978) gives further evidence of this PNBC tendency.[20]

- Community and Economic Development — calling for establishment of a Bureau of Community and Economic Development to stimulate the generation of community service centers.

- Drug Abuse task forces — supporting neighborhood leadership in mobilizing people to fight this enemy.

- Education — supporting the use of tax dollars for public school education, opposing tax breaks for parents who send their children to private schools; support of PUSH.

- Family Life — recommending that churches develop family life programs, conferences, seminars.

- Health Care — recommending that the PNBC go on record in support of National Health Insurance.

- Human Rights; Police Brutality — condemning State of North Carolina and governor for persistent and systematic denial of human rights, with specific reference to the Reverend Ben Chavis and the "Wilmington 10."

- Prayer-a-thon — recommending prayer in local churches for specific PNBC concerns.

- Unemployment — calling for implementation of Humphrey-Hawkins Bill and deprioritization of military spending in favor of creation of jobs.

Numerical and Financial Growth

In 1961, thirty-three people representing twenty-two churches and fourteen states formed the PNBC. The total receipts that first year were $721.26. In 1984 there were 1,050 churches, representing some 430,000 people. Total receipts for this year were $2,200,000.

The rate of growth was steady, though at times a large number of churches joined in one year. In 1969, three hundred churches were added. Between 1974 and 1975, two hundred churches joined. The peak membership year seems to be 1976, with some fourteen hundred churches.[21]

In his report at the Fifteenth Annual Session in Washington, D.C., in 1976, General Secretary Hodges said that PNBCers were requiring city auditoriums for their meetings for the first time in history. He referred to the Fourteenth Session in Atlantic City, 1975. Since that time, small hotel ballrooms have not been large enough to accommodate the thousands of delegates and observers who attend the convention.

Conclusion

This brief survey is only a summary of some of the major events in the PNBC and a sampling of the prophetic visions of its leaders. Many personalities have not been mentioned. An exhaustive history of the Progressive Baptists has yet to be written, though one by founding Pastor Booth's son is in existence.

I hope to have presented some of the flavor and aroma of this dynamic group of Baptist reformers, whose new visions forced them out of their traditional home among National Baptists. The separation was never intended, and it has not been allowed to become a divorce. Indeed, talk is in the air of a reunion as new leadership of the National Baptist Convention, U.S.A., Inc., shares the vision of the PNBC, and as black Baptists consider ever more seriously their need to be good stewards and to combine resources.[22]

It was the wise Dr. Harrison who spoke in his annual address of the pain of division and the hope of merger:

> Progressive Baptists must not accommodate themselves to isolation. We must seek the friendship, cooperation and togetherness of all the other Baptist bodies of America, white and black. Tonight I extend my hand as a symbol of goodwill, brotherly love, Christian fellowship, and peaceful coexistence, which ultimately may terminate in a working program of togetherness with National Baptists, Inc., National Baptists of America, Southern Baptists, and American Baptists working together to do at least one big thing for Christ and the Kingdom of God on earth. There is no place for antipathy, old grudges, revenge of littleness among God's children. Let us begin now to pray, "Thy Kingdom come, Thy will be done, on earth as in Heaven."[23]
>
> Unification of Negro Baptists is not impossible. We must not despair of Him who has all power in Heaven and in earth in his hand, with whom "one day is as a thousand years and a thousand years as one day." Remember the prayer of our Lord?
>
> *"Father keep through thine own name those whom thou hast given me, that they may be one, as we are."* (John 17:11 KJV)

All things are possible with Him.[24]

Notes

1. Robert G. Torbet, *A History of the Baptists* (Valley Forge, Pa.: Judson Press, 1950), 355.

2. Interview with Dr. Thomas Kilgore Jr., past president of the Progressive National Baptist Convention (1977–1978) and pastor of the Second Baptist Church, Los Angeles.

3. *Minutes of the Ninth Annual Session of the Progressive National Baptist Convention, Inc.,* 1970, 74.

4. Interview with Dr. Kilgore.

5. Ibid.

6. *Minutes,* 1970, 74.

7. *Minutes of the Twelfth Annual Session of the Progressive National Baptist Convention, Inc.,* 1973, 78.

8. *Minutes of the Fourteenth Annual Session of the Progressive National Baptist Convention, Inc.,* 1975, 12.

9. The *Worker* is a missionary and education quarterly, begun in 1934 by Nannie Helen Burroughs. It has been the official missionary publication for the National

Baptist Convention for many years. The split of the Progressive National Baptist
Convention from the National Baptist Convention, U.S.A., Inc., did not damage
this arrangement. When the Burroughs school was taken over by PNBC, the *Worker*
became one of the PNBC publications.

10. *Minutes,* 1970, 75.

11. Ibid., 84.

12. *Minutes of the Fifteenth Annual Session of the Progressive National Baptist
Convention, Inc.,* 1976, 92, 96.

13. *Minutes,* 1970, 78.

14. *Minutes of the Tenth Annual Session of the Progressive National Baptist
Convention, Inc.,* 1971, 87–88.

15. Ibid., 248.

16. Ibid., 89.

17. *Minutes of the Seventeenth Annual Session of the Progressive National
Baptist Convention, Inc.,* 1978, 148–49.

18. *Minutes of the Thirteenth Annual Session of the Progressive National Baptist
Convention, Inc.,* 1974, 90.

19. Ibid., 92.

20. *Minutes,* 1978, 94–97.

21. Ibid., 82.

22. Efforts have been made in recent years toward a merger of the National Baptist Convention, U.S.A., Inc., and the PNBC. Leaders of both bodies are doing
small things, like fellowshiping together at conventions, to pave the way for such
a merger. One of the most critical concerns is stewardship. Millions of dollars are
spent by churches to send delegates to these separate conventions that could better
be used by missions.

23. *Minutes,* 1971, 87.

24. Ibid., 85.

Appendix D

Lives at a Glance: Thomas Kilgore Jr. and Jeannetta Miriam Scott Kilgore

THOMAS KILGORE JR.

Early Life

Born February 20, 1913, in Woodruff, South Carolina, the sixth of twelve children of Thomas and Eugenia Kilgore. Received his elementary and secondary education in Woodruff and Brevard, North Carolina, and Asheville, North Carolina.

Became a converted Christian at age nine.

Higher Education

A.B., Morehouse College, 1935

Graduate work, Howard University School of Religion, 1944–45

M. Div., Union Theological Seminary, New York City, 1957

Honorary Degrees

D.D., Shaw University at Raleigh, North Carolina, 1956

D.D., Morehouse College, 1963

D.D., Morris College, 1967

LL.D., Virginia Union University, 1972

LL.D., University of Southern California, 1972

L.H.D., University of Redlands, 1976

D.D., Morehouse School of Religion, 1977

L.H.D., Shaw College at Detroit, 1977

L.H.D., Ottawa University, 1988

Pastorates

New Bethel Baptist Church, Asheville, North Carolina, 1936–38

Friendship Baptist Church, Winston-Salem, North Carolina, 1938–47

Rising Star Baptist Church, Walnut Cove, North Carolina, 1941–47

Friendship Baptist Church, New York, 1947–63

Second Baptist Church, Los Angeles, 1963–85

Professional Activities

Principal, Public Schools in Rutherford and Haywood Counties, North Carolina, 1935–38

Executive Secretary of General Baptist State Convention of North Carolina, 1945–47

Chaplain, Winston-Salem State Teachers College, 1941–44

Board Member of National Public Radio, Washington, D.C., 1977–81

Adjunct Firestone Professor, University of Southern California School of Religion, 1980–82

President, the Gathering (ecumenical clergy group), 1978–82

Trustee, Board Chairman, Morehouse School of Religion, Interdenominational Theological Center

Chairman, Board of Directors, Los Angeles County Opportunities Industrialization Centers (OIC), 1969–70

President and Organizer, Los Angeles Second Baptist Homes, 1969–85

Chairman and Organizer, Board of Directors, Second Baptist Community Homes, 1983–85

Chairman, Board of Trustees, Morehouse College, Atlanta, 1971–91

Organizer of the Concerned Clergy

President, American Baptist Churches, U.S.A., 1969–70

President, Progressive National Baptist Convention, Inc., 1976–78

Vice President, Southern California Baptist Convention, 1969–70

Vice President, Los Angeles Council of Churches, 1966–68

Affiliations

Pastor Emeritus, Second Baptist Church, 1985–98

Member, Board of Directors, Golden State Mutual Life Insurance Company

Member, Omega Psi Phi Fraternity

Member, Board of Trustees, Morehouse College, Atlanta, 1971–98

Chairman, California Sate Attorney General's Commission on Alcohol and Drug Abuse, 1985–87

Advisor to the President and Senior Advisor to the Office of Civic and Community Relations, University of Southern California, 1973–88

First President, Los Angeles Black Agenda, 1981

Board Member, Community Redevelopment Agency, Los Angeles, 1984–93

Board Member, Los Angeles Festival, 1985–88

Board Member, Los Angeles 2000, 1986–88

Board Member, Martin Luther King Legacy Association, 1983–89

Civil Rights Activities

Led in the organization of voter registration and unionization of tobacco workers in Winston-Salem, North Carolina, 1943–44

Organized and directed Prayer Pilgrimage for Freedom, Lincoln Memorial, Washington, D.C., 1957

Supervised the New York Southern Christian Leadership Conference Office, 1959–63

Member of the Administrative Committee and one of the organizers of the March on Washington, 1963

West Coast Director of the Southern Christian Leadership Conference Office, 1964–69

Life Member of the National Association for the Advancement of Colored People

Executive Board Member, Southern Christian Leadership Conference

Led in the organization of an all-day meeting of all segments of the Black community, planning an appropriate memorial service for Dr. Martin Luther King Jr. and developing Operation Unity to prevent violence, April 5, 1968.

Some Contributions

Founder, House of Friendship Community Center, New York City

Organizer, The Heart of Harlem Neighborhood Church Association of the Protestant Council of the City of New York. This organization served as a model for a new city-wide organization structure of the Protestant Council.

Led Second Baptist Church in reopening and staffing Henderson Community Center for youth activities in the Los Angeles South Central area, 1964.

Established Second Baptist Child Development Center, now operated under the auspices of the State Department of Education on an annual budget of $410,000, 1966.

Pueblo Christian Action Center was organized, emphasizing a store-front and street ministry to families and particularly to alienated youths in and around the Pueblo del Rio Housing Complex, 1968.

Established the Los Angeles Second Baptist Homes, a non-profit housing corporation, 1967

The formal opening of Griffith Gardens, a senior citizens housing facility, May 1973

Established the Los Angeles Second Baptist Community Homes, 1984

Founder, University of Southern California Ebonics Support Group (scholarship aid for minority and disadvantaged students), 1976

During the twenty-two years at Second Baptist Church, physical and organizational changes have taken place. A relevant style of community ministries has been instituted, and a new thrust in evangelism is contributing to the spiritual growth of the community. The overall operating budget of the church has increased from $140,000 in 1963 to $1,000,025 in 1985. Benevolent, Christian education, and mission gifts range from $65,000 to $102,000 annually.

Family

Married Jeannetta Miriam Scott in 1936. Mrs. Kilgore is a graduate of Miner Teachers College, Washington, D.C., and has done graduate work at Columbia University. Professionally, she is a public school teacher. For fourteen years she served as Director of Second Baptist Children's Center, 1968–82.

The Kilgores have two daughters: Lynn Elda, who is a graduate of Antioch College, Yellow Springs, Ohio; and Jini Medina, who is a graduate of Occidental College, Los Angeles, and holds a master's degree in journalism, University of California, Berkeley, a master of divinity degree, American Baptist Seminary of the West, and is now an ordained minister.

There are three grandchildren: Robin, Niambi, and Okera, and two great-grandchildren, Justen and Joshua.

Some Awards and Recognitions

1977   Special Man of the Year, Zeta Phi Beta Sorority

Martin Luther King Award, SCLC West, Los Angeles

Most Influential Black Leaders in the United States, *Ebony* magazine

Pioneers of Black Religious Leadership, Brotherhood Crusade, Los Angeles

PUSH for Excellence, Sixth Annual PUSH Convention, Los Angeles

National Communicator's Award, National Association of Media Women

"Our Man of All Time," Laymen's Department, Progressive Baptist State Convention of California and Nevada

Outstanding and Dedicated Leadership, Union Usher Board of Southern California

1978   Invaluable Service Performed for the Black Community, African Institute of Affective Learning

1979   Outstanding Community Service Award, Los Angeles Human Relations Commission

1980   Los Angeles Tribute to Thomas Kilgore Jr., Fifty Years of Religious and Community Service

Recognized by 1980 Bureau of the Census, U.S. Department of Commerce

USC School of Public Administration Award

Pastor of the Year, Progressive National Baptist Convention, Inc.

1981   Special Service Award as Chairperson, Blue Ribbon Advisory Committee, 1978–81, Los Angeles Fire Department

Award of Merit, Information and Referral Federation for the Citizens of Los Angeles

1983   Inducted in Phi Beta Kappa, Delta of Georgia Chapter, Morehouse College, Atlanta

1984   Recognized by *Ebony* magazine, as one of America's 15 greatest Black Preachers

1985   Inducted in Golden Key Honor Society, University of Southern California

1986   Distinguished Christian Service Award, Holman United Methodist Church, Los Angeles

Guardian Angel Award, Young Saints Academy of Performing Arts and Skills

Community Achievement Award, Los Angeles Chapter, NAACP

1989   The Nelson Mandela Humanitarian Award, Compton College, Compton, California

The Thomas Kilgore Jr. $200,000 Endowed Scholarship established by Dr. James Zumberge, President, University of Southern California USC Ebonics

1990   Inducted into the Martin Luther King Jr. International Board of Preachers, Morehouse College

1991   Recipient, Martin Luther King Jr. Award, Anheuser Busch, Inc., Los Angeles

1992   Dedication of the Thomas Kilgore Jr. Center, Morehouse College, February 20

1993   Eightieth birthday celebration sponsored by Mayor Tom Bradley, CRA Chairman Jim Wood, and the friends of the Reverend Dr. Thomas Kilgore Jr. and Frank Kuwahara

1994   Inducted into the Skull & Dagger Honor Society, USC, April 16

JEANNETTA MIRIAM SCOTT KILGORE

Early Life

Born October 26, 19—, in Raphine, Virginia, the fifth of five children of John and Mary Scott. Received her elementary education at Christianburg Institute in Christianburg, Virginia, and her high school education at Dunbar High School in Washington, D.C.

Higher Education

B.S., Miner Teachers College (later named D.C. Teachers College), 1935

Graduate work, Columbia University, New York; UCLA Extension (Early Childhood Education Administration)

Professional Activities

Elementary school teacher, North Carolina; New York

Preschool Director, Second Baptist Church Child Career Center, Los Angeles

Affiliations

Second Baptist Church (serves on several boards and commissions)

National Council of Negro Women, Life Member

Black Women's Forum

NAACP, Life Member

Urban League

Ebonics, University of Southern California

The California Child Development Administrative Association

Southern California's Association for the Education of Young Children

National Association of Ministers' Wives, Life Member

Some Awards and Recognitions

Service Awards, Second Baptist Church, Los Angeles:

- First Director of PIC (Program, Interpretation, Communications) Office
- Editor of Second Baptist Church Informer
- Associate Superintendent of Sunday Church School
- Chair of Ninetieth Church Anniversary Celebration
- Chair of the $10,000 Morehouse College Fund
- Women's Day Speaker twice
- Director of Second Baptist Church's Child Development Center (fourteen years, four months)
- Member of the General Board Executive Committee
- Chair of Elsinore Kilgore Hill Retreat Center Commission
- Coordinator of church bulletin boards
- Member of Historical Commission (church archives)
- Member of Women on the Move

Community Service Award, Los Angeles City Human Relations Commission

Community Service Award, University of Southern California Black Student Union

Minister's Wife of the Year, National Association of Ministers' Wives, New York

Volunteer Award, Los Angeles Chapter of the NAACP, 1988

Mayor's Certificate of Appreciation, 1988

Index

Index entries refer to Part I: Memoirs